Constitutionalism in the Global Realm

This book develops a sociologically informed theory of constitutionalism in the global realm, addressing both national and transnational forms of constitutional ordering. The book begins with the argument that current approaches to constitutionalism remain tied to a state-based conception of constitutions, and overlooks underlying structural transformations that trigger the emergence of constitutional forms of ordering. Poul F. Kjaer aims to address this shortcoming by offering a sociological and historically informed analysis of the evolution of constitutionalism in the face of globalisation. The analysis contextualises ongoing constitutional developments through the use of a long-term historical perspective, which is capable of highlighting the impact of deeper structural transformations unfolding within society.

The book looks at the ways in which national and transnational legal forms have evolved alongside one another. It demonstrates that the formation of global constitutions has not resulted in a corresponding decrease in the power of nation states, but instead, legal and political aspects of both the nation state and the transnational have been reconfigured and intensified in a mutually supportive manner.

In combining insights from a range of fields, this interdisciplinary book will be of great interest to students and scholars of constitutional law, sociology, global governance studies, and legal, social and political theory.

Poul F. Kjaer is Professor at the Department of Business and Politics, Copenhagen Business School. He has published widely on social and legal theory, European integration and global governance. He is the author of *Between Governing and Governance: The Emergence, Function and Form of Europe's Post-National Constellation* (Oxford: Hart Publishing, 2010).

Routledge Research in Constitutional Law

Available titles in this series include:

Weak Constitutionalism
Democratic legitimacy and the question of constituent power
Joel I. Colon-Rios

Engineering Constitutional Change
A comparative perspective on Europe, Canada and the USA
Xenophon Contiades, Centre for European Constitutional Law

Freedom of Speech
Importing European and US constitutional models in
transitional democracies
Uladzislau Belavusau

Colonial and Post-colonial Constitutionalism in the Commonwealth
Peace, order and good government
Hakeem O. Yusuf

Dynamics in the French Constitution
Decoding French republican ideas
David Marrani

Constitutionalism in the Global Realm
A sociological approach
Poul F. Kjaer

Forthcoming titles in this series include:

The Legal Philosophy and Influence of Jeremy Bentham
Essays on 'On the Limits of the Penal Branch of Jurisprudence'
Edited by Guillaume Tusseau

Constitutionalism in the Global Realm

A sociological approach

Poul F. Kjaer

LONDON AND NEW YORK

First published 2014
by Routledge
2 Park Square, Milton Park, Abingdon, Oxon OX14 4RN

and by Routledge
711 Third Avenue, New York, NY 10017

Routledge is an imprint of the Taylor & Francis Group, an informa business

British Library Cataloguing in Publication Data
A catalogue record for this book is available from the British Library

Library of Congress Cataloging in Publication Data
Kjaer, Poul F., author.
Constitutionalism in the global realm : a sociological approach / Poul F. Kjaer.
p. cm. -- (Routledge research in constitutional law)
Includes bibliographical references and index.
ISBN 978-0-415-73373-1 (hbk) -- ISBN 978-1-315-81454-4 (ebk)
1. Constitutional law. 2. Sociological jurisprudence. 3. International cooperation.
4. Social norms. I. Title.
K3165.K567 2014
342--dc23
2013041852

ISBN: 978-0-415-73373-1 (hbk)
ISBN: 978-1-315-81454-4 (ebk)

Typeset in Garamond
by Taylor & Francis Books

Printed and bound in the United States of America
by Edwards Brothers Malloy

Contents

Acknowledgements

This work took form during my years at the Cluster of Excellence, 'The Formation of Normative Orders' at the Goethe University, Frankfurt am Main, and was completed during my time at the Centre of Excellence for International Courts at the University of Copenhagen. Both places provided a stimulating intellectual environment as well as organisational support. I also benefited greatly from the support provided by the Alexander Humboldt Foundation, and, later on, from the Carlsberg Foundation during those years, just as I gained important insights during a research stay at the *École des hautes études en sciences sociales* in Paris.

Many people have a stake in the realisation of this work. To mention just a few: Tilman Allert, Marc Amstutz, Ayelet Banai, Thomas Biebricher, Susana Borrás, Hauke Brunkhorst, Christian Joerges, Karl-Heinz Ladeur, Laura Marin, Aldo Mascareño, Mikael Rask Madsen, Grahame Thompson, Chris Thornhill and Rudolf Wiethölter. But, in particular, the work benefited from the close collaboration with Gunther Teubner, who followed the work with great enthusiasm and a strong sense of purpose.

I thank Chris Engert for an excellent job in relation to the linguistic correction.

Poul F. Kjaer
Copenhagen
September 2013

1 Introduction

The metamorphosis of constitutionalism

1.1 Changing frames

At the Congress of Vienna in 1815, the process which led to the establishment of the first public international organisation, the *Commission Centrale pour la Navigation du Rhin* (CCNR), was initiated.[1] In the same year, the first volume of Friedrich Carl von Savigny's *Geschichte des römischen Rechts im Mittelalter*[2] was published. This work served as a preliminary exercise which subsequently led to the development of the essential principles of modern international private law in his *Systems des heutigen Römischen Rechts* (1840–49).[3] These two developments illustrate that neither public nor private transnationality is a new phenomenon. More importantly, they also indicate that the particular form of modern statehood which materialised in the *époque* which framed the American and French Revolutions has never stood alone, as there have always been substantial structures of ordering, which operate beyond the state. Even more importantly, they highlight that, historically speaking, the consolidation of modern statehood has implied more, and not less, transnationality. In other words, the relationship between nation state and transnational structures has – to date – been characterised by a relationship of mutual increase.

But, in spite of this intrinsic relationship between statehood and transnationality, the latter cannot merely be understood upon the basis of the classical international law and international relation categories. Transnational structures are not only emerging 'in between' states, as a way of achieving a limitation (*Hegung*) of inter-state conflicts.[4] Instead, the transnational space is a structure in its own right, which is reproduced upon the basis of an independent logic. From a sociological perspective, the transnational space must be understood as a conglomerate of Eigenstructures (*Eigenstructuren*),[5] which reproduces an independent form of social patterns. The world is characterised by a plural level of structure-formation with several distinct, but interwoven, logics, all of which operate simultaneously.[6] This plurality is also illustrated by the fact that modern statehood merely acts as an overlay which emerged 'on top' of already existing feudal societal structures which, in many instances, have never ceased to exist. Instead, the preceding societal structures, although increasingly marginalised, continue to operate 'beneath' the structures of the

modern states, as exemplified by the continued existence of constitutional mon-
archies, inherited seats in the British upper house and closed networks of nobility.[7]
Thus, apart from feudal structures and modern statehood, the transnational realm
must be understood as a third layer of social pattern-reproduction unfolding
within world society.

The multiple layers of world society are, however, not adequately reflected
in the mainstream self-understanding of the academic disciplines of law,
political science and sociology.[8] These disciplines remain essentially state-
centred with the consequence that they are methodologically incapable of
grasping the kind of social structures which are being reproduced outside the
realm of the state. From Georg W.F. Hegel[9] to Pierre Bourdieu,[10] the central
emphasis has, instead, been on the totality of the state. The consequence is
that the modern disciplines of law and social science have systematically
sabotaged any attempt to grasp the other layers of world society in their
profundity.

The relationship between nation state and transnational structures has,
however, undergone substantial changes since the middle of the twentieth
century.[11] It is still difficult to assess the depth and long-term consequences
of this re-configuration, but the world might have arrived at a 'tipping
point'[12] indicating a substantial change in the structural texture of world
society. This does not mean that the nation-state layer is bound to disappear,
but it does mean that the relative status and centrality of nation states within
the broader framework of world society is changing. An adequate sociological
understanding of the way in which social order is produced within world
society will, therefore, have to depart from the insight that states only represent
one form of ordering among several. Instead, the contemporary world is
characterised by two dominating forms of ordering which rely on two different
organisational principles: states rely on a territorial principle of organisation,
while contemporary forms of transnational ordering, by way of contrast, rely
on functional differentiation as their central organisational principle. In addition,
pre-modern 'traditional' forms of ordering which rely on segmentary and
stratificatory differentiation continue to play an important role. The development
of a relational perspective aimed at understanding how the different layers of
world society, and the multitude of social orders which operates both within
and in between these layers, interact is, therefore, one of the essential challenges
with which contemporary social and legal theory is confronted.

From where we stand now, the territorially delineated nation states, which,
to a certain extent, were internally stabilised through organisational forms
which rely on stratification as their central inclusion/exclusion mechanism,
and which have, to date, operated upon the basis of the self-proclaimed idea
that all other societal processes are subordinated to the state, seem to reflect a
form of 'transitional semantics'. Classical modernity, which, with a couple of
symbolic dates, can be said to span the period between 1789 and 1989, was
characterised by a double movement in which the emerging functionally
differentiated society was re-stabilised through the development of novel and

distinctively modern forms of territorial and stratificatory differentiation within the different functional systems.[13] To the extent that modernity is defined as the primacy of functional differentiation,[14] it is possible to understand the ongoing developments as representing a radicalisation of modernity, since the exponential expansion of functionally delineated transnational structures in recent decades and the shifting balance between the nation-state layer and the transnational layer indicates that the reliance on functional differentiation in world society is deepening. The functional systems of, for example, the economy, science, the mass media, sport and education gradually free themselves from their internal reliance on stabilisation mechanisms which rely on territorial and stratificatory forms of differentiation, thereby introducing a qualitative break vis-à-vis classical modernity. Both public and private structures, as well as all sorts of hybrid public/private structures which principally rely on functional differentiation, have emerged, as illustrated by organisations and regimes as diverse as the World Health Organization (WHO), the Internet Corporation for Assigned Names and Numbers (ICANN) and the International Organization for Standardization (ISO). Thus, even though the political system in the nation-state form is likely to continue to produce collectively binding decisions, it is increasingly being de-mystified, because of the ability of states to maintain the essentially early modern self-understanding that states are organic or holistic entities which encompass society as a whole is being progressively undermined.

The political and legal systems, in particular, were characterised by a strong internal reliance on territorial delineations in classical modernity. On both accounts, however, this seems to be changing. The emergence of functionally delineated legal and political structures with a truly global reach might still be at an embryonic stage, but, for the first time in history, such structures did emerge in the latter half of the twentieth century, just as the continued expansion of such structures seems to be a credible forecast for the decades to come. Accordingly, it is possible to observe a semantic shift: 'Global law without a state'[15] and 'Cosmopolitan Democracy'[16] have become meaningful statements, thereby indicating that the legal and the political systems are also in the process of freeing themselves from their internal reliance on territorially delineated stabilisation mechanisms.

1.2 The two discourses of transnational ordering

The emergence of new forms of transnational legal and political structures are not, however, likely to imply a simple transfer of nation-state forms of law and politics to the transnational realm through the constitution of a world state or any other form of structure which merely copies the form and function of nation states. Attempts to justify a one-to-one transfer of nation-state norms and institutions to the transnational realm only make sense if they are carried out as a purely philosophical reflection without any sociological foundation.[17] From a sociological perspective, it is impossible to ignore the profoundly different structural composition of the transnational space when compared to the nation-state realm.

The contemporary structure of the transnational layer of world society have partly emerged through a metamorphosis of the kind of public and private inter-state structures, in the form of public international organisations and state-based international private law, which emerged in classical modernity. These structures have, first of all, gained in importance to such a degree that they can no longer be understood as mere reflections of state-based delegation.[18] The evolution of international organisations such as the European Union (EU),[19] the World Trade Organization (WTO) and the World Bank (WB) into extremely complex norm-producing regimes illustrates that these structures have gained a level of autonomy which makes it impossible to understand them as a pure reflections of inter-state bargaining. In addition, the sheer number of such entities has increased dramatically since the middle of the twentieth century.[20] But apart from this transformation of public inter-state structures, new forms of transnational structures, which do not fit into the classical categories of international law and politics, have emerged. Multinational companies,[21] globally operating law firms, think-tanks and leading non-governmental organisations are increasingly operating as autonomous norm-producing entities outside the nation-state framework.[22] They have become autonomous forms of social ordering which constitutes their own cognitive spaces on a global scale. Thus, an exclusive focus on public international organisations does not suffice if one is seeking to describe the current structure of the transnational space.[23]

Within academic scholarship, public and private forms of transnationality are, however, being reflected in two somewhat separate discourses. On the one hand, the vast majority of scholars departing from public law and political science tend to orient their attention towards public international organisations and issues such as the emergence of the global administrative law complex,[24] or the question of how norms of interaction emerge between states. Essentially, this strain of research merely deals with the displacement of public decision-making away from the spheres of the nation states and towards or into the transnational realm. As such, this strand of research, in essence, remains devoted to an ambition of re-formulating the nation-state concepts of law and the political in order to make them compatible with ongoing global developments. In most cases, however, the basic assumptions concerning the form and function of law and political power remain unchanged. On the other hand, a minority group of scholars, who mainly depart from the international private law tradition, is seeking to develop novel concepts concerning how social order is produced in the transnational realm through a deliberate attempt to establish a break with the reliance on classical international law and international relations concepts.[25] The real world processes which the two groups focus upon tend to differ accordingly. As mentioned above, public lawyers and political scientists mainly analyse the dislocation of public power from the nation-state realm to the transnational sphere. In contrast, scholars departing from private law tend to emphasise phenomena such as *lex mercatoria*[26] and *lex digitalis*[27] within the framework of a research programme aimed at conceptualising global forms of social ordering which operate beyond the public realm.

This division of labour is, however, problematical in so far as what can be observed is the emergence of a whole range of functionally delineated config-urations within the transnational space in terms of regulatory conglomerates within areas such as the economy, science, the mass media, sport, the envir-onment and so forth. Conglomerates which are characterised by a highly complex interaction between public and private elements, in terms of public and private international organisations, public and private international courts and court-like tribunals, private companies,[28] think-tanks, non-governmental organisations[29] and so forth. Such conglomerates of social ordering cannot, therefore, be adequately grasped through a one-dimensional emphasis on either the public or the private dimension at the cost of the other.

1.3 The new constitutional agenda

The principle of mutual disregard which seems to guide the relation between the two discourses of public and private ordering in the global realm is all the more puzzling in so far as references to constitutional language can be detected within both discourses, just as their research interest essentially remains the same since the central objective within both discourses is to identify and normatively evaluate the constitutive and limitative structures of social processes unfolding within the global realm. However, in doing so, they act as ships passing each other in the night, since the constitutional concepts to which they refer are markedly different. A large segment of private lawyers tend to orient their work towards the question of the capability of the legal system to frame the transnational dimension of social processes related to, for example, the economy and migration, while systematically downplaying the political aspect of the processes in question.[30] In contrast, scholars departing from a public law or a political science perspective tend to explore the possibility of ensuring the primacy of the political system or – less ambitiously – to investigate the potential for ensuring political accountability of transnational structures.[31] Furthermore, and irrespective of their level of ambition, scholars departing from a public-law and political-science perspective tend to understand law as an instrument which is merely deployed in order to achieve political objectives.

It follows from the above that the development of a theory of constitutionalism in the global realm, which is capable of bridging the gap between public and private perspectives, has become the central challenge for constitutional theory. Such an endeavour cannot, however, take the form of a mere reconciliatory exercise aimed at achieving a compromise between the different positions. Instead, the point of departure must be the insight that law and politics operates in a radically different environment when they are seen as structures which are located in a global context as opposed to a nation-state context. The societal function of law and politics – and thus the position of the systems of law and politics in society and vis-à-vis each other – are substantially different within the transnational dimension of world society when compared to the nation-state setting. Thus, it is essential that an adequate theory of constitutionalism re-configures the nation-state distinction between the public and the private, as well as systematically emphasising the co-evolutionary transformation of law and politics in relation to the increased reliance on functional and sectorial delineations without discarding the existence and continued relevance of the constitutional orders of nation states.

But, even more importantly, such a theory must be built upon the basis of a fundamentally different conceptuality. New context-adequate concepts of law, politics and constitutionalism must be developed upon the basis of a general theory of society (*Gesellschaftstheorie*) capable of describing the basic structures (*Tiefenstrukturen*) of the transnational space, as well as the intertwined relationship between the different layers of world society;[32] a theory which, moreover, must be inductive in nature, since it must be problem-oriented and take a focal perspective which makes it capable of observing how new political and legal forms immanently emerge within broader societal processes. In other words, such a project can only succeed if it is carried out as a genuine sociological project, since sociology remains the only discipline which represents the ambition to describe the structure of society in its entirety.[33]

The developments outlined above have not gone unnoticed within constitutional theory. In recent years, a multitude of positions has emerged that share a common feature, in that they seek to respond to the challenge to constitutional conceptuality emerging from the increasing globalisation. No overarching consensus is in sight, but four main clusters of approaches can be identified.

First, there are those who advocate that the constitutional concept remains intrinsically linked to the concept of the state, and that the invoking of constitutional perspectives in relation to non-state structures represents a category error. Upon the basis of a culturalist world-view, Dieter Grimm advances the argument that the state is the only structure capable of providing a comprehensive frame for society, and that it is, therefore, the only potential constitutional object.[34] A somewhat similar argument has been developed by Martin Loughlin upon the basis of a specific epistemological approach which emphasises that the state expresses an ordered way of grasping the political world. The state is therefore to be understood as a scheme of intelligibility.[35]

Second, there are approaches which, by analogy, identify elements at the transnational level, which resemble corresponding structures within nation states. Three subgroups can be identified here: 1) A group which essentially focuses on the international order from a relatively classical international law outlook. They argue that formal elements of an international order possessing constitutional qualities can be observed through the emergence of global legal regimes which, especially through a shared reliance on human rights, have gained a distinct and relatively coherent set-up. This perspective has been advanced by Jürgen Habermas[36] in particular, but is also being advanced by a quite diverse group of scholars with different substantial interests ranging from social theory,[37] economic law[38] and human rights law,[39] to international public law.[40] 2) A second group that seeks to break with state centredness through a focus on societal constitutional structures while maintaining the analogy with state-based constitutionalism. This leads to a stronger inductive perspective which sees constitutional elements emerging within particularistic segments of global society without making the claim that a singular overarching framework is emerging.[41] 3) Finally, there is a more cautious approach which limits itself to detecting resemblances between specific material features which are observable at both the national and the transnational level.[42]

Third, there is a strand of literature which emphasises the radical pluralist structure of legal arrangements beyond the state, and which argues that this makes the quest for constitutionalism unattainable. Instead, they argue, an entirely different vocabulary has to be developed through the advancement of a legal pluralist perspective.[43] Linked to this group, but still markedly separate, are scholars focusing on global governance in a manner which has indirect relevance for the debate on constitutionalism in the global realm.[44]

1.4 An alternative approach

When compared with the existing positions and approaches, this book takes an alternative route, in so far as it develops the dimensions of a general theory of constitutionalism in the global realm in a manner which is of relevance for national as well as for transnational forms of ordering. The starting-point is the argument that the existing approaches and positions lack a 'deep foundation' because they, in some cases unwillingly, remain linked to a state-based conceptual universe and therefore fail to address the underlying structural transformations and set-ups which have led to the emergence of constitutional forms of ordering in the global realm.

In order to explain the emergence of the *actually* existing constitutional structures, as well as to analyse the *potential* role of constitutionalism beyond the state, four interconnected exercises are needed.

First, a redefinition of the constitutional object. Essentially, all the existing approaches to global constitutionalism depart from the concept of the state, in the sense that the object of study is either positively defined as 'state' or 'state-like', or negatively defined as 'non-state'. Instead, a positive clarification of the *sui generis* character of the object of study must be developed. Upon the basis of a historical argument, it is argued that the constitutional object is normative orders as such, and not states. Instead, states are conceived of as a specific, albeit the most important, type of normative order. Normative orders are defined as social structures that are characterised by a coherent arrangement of rules which reflect specific structures of expectations and which deploy legal sanctions as a means of establishing compliance with the expectations upon which they rely.[45] Moreover, in their modern version, normative orders tend to rely on formal organisation as their concrete operational form.

Second, constitutional transformations need to be analysed in a contextual manner which is capable of systematically linking the evolution of constitutional conceptuality to the deeper transformations of societal structures. As already mentioned, the global set-up is multi-layered, in the sense that three types of ordering exist, each of them operating on a different logic: the transnational, the national and the kind of 'pre-modern' forms that pre-date the state but also continue to be of relevance in the majority of the world. The central novelty to be observed is the re-configuration of the transnational layer, which has been taking place since the middle of the twentieth century, a shift which entailed a move away from a reliance on the centre/periphery differentiation in the form of colonialism, and towards the institutionalisation of legal and political regulatory processes which are primarily functionally differentiated. However, this development does *not* imply a weakening of the state as an entity of collective ordering. Modern statehood emerged hand in hand with transnational forms of ordering in the colonial form, just as statehood first became a global phenomenon in the wake of de-colonisation. Instead of a zero-sum game, the relationship between national and transnational structures is characterised by a relationship of mutual increase. 'More of one' implies 'more of the other', while their inter-connected evolution simultaneously implies an increased marginalisation of 'pre-modern' forms of ordering.

Third, the transformation of transnational structures away from the reliance on the centre/periphery and towards functional differentiation has led to the emergence of novel forms of law and politics. The vast majority of the existing works on law and politics in the global realm assume that the concepts of law and the political remain unchanged. But new context-adequate concepts of law and the political are needed because new forms of cognitivised law and the political have become predominant at the transnational level. The forms of law and the political which can be identified are not primarily driven by normative objectives but are instead *trans-normative*, in the sense that they are oriented towards the facilitation of learning processes with the aim of establishing increased compatibility between normative orders. In addition, the 'infrastructure' upon which such types of law and the political rely is fundamentally different. For example, the transnational form of the political relies on a concept of stakeholders, rather than on the concept of the nation, a concept of transparency, rather than a concept of the public sphere, and a concept of self-representation, rather than a concept of representation.

Although less pronounced, a variant of this development can also be observed at the inter-state level as well as in the relationship between states and transnational structures. The character of interaction between states has escaped the narrow confinement within traditional international law and politics, and is increasingly relying on complex co-ordination and learning-oriented processes which have features that are similar to those pre-dominant at the transnational level. Moreover, within national as well as transnational legal set-ups, specific instruments have emerged to handle the specific interactions with the 'pre-modern' structures.

Fourth, only against the background of the three previous points does it become possible to address the theme of constitutionalism in the global realm. The emergence of constitutional structures and semantics at the trans-national and inter-state levels is intrinsically linked to the emergence of cognitivised forms of law and the political. The normative/cognitive distinction should not, however, be understood as representing a fundamental contra-diction. To the contrary, the distinction is only possible as long as both sides remain in play. The emergence of new forms of cognitivised law and the political does, in fact, establish a *functional need* for a secondary normative stabilisation of such processes, thereby creating a basis for the emergence of constitutional forms of ordering. A more concrete distinction between three dimensions can be made:

1 *Within* the national and the transnational layers, constitutions provide normative orders with a skeleton. They are institutions which, in their political function, frame the *internal* body of rules and norms establishing the formal structure, decisional competences and hierarchically based *locus* of authority within a given normative order at the same time that they, in their legal function, lay down principles for the structuring of conflicts between norms within such orders. Constitutions are, in this sense, laying down the enabling and the limiting rules which guide normative orders internally.

2 The trans-normative legal processes which have emerged are *simultaneously* oriented towards facilitating the transfer of condensed social components (*Sinnkomponente*) such as political decisions, legal judgments, economic products and capital and scientific knowledge *between* normative orders as well as the countering of processes of coalescence, and the igniting of learning-processes among such orders. Rights-based processes of constitutionalisation emerge as the form through which such strongly cognitivised trans-normative law processes are normatively stabilised in the sense that they are the form through which the normative objectives which guide the deployment of cognitive processes are reproduced.

3 Constitutions are oriented towards the inner life of normative orders, and thereby towards the material dimension. Processes of constitutionalisation are, instead, mainly oriented towards the social dimension due to their focus on the kind of trans-normative legal processes unfolding in-between normative orders. It is against this background that the overarching *counter-factual* narratives of constitutionalism emerge, narratives which seek to overcome the contradiction between the internal and external dimen-sions by externalising the difference into the constantly reproduced vision of the future. It is through recourse to the time dimension that the promise of a future which reconciles the material and social dimensions of normative orders is constantly reproduced, thereby establishing a compre-hensive and transcending perspective on the world within each normative order.

As is apparent form the above, the argument presented is a cumulative one. Step by step, a coherent conceptual framework that takes adequate note of real world developments is gradually built up. As such, what follows should be understood as a sociologically informed social and legal theory intervention.

Notes

1 See Christian Walter, 'Constitutionalizing (Inter)national Governance: Possibilities for and Limits to the Development of an International Constitutional Law', pp. 170–201, *German Yearbook of International Law*, 2001, 44, p. 176 *et seq.*

2 Friedrich Carl von Savigny, *Geschichte des römischen Rechts im Mittelalter. Bd. 5*, Bad Homburg: 1961.

3 Friedrich Carl von Savigny, *System des heutigen römischen Rechts* / Bearb. von O. L. Heuser – 2. Aufl., Berlin: 1974.

4 For such a view, see, especially, Georg W.F. Hegel, *Grundlinien der Philosophie des Rechts oder Naturrecht und Staatswissenschaft im Grundrisse*, *Werke Band 7*, Frankfurt am Main: Suhrkamp Verlag, [1821] 1970; Carl Schmitt, *Der Nomos der Erde: Im Völkerrecht des Jus Publicum Europaeum*, Berlin: Duncker & Humblot, 1950.

5 Rudolf Stichweh, 'Strukturbildung in der Weltgesellschaft – Die Eigenstrukturen der Weltgesellschaft und die Regionalkulturen der Welt', in Thomas Schwinn (ed.), *Die Vielfalt und Einheit der Moderne. Kultur-und strukturvergleichende Analysen*, Wiesbaden: Verlag für Sozialwissenschaften, 2006, pp. 239–57; Rudolf Stichweh, 'Das Konzept der Weltgesellschaft: Genese und Strukturbildung eines globalen Gesellschaftssystems', *Rechtstheorie*, 2008, 39, pp. 329–55.

6 Saskia Sassen, *Territory, Authority, Rights: From Medieval to Global Assemblages*, Princeton, NJ: Princeton University Press, 2006; Poul F. Kjaer: 'The Metamorphosis of the Functional Synthesis: A Continental European Perspective on Governance, Law and the Political in the Transnational Space', *Wisconsin Law Review*, 2010, 2, pp. 489–533.

7 See, for example, Simon Deakin: 'The Return of the Guild? Network Relations In Historical Perspective', in Marc Amstutz and Gunther Teubner (eds), *Networks: Legal Issues of Multilateral Co-operation*, Oxford: Hart Publishing, 2009, pp. 53–73.

8 The tendency to methodological nationalism seems, however, to be less profound within sociology. See Daniel Chernilo, *A Social Theory of the Nation-State: The Political Forms of Modernity beyond Methodological Nationalism*, London: Routledge, 2007; Daniel Chernilo, 'Social Theory's Methodological Nationalism. Myth and Reality', *European Journal of Social Theory*, 2006, 9, pp. 5–22.

9 Hegel, *Grundlinien der Philosophie des Rechts oder Naturrecht und Staatswissenschaft im Grundrisse*.

10 See, for example, Pierre Bourdieu, *La Noblesse d'État: Grandes écoles et esprit de corps*, Paris: Minuit, 1989.

11 Neil Walker, 'Beyond Boundary Disputes and Basic Grids: Mapping the Global Disorder of Normative Orders', *International Journal of Constitutional Law*, 2008, 6, pp. 373–96.

12 Sassen, *Territory, Authority, Rights*, p. 9 *et seq.*

13 Poul F. Kjaer, 'The Structural Transformation of Embeddedness', in Christian Joerges and Josef Falke (eds), *Karl Polanyi: Globalisation and the Potential of Law in Transnational Markets*, Oxford: Hart Publishing, 2011, pp. 85–104.

14 Niklas Luhmann, *Die Gesellschaft der Gesellschaft*, Frankfurt am Main: Suhrkamp Verlag, 1997, p. 1143 *et seq.*

15 Gunther Teubner (ed.), *Global Law without a State*, Aldershot, Ashgate Dartmouth Publishing, 1997.

16 Daniele Archibugi and David Held (eds), *Cosmopolitan Democracy: An Agenda for a New World Order*, Cambridge: Polity Press, 1995.

17 For such a philosophical attempt, see Otfried Höffe, *Demokratie im Zeitalter der Globalisierung*, Munich: C.H. Beck Verlag, 1999.

18 Joshua Cohen and Charles F. Sabel, 'Global Democracy?', *NYU Journal of International Law and Politics*, 2005, 37, pp. 763–97.

19 Poul F. Kjaer, *Between Governing and Governance: On the Emergence, Function and Form of Europe's Post-national Constellation*, Oxford: Hart Publishing, 2010.

20 For example, in 2001, the *Yearbook of International Organisations* estimated the number of intergovernmental organisations to be around 7,000 and the number of private international organisations to around 48,000. See, also, www.uia.org/statistics/organisations/11.1.1a.pdf.

21 Larry Catá Backer, 'Economic Globalization and the Rise of Efficient Systems of Global Private Lawmaking: Wal-Mart as Global Legislator', *University of Connecticut Law Review*, 2007, 37, pp. 1739–84.

22 Grahame F. Thompson, *The Constitutionalization of the Global Corporate Sphere?*, Oxford: Oxford University Press, 2012.

23 Christine Schwöbel, 'Whither the Private in Global Governance?', *International Journal of Constitutional Law*, 2012, 10, pp. 1106–33.

24 For a public law-inspired typology of global administrative structures, see Benedict Kingsbury, Nico Krisch and Richard B. Stewart, 'The Emergence of Global Administrative Law', *Law and Contemporary Problems*, 2005, 68, pp. 15–62. For the special case of the European Union, see Poul F. Kjaer 'The Societal Function of European Integration in the Context of World Society', *Soziale Systeme: Zeitschrift für Soziologische Theorie*, 2007, 13, pp. 367–78.

25 Marc Amstutz, 'In-Between Worlds: Marleasing and the Emergence of Interlegality in Legal Reasoning', *European Law Journal*, 2005, 12, pp. 766–84; Marc Amstutz and Vaios Karavas, 'Weltrecht: Ein Derridasches Monster' in Gralf-Peter Calliess, Andreas Fischer-Lescano, Dan Wielsch and Peer Zumbansen (eds), *Soziologische Jurisprudenz. Festschrift für Gunther Teubner zum 65. Geburtstag*, Berlin: Walter de Gruyter, 2009, pp. 645–72; Marc Amstutz and Vaios Karavas, 'Rechtsmutation zu Genese und Evolution des Rechts im transnationalen Raum', *Rechtsgeschichte*, 2006, 8, pp. 14–32; Gunther Teubner and Andreas Fischer-Lescano, *Regime-Kollisionen: Zur Fragmentierung des globalen Rechts*, Frankfurt am Main: Suhrkamp Verlag, 2006; Gunther Teubner and Andreas Fischer-Lescano: 'Regime-Collisions: The Vain Search for Legal Unity in the Fragmentation of Global Law', *Michigan Journal of International Law*, 2004, 25, pp. 999–1046.

26 For example, Tania Liekweg, *Das Recht der Weltgesellschaft: Systemtheoretische Perspektiven auf die Globalisierung des Rechts am Beispiel der lex mercatoria*, Stuttgart: Lucius & Lucius, 2003.

27 Vagias Karavas, *Digitale Grundrechte: Elemente einer Verfassung des Informationsflusses im Internet*, Baden-Baden: Nomos Verlag, 2007.

28 Olaf Dilling, Martin Herberg and Gerd Winter (eds), *Responsible Business: Self-Governance and Law in Transnational Economic Transactions*, Oxford: Hart Publishing, 2008; Larry Catá Backer, 'Economic Globalization and the Rise of Efficient Systems of Global Private Lawmaking: Wal-Mart as Global Legislator', *University of Connecticut Law Review*, 2007, 37, pp. 1739–84.

29 For example, Heike Walk, 'Formen Politischer Institutionalisierung: NGOs als Hoffnungsträger globaler Demokratie', in Jens Beckert, Julia Eckert, Martin Kohli and Wolfgang Streeck (eds), *Transnationale Solidarität: Chancen und Grenzen*, Frankfurt am Main: Campus Verlag, 2004, pp. 163–80.

30 For an important exception, see the work of Christian Joerges. For example, Christian Joerges, 'A New Type of Conflicts Law as the Legal Paradigm of the Postnational Constellation', in Christian Joerges and Josef Falke (eds), *Karl Polanyi: Globalisation and the Potential of Law in Transnational Markets*, Oxford: Hart Publishing, 2011, pp. 465–501; Christian Joerges, 'The *Rechtsstaat* and Social Europe: How a Classical Tension Resurfaces in the European Integration Process', *Comparative Sociology*, 2010, 9, pp. 65–85.

31 For example, David Held and Mathias Koenig-Archibugi (eds), *Global Governance and Public Accountability*, Oxford: Blackwell Publishing, 2005.

32 For the multiple layers of world society, see Kjaer, 'The Metamorphosis of the Functional Synthesis'; Sassen, *Territory, Authority, Rights*.

33 Jürgen Habermas, *Theorie des kommunikativen Handelns, Band 1 Handlungsrationalität und gesellschaftliche Rationalisierung*, Frankfurt am Main: Suhrkamp Verlag, 1981, p. 19 *et seq.*

34 Dieter Grimm, 'The Constitution in the Process of Denationalization', *Constellations*, 2005, 12, pp. 447–63.

35 Martin Loughlin, 'In Defence of Staatslehre', *Der Staat*, 2009, 48, 1, pp. 1–28, p. 7.

36 Jürgen Habermas, 'The Constitutionalization of International Law and the Legitimation Problems of a Constitution for World Society', *Constellations*, 2008, 15, pp. 444–55; Jürgen Habermas, 'A Political Constitution for the Pluralist World Society', in Jürgen Habermas, *Between Naturalism and Religion*, Cambridge: Polity Press, 2008, pp. 312–52.

37 Most notably, Hauke Brunkhorst, *Solidarität: Von der Bürgerfreundschaft zur globalen Rechtsgenossenschaft*, Frankfurt am Main: Suhrkamp Verlag; Hauke Brunkhorst, 'Constitutionalism and Democracy in the World Society', in Petra Dobner and Martin Loughlin (eds), *The Twilight of Constitutionalism?* Oxford: Oxford University Press, 2010, pp. 179–200; Hauke Brunkhorst, 'Cosmopolitanism and Democratic Freedom', in Chris Thornhill and Samantha Ashenden (eds), *Legality and Legitimacy – Normative and Sociological Approaches*, Baden-Baden: Nomos Verlag, 2010, pp. 171–96.

38 Ernst-Ulrich Petersmann, 'Constitutional Theories of International Economic Adjudication and Investor-State Arbitration', in Pierre-Marie Dupuy; Francesco Francioni and Ernst-Ulrich Petersmann (eds), *Human Rights in International Investment Law and Arbitration*, Oxford: Oxford University Press, 2009, pp. 137–94; Ernst-Ulrich Petersmann, 'Multilevel Judicial Governance as Guardian of the Constitutional Unity of International Economic Law', *Loyola International and Comparative Law Review*, 2008, 30, pp. 101–52.

39 Erika de Wet, 'The Role Of European Courts in the Development of a Hierarchy of Norms Within International Law: Evidence of Constitutionalisation?', *European Constitutional Law Review*, 2009, 5, pp. 284–306; Erika De Wet, 'The International Constitutional Order', *International and Comparative Law Quarterly*, 2006, 55, pp. 51–72.

40 For example, Mattias Kumm, 'The Cosmopolitan Turn in Constitutionalism: On the Relationship between Constitutionalism in and Beyond the State', in Jeffrey L. Dunoff and Joel. P. Trachtman (eds), *Ruling the World? International Law, Global Governance, Constitutionalism*, Cambridge: Cambridge University Press, 2009, pp. 258–326; Jan Klabbers, Anne Peters and Geir Ulfstein, *The Constitutionalization of International Law*, Oxford: Oxford University Press, 2009; Anne Peters, 'The Merits of Global Constitutionalism', *Indiana Journal of Global Legal Studies*, 2009, 16, pp. 397–411; Christian Walter, 'Constitutionalizing (Inter)national Governance: Possibilities for and Limits to the Development of an International Constitutional Law', *German Yearbook of International Law*, 2001, 44, pp. 170–201.

41 Andreas Fischer-Lescano, *Globalverfassung: Die Geltungsbegründung der Menschenrechte*, Weilerswist: Velbrück, 2005; Gunther Teubner, *Constitutional Fragments. Societal Constitutionalism and Globalization*, Oxford: Oxford University Press, 2012. For these authors, the absence of a singular framework does not, however, imply an absence of ordering, as they emphasise the network-based interconnectedness of transnational regimes at the same time that they develop a 'constitutional law of collisions' (*Verfassungskollisionsrecht*) which is oriented towards establishing compatibility.

42 Here, the work of Neil Walker stands out: see, for example, Neil Walker, 'Out of Place and Out of Time: Law's Fading Co-ordinates', *Edinburgh Law Review*, 2010, 14, pp. 13–46; Walker, 'Beyond Boundary Disputes and Basic Grids'; Neil Walker: 'A Constitutional Reckoning', *Constellations*, 2006, 13, pp. 140–50.

43 For example, Paul Schiff Berman, *Global Legal Pluralism: A Jurisprudence of Law Beyond Borders*, New York: Cambridge University Press, 2012; Nico Krisch, *Beyond Constitutionalism: The Pluralist Structure of Postnational Law*, Oxford: Oxford University Press, 2010.

44 For example, Anne-Marie Slaughter, *A New World Order*, Princeton, NJ: Princeton University Press, 2004; Sassen, *Territory, Authority, Rights.*

45 This definition highlights the close connection to institutional theory. See, for example, Maurice Hauriou, 'The Theory of the Institution and the Foundation: A Study in Social Vitalism', in Albert Broderick, *The French Institutionalists: Maurice Hauriou, Georges Renard, Joseph T. Delos and Albert Broderick*, Cambridge: Cambridge University Press, 1970, pp. 93–124.

Part I

Structural transformations

2   The implosion of the Eurocentric world

2.1 Introduction

The debate on constitutionalism in the global realm is intrinsically linked to the emergence of dense forms of legally framed social ordering beyond the state. However, this phenomenon is by no means new. Europe's global expansion from the fifteenth century onwards implied, from the very outset, the emergence of extensive forms of transnational ordering in the colonial form. Modern statehood has, therefore, never been the sole form of social ordering in the emerging world society in that modern states have always been embedded in, and interacted with, extensive forms of ordering located beyond the state. Thus, the relationship between statehood and transnational ordering is not a zero-sum relationship. On the contrary, both modern statehood, understood as a limited form of social ordering, *and* transnational ordering emerged hand in hand. The implosion of Europe's global hegemony which started to unfold in the late nineteenth century furthermore implied a structural double movement characterised by a progressive globalisation of modern statehood and a simultaneous expansion of transnational ordering which implied a gradual reduction in the reliance on the centre/periphery differentiation and a move towards an increased reliance on functional differentiation within the transnational layer of world society.

2.2 The long twentieth century

The space (*Raum*) which eventually became known as 'Europe' experienced the gradual emergence of a range of interconnected configurative processes from the eleventh century onwards,[1] and the emergence of a novel form of abstract and generalised political power.[2] A form of power which, due to its reliance on the state form, was distinct from other forms of social power, as was eventually expressed in the state/society distinction introduced by Hegel.[3] The European configurative processes were structured around two deeply interrelated dimensions. First, intense military competition which led to a continued (re-)construction of territories and the populations inhabiting these territories, as a means of increasing the economic resources available for warfare, and the expansion in the density of political power.[4] Second, a successive wave of legal transformations as symbolically compromised in Gregory VII's eleventh-century Papal revolution which led to the introduction of the distinction between public and private law; the sixteenth-century Lutheran- and Calvinist-inspired revolutions which implied the liberation of the individual Christian believer from the subordination to the legal hierarchy of the Catholic Church; the fortification of a generalised legal order within the framework of the emerging state in seventeenth-century England, and, later on, beyond the island of Great Britain; and the self-reflexive and circular linking of modern law and political rule in the wake of the American and French Revolutions in the late eighteenth century through the introduction of the principle of popular sovereignty.[5]

The circular co-evolutionary emergence of modern forms of political power and law within specific territorial segments was conditioned by the existence of a multiplicity of such configurative processes. This multiplicity implied continued mutual observation and increasingly intense transfers of social components such as economic capital and products, scientific knowledge, military technology and organisational techniques between these configurations.[6] As such, inter-configurative competition was the central structural condition which eventually allowed these configurative processes to become self-reinforcing.[7] The emergence and reinforcement of state-centred configurations was, therefore, conditioned by the simultaneous emergence of an overarching configuration of configurations through the constitution of a specific European legal space. Formally speaking, the European configuration of configurations was established with the Peace of Westphalia, which, in praxis, was a complex conglomerate of peace treaties, signed between the 15 May and the 24 October in 1648, which merely provided a legal formalisation of an already existing overarching European configuration of inter-configurational relations which had gradually evolved through century-long processes. The formal framework constituting this configuration of configurations was, moreover, continuously altered and reinforced on occasions, such as the 1713 Peace of Utrecht, the 1721 Treaty of Nystad, which led to the inclusion of Russia into the European legal order, and the Congress of Vienna in 1814–15.

But the emergence of a multitude of configurational processes not only went hand in hand with the simultaneous emergence of a larger European frame within which these processes unfolded. The European configuration of configurations itself only gained its form through the emergence of an increasingly clear-cut distinction between Europe and the rest of the world.[8] As such, the condensation of a specific European legal space was structurally conditioned by the emergence of a world society in the wake of the great discoveries taking place from the late fifteenth century onwards. It follows that the emergence of a multitude of increasingly dense and inter-connected configurational processes within Europe not only implied the emergence of a specific European (legal) space, but also the emergence of a specific (legal) form through which compatibility between this space and the world in its entirety was established. The form of compatibility which emerged was highly asymmetric in nature, in so far as it mainly unfolded through colonialism (*Landnahme*). The configurative processes leading to the emergence of states such as Denmark, France, the Netherlands, Portugal, Russia, Spain and the United Kingdom went hand in hand with the progressive build-up of increasingly vast colonial empires, thereby indicating that the relationship between the interlinked European state-formation processes and the continued expansion of European colonialism were mutually constitutive.[9] However, the colonial endeavours of the European states gained a legal form which was not directly derived from the states in question. Instead a distinct European legal framework aimed at regulating the relations between Europe and the rest of the world emerged. The first expression of this development was the 1494 Treaty of Tordesillas, subsequently complemented by the 1529 Treaty of Zaragoza, which divided the non-European and non-Christian world between Spain and Portugal upon the basis of a Papal bull. Over the following centuries, this framework was continuously altered and expanded, thereby reflecting the continued changes in the relative centrality of different configurative processes within the emerging European space, as, for example, was expressed in the gradual reduction in the centrality of Portugal and Spain and the concurrent increase in the importance of England and the Netherlands from the late sixteenth century onwards. The zenith was reached with the last common European imperialist expansion as agreed upon during the Berlin Conference of 1884–85.[10]

The Berlin Conference not only incarnated the zenith of Europe's world domination, but also provided the basis for its demise. This was the case because one of the central outcomes was the decision by the participating states to recognise King Leopold II's Congo Free State as a sovereign state, thereby establishing the *legal principle* that sovereign states, formally enjoying an equal status with European states, could exist outside the borders of Europe. According to Carl Schmitt, this decision did, however, reflect a *fait accompli* because the actual decision had been taken on the 22 April 1884, some six months before the start of the Berlin Conference. On that date, the government of the United States made the decision to unilaterally recognise the Congo Free State as a sovereign state. With this act, the United States not only broke out of its self-confined sphere of interests, as expressed in the Monroe Doctrine of 1823, which limited the reach of American interests to the New World,[11] but also initiated the breakdown of the European-based world order. This was the case because, for the first time since the emergence of world society, a fundamental change in the legal framework upon which global ordering relied was introduced by a non-European state. With his characteristic mixture of elegance and simplicity, Schmitt, writing in the mid-twentieth century, therefore stylised 22 April 1884 as the defining moment in which the legal and political structure of the contemporary world was established.[12]

Indeed, it is possible to view the major historical world events which occurred in the following 100 years or so in the light of this event, in that they were all related to the continued reduction in the centrality of the European states and the concurrent rise to prominence of, first, the United States, and, later on, Japan and the Soviet Union.[13] The consequence was the replacement of the European legal space, which served as a form for the European domination of the world in its entirety, with a dual US/Soviet form of global ordering during the Cold War era. Essentially, the new order was, however, an extended variant of the preceding European global order. The core upon which global ordering relied was expanded from encompassing Europe to most of the northern hemisphere, while, at the same time, a distinction between the core and the rest of the world was maintained. The core relations were legally stabilised through numerous international arrangements from the Potsdam Agreement of 1945 onwards, while the two superpowers considered it legitimate to fight out the conflict in the rest of the world, as, for example, expressed in their continued engagement in legally largely unregulated proxy wars (for example, Vietnam, Angola, Mozambique, Afghanistan and between Israel and its neighbours) throughout the Cold War period.

In retrospect, the factual and ideological co-dominance of the Russian-dominated Soviet Union (USSR) and the United States in the latter half the twentieth century was, however, a mere transitional phenomenon. This transitional phase came to an end with the implosion of the Soviet Union in 1991 and the peak of the relative power of the United States in the years preceding 15 September 2008, the day when the United States resigned from its role as the guarantor of the global financial system through its acceptance of the bankruptcy of Lehman Brothers.[14] At the time of writing, the world is going through a drastic shift due to the rapid modernisation of Brazil, China and India as well as a vast range of other developing countries. For the first time in human history, a global configuration is emerging, since the majority of the world population is now living within the segment of world society which either has undergone or is likely to go through a profound process of modernisation in the foreseeable future. This development was also reflected in the decision, announced on 25 September 2009, to transform the G8 into the G20. After this day, the states which actively define the basic structure of the global political system represent the majority of the world population for the very first time.[15] As such, the long twentieth century from 22 April 1884 to 25 September 2009 can be understood as the century in which the European configuration, with a short Soviet/US *intermezzo*, was replaced by a global configuration.

2.3 The transformation of 'deeper structures'

The real-world consequences of the still ongoing emergence of a global configuration can hardly be overestimated. In addition, this transformation challenges the world-view upon which the bulk of Western thinking, implicitly or explicitly, has relied since the emergence of modernity to the extent that the distinction between first 'Europe and the rest', and, later on, 'the West and rest' was seen as possessing a constitutive function for the world in its entirety.[16]

Against this background, it is hardly surprising that '[t]he deep structural and conceptual change that this decentring of Euro-centrism has brought about is not yet sufficiently understood.'[17] Indeed, the historical outline in the previous section mainly refers to symbolic dates and 'triggering events' or watersheds of a highly political nature of the kind which is studied by the historical discipline upon the basis of the assumption that political acts and decisions are the central component through which the future of the social world is shaped. Very limited insights concerning the underlying causes of these processes can, however, be derived from the isolated study of such events, just as the assumption of the supremacy of the political within society, as such, remains justifiable.[18] From a sociological perspective, and, in particular, from the perspective of a general theory of society (*Gesellschaftstheorie*), such events must instead be understood as reflections of far more profound transformations of the 'deeper structures' (*Tiefenstrukturen*) of society, in so far as the transformations described reflect fundamental changes in the forms of differentiation which characterise society in its entirety.

The concept of differentiation is a core concept of the sociological discipline since it observes and analyses the paradoxical unity of the differences in the social world. Although differences between dissimilar segments of society have, of course, been observed throughout human history, the breakthrough of modernity in the latter half of the eighteenth century was accompanied by the emergence of abstract theories of differentiation. One of the first moves in this direction was the development of the concept of the division of labour in relation to economic reproduction processes.[19] This line of thinking was adopted by the emerging sociological discipline and given a decidedly different twist through the conception of differentiation as a *structural and systemic* concept which can be used to map and explain the basic structure of society as well as to provide a framework which enables us to gain an understanding of the twilight zone between personal experience and societal expectations.

From the retrospective view of modern sociology, the evolution of social structures has been characterised by a sequential dominance of a limited number of forms of differentiation with each of them enjoying a relative dominance over the other forms within different periods and contexts. In an ideal manner:[20]

1 First, segmentary differentiation, characterised by the principle of *equality* of multiple social systems, such as tribes, villages, clans or families, which are typically demarcated upon the basis of blood relations or physical location.
2 Second, stratificatory differentiation expressing an outright *subordination* of one segment under another upon the basis of rank, as, for example, known from the relationship between the nobility and the non-nobility in early modern Europe.
3 Third, territorial differentiation, implying a construction of a limited and coherent geographical space which is clearly demarcated from other geographical spaces within the framework of the modern nation states.

4   Fourth, the centre/periphery differentiation, which are constituted upon the basis of *asymmetric relations* between different social spheres, for example, between cities and rural areas, or between states and their colonial possessions.
5   Fifth, functional differentiation, which is characterised by the principle of the *equality of different systems* as reflected in the distinction between social spheres such as art, economy, education, health, law, politics and science, with each of them possessing a different quality which cannot be reproduced by the other spheres.

Against this background, modernity can be defined as the supremacy of functional differentiation vis-à-vis the other forms of social differentiation,[21] as is also tentatively acknowledged through the increased focus on functionally differentiated processes from Hegel and onwards.[22] This is the case because modern society can be understood as being characterised by a number of relatively autonomous functionally delineated social 'spheres',[23] 'fields'[24] or 'systems'[25] that reproduce their respective forms of social patterns upon the basis of specific logics and rationalities. One of the many consequences of the increasingly constitutive role of functional differentiation is that society can no longer be conceived of as having a singular centre from which all other dimensions of society are structured. The emergence of the sociological discipline, the discipline of modernity par excellence, can thus be understood as a scientific reflection of the breakthrough of modernity to the extent that one of the central questions posed and analysed by the discipline is that of *how* society can remain integrated under the structural conditions emerging from the increased primacy of functional differentiation.

The degree to which the primacy of functional differentiation has established itself as the primary form of social differentiation is, however, subject to two central and deeply entangled limitations. First, although rapidly expanding its reach, the primacy of functional differentiation has only become a social fact within small segments of world society, since the preceding forms of social differentiation have showed themselves far more resilient than was typically assumed, and because the globalisation of functional differentiation remains a very recent phenomenon. Second, the gradual re-configuration of communicative processes away from the reliance on early modern forms of stratificatory differentiation and towards functional differentiation as the primary form of social differentiation implied the emergence of novel forms of stratification, territoriality and centre/periphery differentiation within the larger framework of functionally differentiated structures.

The complex overlap between the different forms of social differentiation is clearly visible in relation to social stratification. Hegel was the first to highlight the emergence of new forms of social classes in the wake of increased industrialisation and urbanisation. Marx, upon the basis of his concept of the forces of production (*Produktivkräfte*), subsequently elevated the clashes between the different stratified segments into the central form of social conflict. In the broader Marxist tradition, class conflicts were, moreover, conceptualised as a kind of immanent societal contradictions which enabled an understanding of social-class conflict as a central variable which explained societal evolution. However, the Marxist perspective only gained prominence from the mid-nineteenth century to the mid-twentieth century. Moreover, in the segments of world society which have undergone an intense modernisation process, stratification can no longer be understood as an overarching and independent form of structure formation which stands in an orthogonal relationship to functional differentiation and which serves as a constitutive structure for society in its entirety.[26] Instead, stratification has become a particularistic social form which is deployed *within* functionally delineated processes, thus enabling an *internal* stabilisation of such processes through the reproduction of specific asymmetric social roles.[27] Instead of stratification through social-class differentiation, the different functional spheres are internally relying on asymmetric relations between performance roles (*Leistungsrollen*) and audience roles (*Publikumsrollen*) for their internal stabilisation. Central examples of this can be found in the relationship between producers and consumers within the economy, medical staff and patients within health care, clergy and believers within religions, teachers and pupils within education, and politicians and voters within politics.

However, as testified by the discourse of the masses and mass society in the late nineteenth and early twentieth centuries, rapid modernisation implies that social structures are 'in flow' with existing forms of social differentiation being eroded at the same time as new stable forms have not yet gained firm ground.[28] Going beyond a Eurocentric perspective, the massive modernisation processes, as, for example, reflected in the rapid urbanisation and industrialisation taking place in large segments of contemporary Africa, Asia and Latin America, implies that the increased dissolution of stratification as an overarching social category are likely to provoke similar forms of counter-reactions as the ones associated with European Marxism in the late nineteenth and early twentieth centuries. So, even though stratification have ceased to be an overarching category for the constitution of society in its entirety in the most modernised segments of world society, this can hardly be said to be the case in the vast majority of world. An indeterminate state of affairs can be observed in relation to the structural transformation away from a reliance on stratification as an organising principle of society. On the one hand, the dissolution of stratification as an overarching category is rapidly advancing while, on the other hand, it remains far removed from being the case worldwide. As we will turn to in the following two sections, a similar kind of indeterminacy can be observed in relation to the status of modern forms of territoriality within the framework of modern statehood as well as centre/periphery differentiation.

2.4 Limited statehood

Mainstream political and legal theory tends to operate upon the basis of the sociological assumption that statehood not only exists, but that the state is also structurally superior to other societal structures located within its territory.[29] An equally problematical form of reductionism can be detected within large segments of empirical social research, political science and dogmatic legal scholarship, which tend to depart from the assumption that the social world merely consists of polities constituted through territorial differentiation.[30]

The widespread assumption concerning the existence of a polity organised in the form of a state, constituted upon the basis of clearly demarcated territorial boundaries, which possesses supremacy vis-à-vis all other social structures within its territory in that it *de jure* and *de facto* possesses the capability to implement effectively the collective decisions made by the polity,[31] however, reveals a fundamental lack of understanding of the processes resulting in the emergence of modern statehood. Not only is the potential dominance of the state the result of very complex century-long evolutionary processes, but, in addition, one might also argue that both historically and sociologically speaking such a 'supreme state' has *never existed*, since alternative structures of social ordering have *always* existed beneath, beside and above the state. A historical and sociological more adequate understanding of the territorial state therefore implies an understanding of both democratic and non-democratic states alike as very important, but nonetheless *limited*, forms of social ordering, which operates in constant competition with other forms of social ordering. The territorially delineated state is therefore to be understood as a structure which operates within a far broader societal terrain, thereby necessitating an understanding of society – rather than the state – as the central object of study for law, sociology and the social sciences in general.[32]

As already indicated, the first major leap towards the emergence of modern statehood was constituted through the functional separation of the power of the Holy Roman Empire and the power of the Catholic Church, thereby implying that the emerging modern state recognised the legal *and* organisational autonomy of the church.[33] Thus, from the very outset, the state was a *limited* form of collective organisation, which constituted itself vis-à-vis other social structures over which it had only limited *de jure* and *de facto* control. As also previously indicated, the processes of state-building which unfolded in Europe from the eleventh century onwards only led to a progressive construction of – more or less – clearly defined territories and to a high level of physical control over these territories. These processes were characterised by continued bargaining and stabilisation of the relations between the emergent state and a whole range of social structures in the form of the nobility, religious structures, guilds and so forth. Hegel, in *Die Verfassung Deutschlands* (1800–1802), argued that the existence of such privatistic intermediate structures was the central reason why Germany had not transformed itself into a modern state similar to France or the United Kingdom.[34] Thus, according to Hegel, building on Rousseau, the pre-condition for statehood was, as also argued by Dieter Grimm today,[35] a 'pure' relationship between the state and its citizens. From a Hegelian perspective, the modern state has a *single* centralised force of authority, namely, the sovereign people which establish a circular form of self-rule in which the *pouvoir constituant* and the *pouvoir constitué* are interlocked in an immediate fashion within the form of the territorial state.

However, the progressive realisation of this form of statehood only came about through a gradual process which implied that the state gained a distinctive organisational form through the establishment of a functionally delineated and specialised system of political rule and its capability to deploy a unique form of political power characterised by its generalisability and its abstracted detachment from particular individuals. By the mid-nineteenth century, only a handful of modern states covering an extremely small part of the world existed. More importantly, these states were not established through a conscious and clearly identifiable act, but instead emerged in the form of a metamorphosis from *within* the already existing feudal structures.[36] This paves the way for an understanding of modern territorial states as Eigenstructures (*Eigenstrukuturen*), in the sense that their emergence was structurally conditioned by a reliance on the previously existing structures at the same time as they increasingly marginalised these structures over time.[37]

A clear example of this process can be observed in relation to the United Kingdom, a state characterised by a considerable degree of institutional continuity. Even today, the British feudal order remains firmly in place, as illustrated in the form of the continued existence of the monarchy and inherited seats in the upper house. Instead of disappearing, the monarchy and nobility-based feudal order have merely been gradually marginalised, in the sense that the modern-state structures which grew out of this order have progressively drained the feudal structures of their substantial functions without actually eradicating these structures in their entirety. Thus, the state-building process of the United Kingdom is characterised by an evolutionary development in which two fundamentally distinct, but deeply intertwined, logics have co-operated in a hybrid manner for centuries, at the same time as the logic of the modern state has only gradually marginalised the logic guiding the feudal order.

Even in the case of France, a state characterised by stronger and more frequent ruptures than the United Kingdom, and thus a more fundamental elimination of feudal structures, the emergence of a 'strong state' was only realised by the end of the nineteenth and during the early twentieth century. Only at this point in time did the French state obtain effective control over its territory and establish a density of *symbolic power* enabling it *de facto* to re-constitute its subjects within an overall discursive frame in a relatively comprehensive manner.[38] Thus, it was first in this period that the most advanced states achieved a capacity to reconstruct their citizens in their own image through the development of highly intrusive, disciplining and hegemonic 'imagined communities'.[39]

But the argument might even be radicalised to the extent that the realisation of the overarching physical *and* symbolic[40] control over society by the state only came into existence between 1914 and 1918, when the war effort led to a massive dislocation of the boundaries of the state, in the sense that ever more societal spheres became subject to direct state control (e.g. in the form of the regulatory regime of the *Kriegsökonomie* or war economy).[41] Against this background, it is hardly surprising that the welfare state must also be understood as a phenomenon which emerged from the efforts to mobilise resources for warfare during the two world wars.[42] As such, it is not only law,[43] but also modern welfare regimes that have a 'dark legacy' which needs to be confronted.

But even this type of state was a very limited phenomenon. As argued by Chris Thornhill, the (West) German state, for example, did not achieve a capability to deploy its power throughout its territory in an unquestioned and generalised manner before sometime in the mid-twentieth century, after the nobility based form of privatistic ordering had finally collapsed in the wake of National Socialism and the Second World War.[44] In a similar manner, the US Federal Government did not gain unquestioned authority in the Southern states of the USA before sometime in the mid-twentieth century, since, until this point, federal power was continuously challenged by localistic counter-movements. Furthermore, in places such as Southern Italy, South-eastern Turkey and the Basque country similar counter-movements continue to be vibrant today, just as the strong presence of localistic power structures remains the normality in most parts of Africa, Asia and Latin America. Thus, the vast majority of the world has not (yet) been subject to a successful Hegelian codification of society in its entirety by the state. In the vast majority of the world, the state only acts as a thin layer of varnish which serves to 'cover up' very persistent privatistic and localistic forms of 'pre-modern' social ordering operating beneath the state.

Hegels's statement that the 'supreme state' embodies 'God's march through history'[45] only became a historical reality in the first half of the twentieth century within the small segments of world society occupied by North-western Europe and North America. But, more importantly, this state disintegrated at the moment in which it came into being. An extreme form of disintegration emerged through totalitarianism. In contrast to common conceptions, totalitarianism did not imply the totality of the state, but, rather, its dissolution, in the sense that the distinction between the state and other parts of society disappeared and were replaced by highly obscure and arbitrary forms of privatistic power.[46] Totalitarianism implied a forceful combination of a re-emerging form of privatistic feudal-like power and modern organisational capacities.[47]

But also in non-totalitarian settings the unity of the state was increasingly undermined due to the massive and continuing expansion of the state throughout the twentieth century. The constitutional set-up of the state, which became formalised during the American and French Revolutions, was oriented towards states which were extremely limited in terms of organisational size and capacity. However, such states have little in common with the extremely complex organisational conglomerates of present-day administrative welfare- and risk-regulating states.[48] It follows that, in the most modern parts of the world, the size of the state in terms of economic resources, manpower and the amount of policy areas which it regulates are larger than ever before, at the same time that its internal consistency is increasingly strained. The state has mutated into a hyper-complex conglomerate consisting of a whole range of partly reinforcing and partly contradictory dimensions, increasingly making the idea of states as coherent and unitary organisational entities an illusion.[49]

One consequence of this development is that, in the most functionally differentiated parts of world society, the greatest threat to state-based democracy today is not coming from the danger of enemy *panzers* rolling over the borders, the risk of occasional attacks from terrorist networks or the dislocation of political power to transnational structures. Instead, the far more profound challenge to state-based democracy is to be found in the *immanently* unfolding structural transformation of the state itself. The massive increase in the internal complexity (*Eigenkomplexität*) of the state implies an ever-increasing displacement between political and administrative rationality in favour of the latter. Or to express it differently: the real threat to state-based democracy is that the state sinks under its own complexity and that the already existing discrepancy between the functional demand for decision-making and what can be adequately processed through democratic decision-making continue to expand, thereby triggering 'decisional outsourcing' to other forms of decisional structures.[50] Thus, the real danger to democracy is that it turns out be an evolutionary obsolescent model of decision-making which only gained prominence in a societal setting which is characterised by a relatively limited level of social complexity.[51]

But, even in the course of the nineteenth and early twentieth centuries, the state did not merely evolve through a singular expression of the will of the people through elected representatives operating within the form of the state. As already touched upon, the emergence of the modern functionally differentiated society, which included – but was not limited to – the emergence of a specific economic system operating on its own logic,[52] implied the emergence of new forms of social stratification. This was again reflected in the emergence of specifically-modern forms of intermediate structures, in the form of late nineteenth- and early twentieth-century corporatism and post-war neo-corporatism, which served as inter-systemic frameworks of stabilisation between the increasingly differentiated spheres of politics and the economy. Thus, the idea, as advocated by both conservative and progressive approaches alike, that the state and its citizens engage in an immediate fashion is also, in this respect, problematical. The twentieth-century welfare states were instead characterised by very complex and versatile relations where non-state societal forces were either co-opted and integrated into the state or by processes in which the state stabilised its relations with the other parts of society through institutionalised arrangements in the form of (neo-)corporatist negotiation systems (*Verhandlungssysteme*).[53] Even in its most mature form, the state never possessed the power merely to decide and subsequently implement collectively binding decisions through a stringent circular democratic process which only involved the state and its citizens. The state has *always* muddled through upon the basis of more or less formalised co-ordination and bargaining processes with complex conglomerates of private power which operate outside the state. In addition, the state has continuously been 'captured' by special interests, thereby making it an instrument with *de facto* partial and privatistic features.[54] Apart from short moments of evolutionary overshooting under the reign of Robespierre, Pol Pot and consorts, in which the concept of *volonté générale* was taken literally, instead of being understood as an abstract construction developed within the symbolically generalised medium of power,[55] society has never been a political community in its entirety. The modern form of politics remains linked to a specialised and institutionalised system of politics, which reproduces very fundamental – but also quite specific – social functions.

It follows, as we will return to in Chapter 6, that the sort of 'higher order' associated with the nation state cannot be understood as a purely state-based order. Instead, national configurations are far more complex conglomerates which bundle a whole range of dimensions which are mutually oriented vis-à-vis one another.[56] The consequence is that the state has never been the sole source of authority, but has always been a structure which has operated in a social environment characterised by 'co-optation', in the sense that the state continuously have been forced to build alliances with and compete with other societal structures. The role of the Catholic Church in states such as Ireland, Italy, Poland and, until recently, Spain, or the role of the trade unions in France, the persistent presence of the mafia in Southern Italy or the influence of the financial industry in the UK, all serve to illustrate that alternative centres of authority and, therefore, competition for allegiance, has been the rule, rather than the exception.

That the mainstream understanding of the territorially delineated political system as a structure which enjoys a privileged position vis-à-vis other societal structures rests on a simplified understanding of the function and position of the political system in society becomes clearer when one compares the difference in the *internal* composition of different function systems. The relative importance of (self-)reflection, the operations undertaken by a system in order to maintain itself, the prestation (*Leistung*) which a system produces vis-à-vis other partial systems in society, and societal function towards society as a whole, differs from system to system. The consequence is that different function systems produce different forms of effects vis-à-vis their social environments. For example, within the systems of art, intimacy and certain strands of religion and science (*Wissenschaft*) reflection plays a relatively more important role than within other functional systems, due to the porous and very 'fluid' media of communication upon which these systems rely. The consequence is that the forms of communication of which these systems consist tend to emerge as irritations within the most unexpected settings in their social environments. This again creates a tendency within these systems to elevate momentary – but creative – forms of de-differentiation into a systemic imperative (*Systemziel*), in the sense that art systematically seeks to break boundaries just as true love is supposed to defy all restrictions. Moreover, as expressed in the strong reliance on a semantic of subjectivity, experiences (*Lernerfahrungen*) tend to be framed in a personalised 'existentialist' manner within these systems.[57]

For the legal system producing prestations vis-à-vis specific sections of society are the most dominating trademark in that it acts as the social trans-action cost system par excellence. Almost all forms of the operationability of social systems rely upon a legal framing, or, at least, on the potential reference to legal instruments in their internal operations as well as in their reflections of their respective environments. Thus, the legal system provides a sort of specialised 'services' to the remainder of society. The economic system also has a strong focus on prestation towards other partial segments of society. Intimacy and certain forms of religion are probably exceptions which confirm the rule that functional systems cannot operate without relying on a continued flow of economic resources, and thus a very strong reliance on the economic system. But, whereas the legal system, in most cases, merely provides an overall framing and, as such, tends to remain a 'back-up' system which is only activated in cases of profound conflicts, the money medium, in sharp contrasts, enjoys a far more widespread use in everyday life.

In contrast to the legal and economic systems, the political system, in the state form, is characterised by a relatively stronger emphasis on the function that it produces vis-à-vis society in its entirety. When the political system operates in the state form, the strong emphasis on societal function is expressed through its orientation towards the construction of territorial deli-neations and the production of collectively binding decisions. However, the relatively stronger focus on societal function does not provide the political system with any outright superiority. This is, first of all, the case because no hierarchy exists between function, prestation and reflection. The integration of society in its entirety remains conditioned by the simultaneous existence of all three forms within all functional systems. The three dimensions are not related to one another in the style of Russian dolls, in which each one is contained in another. Second, although the tasks which the political systems reproduces are of a very fundamental nature, the relatively higher focus on the reproduction of functions vis-à-vis society as a whole is reflected in an equally strong reduction of the range of tasks which the political system in the form of states deals with.[58] The political system might produce more compact components than systems with a stronger emphasis on reflection, but the price paid is that the reach of political language remains limited, a limitation that subsequently tend to be 'covered up' through the kind of ideological semantics which, on paper, remain oriented towards society in its entirety. The claim that the state is a supreme structure is based upon a peculiar paradox and fundamental indeterminacy, in the sense that the state – at the same time – is assumed to be both distinct from the other segments of society and in control of those other segments of society.

It is against this background that territorial differentiation can, at best, be described as an internal form of stabilisation of the political system, which cannot be extended to other social areas in a one-to-one manner. The legal system, due to its tight coupling to the political system, has also tended to rely on territorial differentiation, but, as we will return to, the massive expansion in the juridification of global processes in recent decades implies that the structurally boundedness of the legal system to territoriality seems to be less profound than is the case for the political system. Other systems, such as those related to art, the economy and science do not follow the logic of territoriality.[59]

In addition, even if states do possess a factual monopoly of the legitimate exercise of physical power, this does not imply an ability on the part of these states to control the logics and structures of expectation which guide other social processes. Artistic evaluations, economic exchanges, religious beliefs and scientific discoveries continue to unfold on their own logics since political power remains fundamentally incapable of defining or controlling the meaning and normative value which these segments of society articulate. Political supremacy only exists in relation to the specific, albeit very fundamental, social functions of political power, such as the legitimate exercise of physical violence and the production of collectively binding decisions. This structural inability can also be observed in relation to the totalitarian regimes of the twentieth century. These regimes did not manage to eradicate the existence of independent sources of meaning (*Sinn*) within the realm of art, science, religion and economy, but merely suppressed these spheres of society and forced them into an underground existence.[60] Another consequence of the structural limitation inherent to modern political power is that the idea of 'radical democracy', if it is understood as an extension of the form of collective decision-making which characterises democratic political systems to all social structures, remains a Fata Morgana. This kind of democratic decision-making remains an institutional form which is intrinsically linked to the particularities of the medium of political power.

As we will return to in detail later, the attempt to reserve the constitutional concept for territorial states and states alone is, therefore, not taking adequate account of the complexity of the societal setting within which states operate. Dieter Grimm, for example, reproduces a narrative of the state as an entity which, at one point, possessed the capability of forging a unity of society in its entirety which falls well behind the insights offered by contemporary sociology concerning the persistent hybridity between modern statehood and pre-modern forms of social ordering, as well as the functional limitation to modern political power.[61] Martin Loughlin offers a more refined statist perspective by arguing that the state provides a comprehensive way of seeing, understanding and acting in the world.[62] The problem with this perspective is, however, that modern statehood is not the only social entity which provides such a comprehensive perspective. One merely has to cast a brief look at the self-understanding of the Roman Catholic Church, or, in fact, any major religious organisation to see this. Moreover, the 'universality' of the state is paradoxically particularistic, in that the state/society distinction and territorial delineations implies that the vast majority of the world remains beyond the reach of any particular state.

Modern states are characterised by a form of 'epistemological self-delusion' which leads them to assume that they offer a comprehensive form of ordering of society in its entirety.[63] That the totality of a state-based world-view remains an illusion, in spite of the reliance on holistic ideological articulations, can be clearly observed in relation to the epistemological framework guiding international law. International law, the form through which states frame their external interactions, was established in the late nineteenth century and provided an understanding of international law as public law on the basis of the idea that world society exclusively consists of states. This epistemological framework subsequently enabled states conceptually to ignore the fact that, from the very beginning, transnational ordering was just as much a private law phenomenon as a public law phenomenon,[64] at the same time as the real existing intersections with private ordering were continually accommodated through pragmatic ad hoc solutions which enabled the maintenance of the illusion of transnational ordering as being an exclusively public law phenomenon.[65]

2.5 The co-evolution of statehood and transnational ordering

The argument presented above addresses the weak sociological foundations of the concept of the state, from which state-centric perspectives on constitutional ordering depart. But the understanding of the state as a limited form of social ordering does *not* imply that a weakening of statehood is taking place. Essentially, all contemporary approaches to constitutionalism in the global realm explicitly or implicitly depart from the assumption that a weakening of statehood can be observed, and that this development is one of the primary reasons for the emergence of constitutionalism beyond the state.[66] But this perspective also reflects, in several ways, a crude and simplified understanding of statehood. From a purely numerical perspective, the number of states has continued to expand rapidly throughout the last two centuries, and, in particular, throughout the last 50 years. Furthermore, in terms of its reach, the phenomenon of statehood has only gained global status very recently, namely, in the wake of the de-colonisation processes of the mid-twentieth century.[67] Thus, when observed from a long-term historical perspective, an unprecedented quantitative expansion in statehood has taken place in recent historical times. But qualitatively statehood has also kept expanding. If one characterises a 'strong state' as a form of limited statehood which is based upon a formal as well as an operational distinction between the state and other segments of society, a fairly stable institutional set-up and an extensive, although not necessarily exclusive, capability to deploy political power in a generalised manner, then it is possible to argue that a larger part of the planet is characterised by strong statehood today than in any previous historical period.[68] Thus, statehood is, at the same time, a far more limited social phenomenon than is commonly assumed by state-centrist approaches and far more vibrant than has been assumed within the globalisation discourse of the last two decades.

Within the globalisation discourse, statehood and transnational ordering are typically conceived of as being characterised by a zero-sum relationship, in which more of one implies less of the other. A historical view, however, reveals that statehood and extensive forms of transnational ordering emerged hand in hand, and that the two forms of ordering are, in fact, mutually constitutive. As already indicated, an intimate relationship exists between statehood and transnational forms of ordering. From England and the Netherlands in early modernity, to the United States today, all mature states have been structurally linked to dense forms of transnational ordering either through colonialism, or, as is the case today, through their embeddedness in dense and increasingly global governance networks.

From the outset, colonialism was, to a large extent, organised around chartered private companies, which, over time, became rulers of vast territories, possessing their own armed forces, legal systems and bureaucratic structures. Not surprisingly, the emergence of colonialism was, therefore, intrinsically linked to the emergence of a dense vocabulary of private rights in relation to property, contract and exchange, not only enabling a justification and stabilisation of the privately based colonial expansion, but also laying the foundational framework for the unfolding of increasingly globalised social processes until this day.[69]

A second phase emerged with the increased state-centredness of colonialism from the mid-nineteenth century onwards, in which the states increasingly took direct control over the colonial territories. This phase was, however, rather short in that it only unfolded from the mid-nineteenth to the mid-twentieth century. Moreover, both phases of colonialism were characterised by a strong transnationally operating 'civil society' in the form of, for example, church organisations and anti-slavery organisations, thereby making it into something that was far more than a purely economic phenomenon.

The decolonisation processes of the mid-twentieth century triggered a third transformation in transnational ordering characterised by an exponential expansion of public and private transnational entities. This move came about through a contracted process. As noted, the first public international organisation the *Commission Centrale pour la Navigation du Rhin* was established in 1831 and followed by the International Telegraph Union (now the International Telecommunication Union) in 1865 and the General Postal Union (now the Universal Postal Union) in 1874.[70] A similar trend can be observed in relation to private international organisations. The International Committee of the Red Cross was established in 1863, and the first private international intellectual property organisation, the *Association Littéraire et Artistique Internationale*, in 1878. From this slow start, the number of transnational sites of ordering have, especially throughout the last 60 years, rapidly mutated through the establishment of functionally delineated public organisations such as the International Monetary Fund (IMF), the World Bank (WB), the World Health Organization (WHO) and the World Trade Organization (WTO), hybrid public/private organisations such as the International Organization for

Standardization (ISO) and the Internet Corporation for Assigned Names and Numbers (ICANN) as well as a vast host of purely private organisations in the form of trade associations and non-governmental organisations. Today, as also noted, some 250 public and around 40,000 private international organisations exist, to which one can further add multinational firms and globally operating law firms.

The protracted expansion of both statehood and transnational sites of ordering took place simultaneously, thereby indicating that the two forms of social ordering are structurally linked. As we will return to in detail in the following chapter, this structural boundedness can be traced back to the different societal functions which they reproduce within world society at large. For the present, the insight suffices that a dual movement can be observed through a *simultaneous* expansion and globalisation of statehood, and a conversion of transnational forms of ordering away from a reliance on the centre/periphery differentiation in the colonial form and towards an increased reliance on functional differentiation.

It follows that the vibrant debate on 'global and multi-level governance'[71] needs, from a historical perspective, to be seen as intrinsically linked to the former version of colonial transnational ordering. In the same manner in which modern statehood grew out of the preceding feudal orders, contemporary global-governance structures grew out of the colonial form of ordering. For example, one of the core functions of the League of Nations was to administrate mandated territories, the former German colonies and parts of the former Ottoman Empire, at the same time that these territories were *de facto* included in the colonial possessions of the First World War allies. Furthermore, the United Nations furthermore had de-colonisation as one of its central – and, to this day, most accomplished – objectives. Even the emergence of the European Union as a regional form of transnational ordering needs to be understood against this background, to the extent that the European integration process was a direct response to Germany's failed attempt to establish an empire *and* the implosion of the actually existing empires of France and the United Kingdom. This is most evident not only in relation to the Common Market, which served as a substitute for the loss of 'market access' in the former colonies, a central motive for Britain to seek inclusion in the European integration process,[72] but also goes beyond purely economic concerns in so far as similar developments can be observed in relation to the increased integration within areas such as science and technology, and environmental and foreign policy. In a deeper structural sense, the emergence of the European Union and its preceding institutions are, therefore, to be understood as a reaction to the implosion of Europe's global hegemony, with common European policies serving as instruments aimed at offsetting the continued reduction in the global standing of the major European states. Thus, it might be argued that the central driving-force of the integration process is not the striving for French/German reconciliation or other internal European issues, but the structural re-configuration of the relations between Europe and the rest of the world.[73]

The insight that contemporary forms of transnational ordering emerged from within the colonial form of transnational ordering and the fact that they continue to rely upon institutional forms originally developed in a European context, serve as the basis for the argument that contemporary transnational structures are nothing more than substitutes of colonialism.[74] From a structural perspective, these structures can, indeed, be understood as 'functional equivalents' in that one form of ordering replaced another, and since both, as we will return to, share a common function vis-à-vis world society in its entirety, since they serve as transfer structures between different contexts. This perspective is also reinforced by the observation that contemporary transnational structures remain characterised by the centre/periphery dimension, as expressed in the often used (but geographically rather imprecise) North/South distinction. However, two major differences between the previous colonial regimes and contemporary transnational structures do minimise (without completely eradicating) the strong, asymmetric power relations that are inherent in any kind of centre/periphery differentiation. First, since the European space – and, with it, Europe's global hegemony – imploded in the first half of the twentieth century, it has been possible to observe a slow, but progressive, expansion of the parts of the globe which belong to the centre. For example, whereas the General Agreement on Tariffs and Trade (GATT) was a hegemonic American enterprise, the World Trade Organization (WTO) became a bipolar structure with the United States and the EU in the defining roles. Moreover, the drawn-out battle over the World Trade Organization's DOHA Development Agenda reflects a gradual, but very fundamental, move towards a multi-polar order, in which China in particular, but also countries such as Brazil, Russia and India (BRIC), are increasingly becoming central players. As noted, a similar development can be observed in relation to the G8, which has recently been replaced by the G20 as the central mechanism of co-ordination between the leading states. Second, the normative values and the sort of justifications produced are fundamentally different within colonialism and contemporary forms of transnational ordering. Third, at a more profound structural level, it is possible to observe that the centre/periphery differentiation has been increasingly re-configured away from an overarching form of social differentiation which is constitutive for world society in its entirety, towards an internal form of stabilisation deployed *within* globally operating functional delineated regimes. For example, within higher education, a global cognitive space has been constituted through the emergence of increasingly dense global standards which the majority of the world's higher-education institutions seek to aspire to at the same time as the US Ivy League and the UK 'Oxbridge', to a high degree, define these standards, thereby introducing highly asymmetric relations between the centre and the periphery.[75] Similar asymmetric relations can be observed within global finance in which the City of London and Wall Street continue to set the standards for other segments of the global financial system. Such centres, adhering to different functional segments of world society, tend to be structurally linked and engage in mutually reinforcing exchanges, as, for example, can be observed through the recruitment of graduates from the top universities by the financial industry, and by the endowments provided by the industry and its employees to these universities. Such links provide the case for an understanding of these inter-linkages as constituting hegemonic power structures. But, at the same time, they remain separate social processes which fulfil different societal functions. Furthermore, high degrees of coalescence and de-differentiation tend to undermine the integrity and long-term vibrancy of the social entities in question, thereby providing a *functional need* for the development of internal constitutional frameworks within different segments of world society. Frameworks which are capable of simultaneously separating and re-connecting different spheres in a manner which allows for a limited transfer of condensed social components between these spheres, without this leading to a mutual degeneration of the spheres in question. As we will return to in Chapter 6, moves towards de-differentiation tends to lead to self-destruction in the long run, thereby indicating the limited long-term viability of hegemonic enterprises.[76]

To sum up, also in relation to the centre/periphery differentiation, widespread indeterminacy can be observed since a move towards a reduction in the centre/periphery differentiation as an *overall* form of transnational ordering can be detected at the same time as new interconnected forms of the centre/periphery differentiation has emerged within functionally delineated processes with a global reach.

2.6 Conclusion

One core argument which has been pursued in this chapter is that the implosion of the Eurocentric form of global ordering is the central structural change with which ongoing debates on globalisation and constitutional transformation are dealing. This implosion is furthermore to be understood as a consequence of a protracted, but nonetheless countervailed, drive towards an increased reliance on functional differentiation as the central principle of social organisation throughout world society. In concrete, the implosion of Eurocentrism has manifested itself through an intertwined and mutually constitutive double movement. First, the expansion and increased globalisation of modern statehood, understood as a limited form of social ordering which refers to the reproduction of a restricted number of social functions which are stabilised through reliance on territorial differentiation. The upholding of this form of statehood is furthermore conditioned by the maintenance of a formal, as well as operational, distinction between the state and the rest of society. Second, an increased re-configuration of transnational processes away from a reliance on the centre/periphery differentiation, as was known from the period of colonialism, and towards an increased reliance on functional differentiation, at the same time as new forms of the centre/periphery differentiation have emerged within increasingly globalised functionally delineated social processes.

Notes

1 Norbert Elias, *Über den Prozeß der Zivilisation. Band 2: Wandlungen der Gesellschaft. Entwurf zu einer Theorie der Zivilisation*, Frankfurt am Main: Suhrkamp Verlag, [1939] 1997.

2 Niklas Luhmann, *Macht*, Stuttgart: Enke Verlag, 1975; Chris Thornhill, 'Towards a Historical Sociology of Constitutional Legitimacy', *Theory and Society*, 2008, 37, pp. 161–97.

3 Georg W.F. Hegel, *Grundlinien der Philosophie des Rechts oder Naturrecht und Staatswissenschaft im Grundrisse, Werke Band 7*, Frankfurt am Main: Suhrkamp Verlag, [1821] 1970.

4 Michael Roberts, *The Military Revolution, 1560–1660*, Belfast: Boyd, 1956; Charles Tilly, *Coercion, Capital, and European States*, AD 990–1990, Oxford: Blackwell Publishing, 1990; Jeremy Black, *A Military Revolution? Military Change and European Society, 1550–1800*, Basingstoke: Macmillan, 1991.

5 Hauke Brunkhorst, 'Machbarkeitsillusionen, feierliche Erklärungen und Gesänge: Zum Verhältnis von Evolution und Revolution im Recht', in Gralf-Peter Calliess, Andreas Fischer-Lescano, Dan Wielsch and Peer Zumbansen (eds), *Soziologische Jurisprudenz: Festschrift für Gunther Teubner zum 65. Geburtstag am 30. April 2009*, Berlin: Walter de Gruyter, 2009, pp. 447–64.

6 Norbert Elias, *Die höfische Gesellschaft*, Frankfurt am Main: Suhrkamp Verlag, [1969] 2002. For the concept of transfer of social components, see Rudolf Stichweh, 'Transfer in Sozialsystemen: Theoretische Überlegungen'. Paper, 12, 2005. Available at: www.unilu.ch/deu/prof._dr._rudolf_stichwehpublikationen_38043.html.

7 Chris Thornhill has launched a radical counter-perspective to the inter-configurative perspective with the argument that the evolution of modern political power is to be understood as purely internalistic process in which the drive towards the separation of public and private power at the same time was the central driving-force and result of European state-building processes. However, in his analysis of the breakdown of the public/private distinction in large parts of Europe in the interwar period, he concedes that the effects produced by the First World War, and thus inter-state competition, provided the structural setting within which the breakdown unfolded. For this perspective, see Chris Thornhill, *A Sociology of Constitutions: Constitutions and State Legitimacy in Historical-Sociological Perspective*, Cambridge: Cambridge University Press, 2011, p. 275 *et seq*. The tension between internal and external perspectives on state-building processes points to the need to develop a 'two-dimensional theory' capable of taking adequate account of endogenous as well as exogenous factors, and, in particular, the intertwinedness between the two dimensions. For theoretical reflections on this issue, see, also, Poul F. Kjaer: 'Systems in Context: On the Outcome of the Habermas/Luhmann Ddebate', *Ancilla Iuris*, 2006, September, pp. 66–77; Poul F. Kjaer, 'Law of the Worlds – Towards an Inter-Systemic Theory', in Stefan Keller and Stefan Wipraechtiger (eds), *Recht zwischen Dogmatik und Theorie: Marc Amstutz zum 50. Geburtstag*, Zurich: Dike Verlag, 2012, pp. 159–75.

8 Niklas Luhmann, 'Europa als Problem der Weltgesellschaft', *Berliner Debatte*, 1994, 2, pp. 3–7.

9 James Tully, 'The Imperialism of Modern Constitutional Democracy', in Martin Loughlin and Neil Walker (eds), *The Paradox of Constitutionalism: Constituent Power and Constitutional Form*, Oxford: Oxford University Press, 2007, pp. 315–38.

10 Martti Koskenniemi, *The Gentle Civilizer of Nations: The Rise and Fall of International Law 1870–1960*, Cambridge: Cambridge University Press, 2001, p. 121 *et seq*.

11 Carl Schmitt argues that the existence of independent states in the Americas from the late eighteenth century onwards was treated as a legal anomaly by the European powers, which could be conceptually confined as long as the United States maintained its self-declared intention not to question European hegemony outside the Americas. As long as that was the case the United States, and the other independent states in the Americas, did not fulfil a constitutive role in relation to the maintenance of global order. See Carl Schmitt, *Der Nomos der Erde: Im Völkerrecht des Jus Publicum Europaeum*, Berlin: Duncker & Humblot, 1950.

12 Schmitt, *Der Nomos der Erde*, p. 200 *et seq.*

13 Russia lost its status as a European power in the wake of the Bolshevik takeover in 1917. The confinement of communist rule to the Soviet Union during the interwar period enabled the leading European states to treat it as yet another anomaly which did not question the European world order. One particularly clear consequence of the exclusion of the Soviet Union from the European order was Nazi Germany's decision that the constraints provided by international law should not be applied on the Eastern front during the Second World War, constraints which formally, but, of course, not in practice, were maintained on the Western front. Nazi Germany's treatment of the Soviet Union as a 'non-civilised nation' meant that it was considered as being on equal footing with the non-European parts of the world which had been the object European colonisation throughout the preceding centuries.

14 For the relationship between the 2008 financial crisis and ongoing global transformations see Poul F. Kjaer, 'Law and Order within and Beyond National Configurations', in Poul F. Kjaer, Gunther Teubner and Alberto Febbrajo (eds), *The Financial Crisis in Constitutional Perspective: The Dark Side of Functional Differentiation*, Oxford: Hart Publishing, 2011, pp. 395–430, at 413 *et seq.*

15 In the G20 configuration, Africa is the only continent which is severely under-represented, in that South Africa is its only member.

16 For example, Immanuel Kant, *Zum ewigen Frieden*, Hamburg: Felix Meiner Verlag, [1795], 1992.

17 Hauke Brunkhorst, 'Constitutionalism and Democracy in the World Society', in Petra Dobner and Martin Loughlin (eds), *The Twilight of Constitutionalism?*, Oxford: Oxford University Press, 2010, pp. 179–98, at 185. See, also, Hauke Brunkhorst, *Solidarität: Von der Bürgerfreundschaft zur globalen Rechtsgenossenschaft*, Frankfurt am Main: Suhrkamp Verlag, 2002, p. 146 *et seq.*

18 Niklas Luhmann, *Politik der Gesellschaft*, Frankfurt am Main: Suhrkamp Verlag, 2000.

19 Rudolf Stichweh, 'The History and Systematics of Functional Differentiation in Sociology', Paper 02/2012. Available at: http://www.unilu.ch/deu/prof._dr._rudolf_stichwehpublikationen_38043.html.

20 For an attempt to link international relations theory to theories of differentiation see Barry Buzan and Mathias Albert, 'Differentiation: A Sociological Approach to International Relations Theory', *European Journal of International Relations*, 2010, 16, 3, pp. 315 – 337.

21 Niklas Luhmann, *Die Gesellschaft der Gesellschaft*, Frankfurt am Main: Suhrkamp Verlag, 1997, p. 743 *et seq.*

22 For the classical works, see Georg W.F. Hegel, *Grundlinien der Philosophie des Rechts. Oder Naturrecht und Staatswissenschaft im Grundrisse. Werke Band 7*, Frankfurt am Main: Suhrkamp Verlag, [1821] 1970; Émile Durkheim, *De la division du travail social*, Paris: Presses universitaires de France, [1893] 1973; Georg Simmel, 'Über sociale Differenzierung. Sociologische und psychologische Untersuchungen', in Georg Simmel, *Aufsätze 1887–1890*, Frankfurt am Main: Suhrkamp Verlag, [1890] 1989; Talcott Parsons, *The System of Modern Societies*, Englewood, NJ: Prentice-Hall, 1971; Luhmann, *Die Gesellschaft der Gesellschaft*, p. 595 et seq.

23 Georg W.F. Hegel, *Grundlinien der Philosophie des Rechts*, Frankfurt am Main: Suhrkamp Verlag, [1821] 1970.

24 Pierre Bourdieu, *La Distinction. Critique sociale du jugement*, Paris: Les Editions de Minuit, 1979.

25 Niklas Luhmann, *Soziale Systeme. Grundriß einer allgemeinen Theorie*, Frankfurt am Main: Suhrkamp Verlag, 1984.

26 Rudolf Stichweh and Paul Windolf (eds), *Inklusion und Exklusion. Analysen zur Sozialstruktur und sozialen Ungleichheit*, Wiesbaden: VS Verlag für Sozialwissenschaften, 2009.

27 Ralf Dahrendorf, *Soziale Klassen und Klassenkonflikt in der industriellen Gesellschaft*, Stuttgart: Ferdinand Enke Verlag, 1957.

28 Christian Borch, *The Politics of Crowds: An Alternative History of Sociology*, Cambridge: Cambridge University Press, 2012.

29 In the work of John Rawls, one, for example, finds the assumption of the existence of a 'well-ordered' society in the state form. See John Rawls, *A Theory of Justice*, Oxford: Oxford University Press, 1972, p. 54 *et seq.*

30 For explorations of the changed status of the state in society, see the contributions in Stephan Leibfried and Michael Zürn (eds), *Transformations of the State?* Cambridge: Cambridge University Press, 2005.

31 For a brilliant reconstruction of the historical origins of this assumption, see Ulrich K. Preuß, 'Disconnecting Constitutions from Statehood: Is Global Constitutionalism a Viable Concept?', in Petra Dobner and Martin Loughlin (eds), *The Twilight of Constitutionalism?* Oxford: Oxford University Press, 2010, pp 23–46.

32 Peer Zumbansen, 'Law and Legal Pluralism: Hybridity in Transnational Governance', in Paulius Jurčys, Poul F. Kjaer and Ren Yurakami, *Regulatory Hybridization in the Transnational Sphere*, Leiden: Brill Publishing, 2013, pp. 49–70.

33 Richard Garnett, 'The Freedom of the Church', *Journal of Catholic Social Thought*, 2007, 4, pp 59–86.

34 Georg W.F. Hegel, *Die Verfassung Deutschlands, Werke 1*, Frankfurt am Main: Suhrkamp Verlag, [1800–802] 1971.

35 Dieter Grimm, 'The Constitution in the Process of Denationalization', *Constellations*, 2005, 12, pp. 447–63.

36 Niklas Luhmann, 'Verfassung als evolutionäre Errungenschaft', *Rechtshistorisches Journal*, 1990, 9, pp. 176–220.

37 Rudolf Stichweh, 'Strukturbildung in der Weltgesellschaft – Die Eigenstrukturen der Weltgesellschaft und die Regionalkulturen der Welt', in Thomas Schwinn (ed.), *Die Vielfalt und Einheit der Moderne*, Wiesbaden: Verlag für Sozialwissenschaften, 2006, pp. 239–57.

38 Eugen Weber, *Peasants into Frenchmen: The Modernization of Rural France, 1870–1914*, Stanford CA: Stanford University Press, 1976.

39 Benedict Anderson, *Imagined Communities: Reflections on the Origin and Spread of Nationalism*, London: Verso [1983], 2006.

40 Pierre Bourdieu, 'Rethinking the State: Genesis and Structure of the Bureaucratic Field', *Sociological Theory*, 1994, 12, pp. 1–18.

41 Chris Thornhill, 'The Future of the State', in Poul F. Kjaer, Gunther Teubner and Alberto Febbrajo (eds), *The Financial Crisis in Constitutional Perspective: The Dark Side of Functional Differentiation*, Oxford: Hart Publishing, 2011, pp. 357–93, at 369 *et seq.*

42 Bruce D. Porter, *War and the Rise of the State. The Military Foundations of Modern Politics*, New York, N.J.: The Free Press, 1994, p. 149 et seq.

43 Christian Joerges and Navraj Singh Ghaleigh (eds), *Darker Legacies of Law in Europe: The Shadow of National Socialism and Fascism over Europe and its Legal Traditions*, Oxford: Hart Publishing, 2003.

44 Chris Thornhill, *A Sociology of Constitutions. Constitutions and State Legitimacy in Historical-Sociological Perspective*, Cambridge: Cambridge University Press, 2011, p. 335 et seq.

45 Georg W.F. Hegel, *Grundlinien der Philosophie des Rechts*, Frankfurt am Main: Suhrkamp Verlag, [1821] 1970, § 256.

46 Franz L. Neumann, *Behemoth: The Structure and Practice of National Socialism 1933–1944*, Washington, DC: Octagon, [1944]1983, p. 467 *et seq.* This argument is, moreover, supported by the insight that totalitarianism was successful in areas such as Germany, Italy and Spain, where the state was weak and pre-modern structures still maintained substantial societal standing. See, also, Chris Thornhill, 'Towards a Historical Sociology of Constitutional Legitimacy', *Theory and Society*, 2008, 37, pp. 161–97.

47 Zygmunt Baumann, *Modernity and Holocaust*, Cambridge: Polity Press, 1989.

48 Edward L. Rubin, 'Getting Past Democracy', *University of Pennsylvania Law Review*, 2001, 149, pp. 711–92.

49 Anne-Marie Slaughter, *A New World Order*, Princeton, NJ: Princeton University Press, 2004, p. 12 *et seq.*

50 The is particular visible in relation to the European Union, where decision-making is, to a large extent, outsourced to different forms of governance structures, in the form of regulatory agencies, Comitology and the Open Method of Co-ordination processes (OMC). See, also, Poul F. Kjaer, *Between Governing and Governance: On the Emergence, Function and Form of Europe's Post-national Constellation*, Oxford: Hart Publishing, 2010, p. 46 *et seq.*

51 Niklas Luhmann, *Rechtssoziologie. 2 Bände*, Opladen: Westdeutscher Verlag [1972], 1983, p. 339 *et seq.*

52 For the differentiation of the economic system from the rest of society, see Karl Polanyi, *The Great Transformation: The Political and Economic Origins of our Time*, Boston, MA: Beacon Press, [1944] 2001.

53 Helmut Wilke, *Ironie des Staates*, Frankfurt am Main: Suhrkamp Verlag, 1992.

54 Pierre Bourdieu, *La Noblesse d'état: grandes écoles et esprit de corps*, Paris: Minuit, 1989.

55 Luhmann, *Politik der Gesellschaft*, p. 18 *et seq.*

56 Kjaer, 'Law and Order within and beyond National Configurations', at 408 *et seq.*

57 The strong existentialist dimension within art and love means that one might also understand their system-imperatives as 'fantasies' of self-transcendence.

58 Thornhill, 'Towards a Historical Sociology of Constitutional Legitimacy'.

59 For these systems, the external constraints of law and politics might, however, lead to an increase in the transaction costs of cross-border social exchanges when compared to domestic exchanges, and thus to an increase in their orientation towards domestic solutions.

60 Gunther Teubner, *Constitutional Fragments: Societal Constitutionalism and Globalization*, Oxford, Oxford University Press, 2012, p. 21 *et seq.*

61 Dieter Grimm, 'The Constitution in the Process of Denationalization', *Constellations*, 2005, 12, pp. 447–63.

62 Martin Loughlin, 'In defence of Staatslehre', *Der Staat*, 2009, 48, 1, pp. 1–28.

63 One, however, has to acknowledge that such self-delusions are real-world phenomena which have an independent impact on society, just as they can be incredibly forceful, as is testified by the extreme vibrancy of holistic political ideologies such as Islamism, nationalism, socialism and the ecology movements throughout modernity.

64 Martti Koskenniemi, 'Empire and International Law: The Real Spanish Contribution', *University of Toronto Law Journal*, 2011, 61, pp. 1–36. More generally concerning the structure of international law: Martti Koskenniemi, *From Apology to Utopia: The Structure of International Legal Argument*, Cambridge: Cambridge University Press, [1989] 2005.

65 Jan Klabbers, 'Of Round Pegs and Square Holes: International Law and the Private Sector', in Paulius Jurčys, Poul F. Kjaer and Ren Yurakami (eds), *Regulatory Hybridization in the Transnational Sphere*, Leiden: Brill Publishing, 2013, pp. 29–48.

66 For an illustrative example, see Jan Klabbers, Anne Peters and Geir Ulfstein, *The Constitutionalization of International Law*, Oxford: Oxford University Press, 2009.

67 Rudolf Stichweh, 'Dimensionen der Weltstaat im System der Weltpolitk', in Mathias Albert and Rudolf Stichweh (eds), *Weltstaat und Weltstaatlichkeit: Beobachtungen globaler politischer Strukturbildung*, Wiesbaden: Verlag für Sozialwissenschaften, 2007, pp. 25–36, at 26 *et seq.*

68 Poul F. Kjaer, 'The Concept of the Political in the Concept of Transnational Constitutionalism', in Christian Joerges (ed.) in co-operation with Tommi Ralli, *After Globalization: New Patterns of Conflict and their Sociological and Legal Re-construction*, Oslo: Arena, 2011, pp. 285–321.

69 Martti Koskenniemi, 'Empire and International Law: The Real Spanish Contribution', *University of Toronto Law Journal*, 2011, 61, pp. 1–36.

70 Christian Walter, 'Constitutionalizing (Inter)national Governance: Possibilities for and Limits to the Development of an International Constitutional Law', *German Yearbook of International Law*, 2001, 44, p. 176.

71 For an overview over the ever-expanding literature, see Henrik Enderlein, Sonja Walti and Michael Zürn (eds), *Handbook on Multi-level Governance*, Cheltenham: Edward Elgar Publishing, 2011.

72 Alan S. Milward, *The European Rescue of the Nation-State*, London: Routledge, 1999, p. 345 *et seq.*

73 Luhmann, 'Europa als Problem der Weltgesellschaft'.

74 For example, James Tully, 'The Imperialism of Modern Constitutional Democracy,' in Neil Walker and Martin Loughlin (eds), *The Paradox of Constitutionalism: Constituent Power and Constitutional Form*, Oxford: Oxford University Press, 2007, pp 315–38.

75 Rudolf Stichweh, 'Centre and Periphery in a Global University System'. Paper [08/2009]. Available at: www.unilu.ch/deu/prof._dr._rudolf_stichwehpublikationen_38043.html.

76 See Kjaer, 'Law and Order Within and Beyond National Configurations'.

3 The multiplicity of normative orders in world society

3.1 Introduction

Only one society exists and that is world society, in that the ultimate horizon of all humans today is the world as such and not a confined segment of this world. One of many consequences following from this insight is that states cannot be understood as overarching and closed entities. When viewed from a world-society perspective, states instead appear as particularistic entities which are located within a far broader societal terrain. But, although the category of states is too narrow and therefore cannot serve as the ultimate unit of analysis for law and the social sciences, the concept of world society remains too broad and under-determined. As an alternative, the concept of normative orders is introduced. A normative order is defined as a social structure that is self-sufficient in so far as it reproduces independent sources of meaning (*Sinn*), which enable it to constitute a comprehensive and condensed universe through the integration of functions and norms over time, thereby providing a framework through which an unknown future can be addressed. In practice, the concept of normative orders serves as a meso-level concept, capable of including social structures as different as organisations, regimes, ethnic and religious communities and states. A further advantage of the concept of normative orders is that it, in contrast to the system-theoretical world-society perspective, enables a dynamic understanding of the relationship between cognitive and normative structures of expectations as a relation of mutual increase in which more of one implies more of the other. Finally, the existence of multiple normative orders in world society means that exchanges, in terms of collisions and transfers, between normative orders become a central focus point. Governance structures, defined as frameworks of transfer located in between normative orders which are characterised by legal and organisational heterarchies, are identified as the institutional form aimed at stabilising such exchanges.

3.2 The concept of world society

As early as in 1971, Niklas Luhmann introduced the concept of world society, thereby foregoing contemporary globalisation debates by several decades.[1] The idea of world society implies a co-extensiveness of the world with a singular society, meaning that only one society exists in the world. One of many implications of this perspective is that states are considered to be sub-divisions of the global political system and the global legal system, and not closed units which constitute societies through a framing and control of non-political and non-legal communication within a given territory. The concept of world society is therefore explicitly linked to the already developed idea that the political and legal systems do not possess a privileged position vis-à-vis other segments of society such as the economy, religion or the sphere of art.

In terms of historical origin, the early Luhmann advanced the thesis that the realisation of world society is a relatively new phenomenon which has emerged through a progressive merger of the horizons which individuals operate within, thereby leading to a convergence of expectations. In world society, an individual who is transplanted from one part of the world to another will find most of the things he or she encounters to be similar or, at least, recognisable when compared to the experiences gained in the original context.[2] To the extent that society is understood as consisting of communication rather than human beings, a perspective advanced by the late works of Luhmann, then one can also understand world society as existing if all communications existing in a given moment are, in principle, capable of linking up with all other communications unfolded in the same moment.[3] This possibility for worldwide communication has been and continues to be radically increased through the gradual expansion of the reach and speed of information technology from Gutenberg to the Internet. In practice, the realisation of world society is therefore closely linked to the historical evolution outlined in the previous chapter, involving a gradual move towards a globalisation of specifically modern societal logics that originally emerged in the European context and which, in a modified form, have been transplanted to the rest of the world, thereby leading to the establishment of a global configurative process.

The concept of world society provides a useful overall framework for a theory of constitutionalism in the global realm in that it highlights the universal character of the world. In particular, the concept undermines the central claim of holistic perspectives on constitutionalism. This is the case because, when departing from the world as such, states must also be understood as particularistic entities which rely upon extensive exclusion mechanisms. From a world-society perspective, a given state only encompasses a small and very selective segment of the world. This perspective is being further amplified by the insight that the horizon of a state is, in fact, not delineated along territorial lines, but, instead, along the lines of a legally constructed multitude which consists of the agglomeration of individuals upon which the state in question has conferred a special status through the social role of a citizen. Thus, the borders of states are borders of meaning (*Sinngrenzen*) and not geographical borders even though these borders are symbolically manifested through geographical references.[4] The illegal immigrant living within the territory of a given state remains outside the horizon of the state, just as widespread migration typically implies the *de facto* existence of parallel communities thereby factually undermining the claim to comprehensiveness along territorial boundaries enshrined in classical constitutional semantics. The concept of world society can thus be understood as a way to challenge the 'methodological nationalism'[5] which not only classical constitutional theory but also normative legal and political theory more generally – as well as the majority of empirical social research – tend to depart from, since it undermines the ontological assumption concerning the existence of a polity, in the nation-state form, and the idea that only the state can serve as the basic unit of study for the social sciences and law. But, at the same time, the concept of world society provides an insufficient point of departure for reasons we will turn to in the following three sections.

3.3 The re-configuration of cognitive and normative expectations

A key insight which Luhmann derives from the concept of world society is that the progressively more globalised structures of world society are characterised by an increased reliance on cognitive based structures of expectations, understood as expectations which are subject to revision in cases of disappointment, and a concordant reduction in the reliance on normative-based structures of expectations, understood as expectations which are upheld in spite of disappointment.[6] This dislocation is seen as linked to a relative increase in the centrality – within world society – of social processes with a strong cognitive component, such as those related to science, technology and the economy, and a concordant relative decline in the relevance of social processes with a strong normative component, such as those related to morality, politics, religion and law in the global realm.[7]

This perspective is both too limited and goes too far at the same time. It is too limited because, instead of a decline in the relevance of moral, legal and political forms of communication, it is possible to observe a fundamental transformation in the core fabric of law and the political, since law and the political themselves are increasing their reliance on cognitive structures of expectations. From the Open Method of Co-ordination (OMC) to Corporate Social Responsibility (CSR) measures and science-based risk regulation, it is possible to observe the emergence of novel forms of political and legal regulation with a strong cognitive component at the transnational level of world society. This development is not, of course, limited to the transnational segment, but is, instead, a far more profound development which can also be observed at the nation-state level of world society.[8] But, as we will return to in detail the following two chapters, due to the strong reliance on functional differentiation at the transnational level of world society, rather than the kind of territorial differentiation which remains a strong feature at nation-state level, inclusion/exclusion processes unfold in a far more dynamic manner at the transnational level, thereby leading to systematic uncertainty concerning who is included and who is excluded. Thus, the structural pressure for far more flexible frameworks and for a move towards an increased reliance upon cognitive-based frameworks is particularly strong in relation to transnational structures.

The system-theoretical perspective on the relationship between cognitive and normative expectations is, however, not only problematical due its prediction of a reduction in the relevance of legal and political communication, at the same time as it assumes that the very nature of law and the political remains unchanged. It is also too limited because it frames the relationship between cognitive and normative structures of expectations as a zero-sum game. From the perspective of logics, the two sides of the distinction are *mutually constitutive* since the existence of one of the two dimensions is logically conditioned by the existence of the other.[9] But also in terms of their historical development both cognitive and normative expectations are the product of co-evolutionary developments in which the increased vibrancy of one dimension is conditioned by the increased vibrancy of the other dimension. Rather than a reduction in normative-based communication, a re-configuration can be observed, which implies an increased cognitivisation at the operational level, that is to say, at the level of tactics rather than at the level of strategy, at the level of method rather than at the level of theory, at the level of policy rather than at the level of politics, at the same time as normative-based communication increasingly assumes a strategic role.

For instance, the social phenomenon of morality, one of the prime examples of normatively based communication, has undergone a massive transformation in the wake of increased functional differentiation. It has pulled back and ceded its role as the initiator and medium of the 'community terror of village life' ('*Gemeinschaftsterror des dörflichen Zusammenlebens*'),[10] and become a far more reflexive form of communication. In its most modern form, morality merely fulfils an alarm function, reproduced along the boundaries of social systems which are activated in two instances. The first instance is related to integrity preservation: when a social system sees itself as being the victim of the asymmetries, crowding-out effects and colonising tendencies which emerge from its environment in the form of, for example, doping, corruption, prostitution or pollution, which threatens the coherency of the system. In such cases, modern forms of moral communication fulfil the function of awareness-raising which is aimed at countering processes of coalescence and boundary dissolution which are the central trademarks of crises in modernity.[11] The second instance is specific to function systems and is expansionist in nature: within function systems, in contrast to organisation and interaction systems, logics of 'complete inclusion' (*Vollinklusion*), which are characterised by a striving towards a coupling of all human beings with specific social roles (producing or audience roles) that correspond to the system in question, can be observed.[12] Missionary religions seek to convert all human beings worldwide into believers, the capitalist economy seeks to transform all humans into producers and consumers, and the global human-rights agenda is oriented towards a formal as well as factual inclusion of all humans under the human-rights umbrella. But as long as such striving remains contra-factual, rather than factual, through the exclusion of a significant number of individuals, moral communication tends to emerge as, for example, highlighted by the strong reliance on moral argumentation within the discourse on global poverty and the high levels of socio-economic inequality which characterise the globe.[13] Moral communication, in this instance, fulfils the function of pointing to an 'untapped potential' which can be a source of further expansion of meaning production (*Sinnproduktion*), in the sense that the levelling of such differences is addressed through attempts to increase the scale of inclusion into the formalised frameworks of the economy, law, education and so forth.

In a similar fashion, the retreat of politics from hands-on control over large segments of society in recent decades implies a re-configuration of the political rather than a diminished impact of political forms of communication. As the Foucaultians teach us, the emergence of more refined, indirect and, thus, in their abstraction, less-visible ways of exercising power through new public management and other forms of strongly cognitivised forms of policy-making and policy-implementation reinforces, rather than minimises, the scope for exercising power. Thus, as is also testified by the emergence of managerialism at the transnational level of world society,[14] it is difficult to argue that a relative decline in the relevance of political and legal forms of communication can be observed. Furthermore, even though the term managerialism highlights the increased cognitivisation of law and the political, it nonetheless remains impossible to claim that strongly cognitivised regulatory processes, within areas as different as trade, health, food safety or the Internet, are no longer relying on normative structures of expectations, since they all are linked to the realisation of internally defined normative and essentially political visions concerning the establishment of non-discriminatory free trade, access to health, appropriate levels of food security and access to Internet-based communication on a worldwide basis.

It follows from the above that the constitutive distinction of social phenomena, including those operating within the global realm, is the doubling of reality (*Realitätsverdopplung*) between facticity and normativity as expressed in the distinction between the factual existing order and the internally reproduced, and equally real, idea concerning how the order in question ought to look like.[15] As all social phenomena are process-based, this distinction is, however, of a dynamic nature. Normative visions are not fixed in time, but also change over time, although they only do so at a slower pace than actually unfolding, and increasingly cognitivised, social operations of a given order. A time gap exists between the two dimensions, and bridging this gap is, as we will return to, the central function of law.

3.4 Normative orders as basic units of study

Apart from the zero-sum perspective on cognitive and normative expectations, another shortcoming associated with the concept of world society is the assertions that the increasing possibility for all communications to link up with all other communications and that the singular world is the common horizon of all communications[16] is a sufficient characteristic of a society. In its present form, the concept of world society remains under-determined (*unterdeterminiert*),[17] since a society first emerges when, through complex institution-building, a possibility of self-governing (*Selbststeuerung*) appears. Thus, the world cannot be understood as a singular society as long as a singular form of order (*Ordnungsform*) does not exist.[18] Or to use the words of Talcott Parsons: 'Perhaps the most general function of a societal community is to articulate a *system* of norms with a collective organization that has unity and cohesiveness.'[19] It is this general function of society which is not being reproduced for the world in its entirety.

Instead, the reproduction of this sort of integration unfolds at a 'lower level', within fiduciary and value-based forms of pattern maintenance such as organisations, professions, clans, networks, ethnic communities, regimes, religious congregations and states. These are the sorts of autonomous Eigen-structures[20] which generate themselves over time upon the basis of their own logics, and which integrate functions, norms and principles for approaching the future as a coherent whole. They are the kind of universes which Kuhn, in relation to science, described with the concept of paradigms to the extent that paradigms are characterised by integration of method, belief and propositions.[21] Or, to put it into system-theoretical language: the integration of the material, social and time dimensions of a given social structure. Thus, the comprehensive view of the world, which traditional concepts of constitutionalism only consider to be manifested in the state,[22] is a feature that can be observed at many different sites within world society. As we will return to, 'constitutional ability' is therefore not a prerogative of states.

Eigenstructures can also be described as a '*nomos*' which establishes coherency with the help of narratives.[23] However, the emergence of a *nomos* is, as argued by Carl Schmitt, not linked to the concrete occupation (*Landnahme*) of a geographical space (*Raum*) through the establishment of physical borders.[24] Instead, *nomoi* are constituted through the introduction and maintenance of boundaries of meaning (*Sinngrenzen*) in that 'the concept of meaning refers to the form of ordering (*Ordnungsform*) of human experiences'.[25] Whereas states, as previously mentioned, tend to deploy symbolic references to geographical borders when delineating boundaries of meaning, phenomena as different as the *Ummah*, the commonwealth of Muslim believers, and the global financial industry, operate without such references.

It follows that the world consists of many worlds, in the sense that a multiplicity of worlds of meaning (*Sinnwelten*) exists. Keeping the constitutive function of the distinction between the factual and counter-factual dimensions of social phenomena in mind, and adding the criteria of comprehensiveness, which, as we will return to in the next chapter, implies that such orders obtain a generalised legal form, makes it possible to argue that the basic unit of study for social sciences and law is not nation states, but normative orders as such. Such orders can be defined as social structures which are self-sufficient to the extent that they reproduce independent sources of meaning which enable them to constitute a comprehensive and condensed universe through the integration of functions and norms over time, thereby providing a framework through which an unknown future can be addressed.

The degree to which the structures of expectation of a given normative order are static or dynamic varies from order to order. The emergence and gradual expansion of specifically modern structures have, however, implied a general increase in temporalisation, thereby reinforcing the idea that the expectations which exist at given moments are constituted upon the basis of the distinction between the past and the future.[26] It follows that internal teleologies appear in the sense that regulatory principles of selection emerge which are linked to a *contra-factual* vision of an ultimate end-goal and which fulfil the function of stabilising the structure in question over time. Teleologies that serve as formulae through which the unity of the distinction between the past and the future is maintained from operation to operation.[27] For example, a state such as France, '*La Grande Nation*', is constructed around a narrative which points to the future upon the basis of the past in the sense that the self-understanding of the French state is closely linked to the continued striving for the realisation of the ideals of the French Revolution on a global scale. The German Federal Republic was, moreover, founded upon the basis of an imperative of increased *Westbindung*, the (re-)integration of Germany in the Western community of states, upon the basis of a narrative which had the avoidance of a future repetition of Germany's recent history at its core.[28] Both of these narratives have become increasingly strained in recent years as a result of the profound structural transformations which have unfolded since the fall of the Berlin Wall, which created a widespread sense of uncertainty. But similar logics can also be found elsewhere. The European Union, in spite of continued resistance from its social environment, reproduces itself upon the basis of the logic of an 'ever-closer Union' thereby making increased integration an end in itself.[29] Functionally delineated transnational regimes also rely on such teleologies; for instance, the world-trade regime might be conceived of as relying on a self-understanding which is oriented towards a worldwide abolition of barriers to trade, just as the global human-rights regime could be seen as having not only the principle but also the factual establishment of a space of law (*Rechtsraum*) comprising the world in its entirety as its ultimate aim. As previously indicated, it is the handling of this doubling of reality (*Realitätsverdoppelung*) – between the factually existing world and an *immanently constructed*, but nonetheless real, idea concerning how the world should be[30] – which establishes the core contribution of law to society.

The status of normative orders as autonomous social structures implies that they are faced with a demand from their environments to justify why a specific operation is selected and why others are not selected.[31] Such justifications are, however, paradoxical in nature since they are always *self*-justifications. On the one hand, they refer to external structures, in the sense that justification is about providing reasons to the wider world concerning why a specific operation is selected. In practice, on the other hand, normative orders create internal images of their environments which are used in order to frame such justifications. Each order produces semantic artefacts which they can claim are external in nature. For example, the political system traditionally refers to the state as a holistic whole which encompasses society in its totality, or (within democracies) to an internally constructed image of the 'will of the people'. The legal system refers to internally developed universal and 'self-evident' (natural) rights. In order to fulfil similar objectives, the economic system refers to the concept of market demand, and the religious system to the will of God. Thus, within all spheres of society, it is possible to observe the unfolding of strategies which are aimed at 'covering up' the paradoxical nature of their justifications upon the basis of metaphors which are assigned a foundational and transcendental quality, in the sense that they are internally described as having validity for society as a whole. Despite being internal in nature, such self-justifications are, however, relevant for the structures operating in the environment of a given social system. This is the case because strategies of justification tend to be based upon a more or less coherent and relatively stable set of principles, which serve as regulatory ideas in the continued selection of operations. Hence, such principles provide a basis for a stabilisation of the expectations emerging in the environment vis-à-vis a given normative order in the sense that they increase the probability of correctly predicting which type of operations will be selected. This again increases the ability of other normative orders to adjust their internal selections of operations.

The teleologies of social systems are not given by nature or, in any other sense, carved in stone as was often assumed in early modern philosophy. At the semantic level, justifications tend to emerge, which claim that higher forces underlie such teleologies, but, from an operational perspective, they remain temporal and contingent. Or to put it more precisely: contingent because they are temporal, thereby making them the result of unpredictable evolutionary developments. Nonetheless, they are more than just programmes in the Luhmannian sense. Luhmann distinguishes between codes and programmes. Whereas codes are unchangeable, in the sense that a change of the code would mean one was dealing with a fundamentally different system,[32] programmes are changeable and might or might not be deployed in a given operation. Teleologies can, in this sense, be understood as 'hegemonic programmes', in the sense that they are frames which are characterised by a high level of stability over time, just as they establish a sense of overall coherence through narrative framings with strong normative implications. Whereas *alterability* is often understood as an essential feature of a normative world, in the sense that the possibility of thinking of or imagining a different world always exists, teleologies function, instead, as forms through which the varieties of potential selections are reduced in the sense that 'alternative languages' are being systematically marginalised. A normative outlook does not only imply a striving for alterability, but also, and equally so, a condensation, established through re-iteration, of an already established view of the world. Thus, the normative architecture of such worlds might be reinforced just as its reach might be expanded, but the principles and objectives which it promotes tend to be far more static and resistant to change. Or to express it differently, the imaginary realities also change over time but they tend to do so at a slower pace than the factually existing structures which characterise a given world.

Making the concept of normative orders the central point of departure enables one to walk a thin line between the multiple-modernities paradigm and the world-society perspective advanced by systems theory. The paradigm of multiple modernities advanced by Shmuel Eisenstadt rightly challenges the Eurocentric and Western-centric perspective which dominates social scientific enquiry. However, it remains limited to a very general macro-sociological enquiry which sees the major civilisations of the world as the central units of study, thereby underplaying the continued interaction and entangledness of civilisations.[33] In addition, due to its sheer broadness and focus on culture, it is not sufficiently concise to illuminate the specific logics which characterise different social processes such as those related to, for example, law, the economy, science and religion, just as the structural transformations through changes in the 'deeper structures' of society in terms of the forms of social differentiation which different segments of society rely upon remain essentially out of reach for this school of thought.

Systems theory, by way of contrast, has an inherent tendency to provide a somewhat reductionist picture of society through its ambition to grasp society in its entirety by means of a purely systemic perspective. The systemic component is, however, only one of several aspects of society, since systems always operate within broader cultural contexts. They are, in many ways, parasites which are conditioned by the existence of latent socio-cultural structures from which they can distil their components. It follows that autopoietic processes cannot be considered to be 'pure' processes merely reproducing themselves upon the basis of recursive operations. Moreover, the socio-cultural universes in which social systems are embedded serve as the resource which allows inter-penetration between the different systems to take place because successful inter-penetration is conditioned by the existence of a common world of meaning (*Sinnwelt*). Thus, the system-theoretical claim that the theory is capable of describing society in its entirety is a considerable overestimation. Just like human beings,[34] society is characterised by an infinite complexity (*Unendlichkeit*) which cannot be adequately grasped by the existing system-theoretical vocabulary.

The concept of normative orders is located within the two extremes of the civilisation approach and systems theory, enabling a combination of the systemic dimension with its relation to the broader and rather intangible socio-cultural terrains within which social systems operate. In this sense, normative orders can also be understood as hybrids which establish the unity between systemic structures and their respective contexts. In addition, the level of analysis is different. Not only the civilisation approach, but also systems theory's focus on globally operating function-systems, implies a macro approach which tends to make them less-capable frameworks for detailed empirical analysis. The concept of normative orders, in contrast, provides a basis for meso-level analyses of, for example, organisations, networks and communities, and thus a level of analysis which, as we will return to, is far more in alignment with the location of actually existing constitutional structures.

3.5 The entangled vertical and horizontal logics of world society

Furthermore, the system-theoretical concept of world society, with its focus on the horizontal relations between function systems, is inadequate because it does not sufficiently acknowledge the independent value of the vertical dimension of structure formation in world society, as reflected in the fundamentally different organisational principles and logics which characterise local, national and transnational forms of social ordering in the global realm.[35] Clusters of functions related to, for example, law, politics and religion might be identified within all three layers, thereby building a case for the unity of function systems across vertical boundaries. But such components always engage in the sort of hybrid relations with their broader contexts which are the trademark of normative orders. Thus, identical functional components produce substantially different effects within different contexts. It follows that local, national and transnational structures cannot be considered to be functional equivalents vis-à-vis each other. They do not possess a quality which makes them mutually substitutable since the functional components themselves undergo a transformation when the context in which they are located changes.[36] The widespread tendency within social sciences and law to transpose concepts from one layer of world society to another in a one-to-one manner is therefore inherently problematical.[37] Legal pluralist accounts developed through studies of local communities cannot be transposed to the transnational level,[38] and the conceptual framework for analysing the European Union cannot be derived from the nation-state universe,[39] just as the constitutional vocabulary of nation states cannot be transposed to the transnational level in a one-to-one manner.[40] As previously indicated, this is also reflected in the substantially different evolutionary paths of local, national and transnational forms of ordering. The complex constitutional conglomerates, which, in everyday language, are described as nation states, grew gradually, through a metamorphosis, out of the already existing feudal orders. Similarly, contemporary transnational regimes primarily emerged from within the colonial form of transnational ordering,[41] through the re-configuration of transnational processes of structure formation away from reliance on the centre/periphery differentiation and towards an increased reliance on functional differentiation as their central organisational principle.

But, although local, national and transnational forms of ordering are substantially different, they do not operate independently from each other.[42] They are different organising logics which 'co-operate', in the sense that they operate in a mutually fixed manner over time.[43] Just as state-based and pre-state structures are distinct but deeply entangled, transnational structures are likewise autonomous structures which remain deeply entwined with the other two layers of world society. In most cases, these different logics rely upon the same material substance. Nation-state organisations, for example, tend to develop an additional transnational dimension which enables them to interact and to compare themselves reflexively with their counterparts in other national contexts. National courts engage in juridical cross-fertilisation,[44] and state bureaucracies engage in reflexivity-increasing exercises aimed at enhancing mutual observation, as, for example, is the case in relation to European Union, the International Monetary Fund (IMF) and the Organisation for Economic Co-operation and Development benchmarking exercises.[45] This development reflects the disaggregation of the state, which is a reflection of the conversion of ever more states into modern states which internally mirror the functionally differentiated nature of the social environment within which they operate. Consequently, the different functionally defined dimensions of states tend to fulfil different functions and pursue different objectives in a relatively unco-ordinated manner, at the same time as these dimensions establish institutionalised relations to their counterparts in other states as well as to other public and private structures operating in the global realm.[46] Both internally and externally, state organisations, furthermore, appertain to different problem constellations, norms and procedures, thereby making the challenge of establishing internal coherency between the different sets of expectations a central challenge for modern state organisations.

In a similar manner, most multinational firms remain closely linked to the business culture and legal regime of their country of origin. Wal-Mart remains a very American company and Toyota a very Japanese company. But, at the same time, they are engaged in business operations on a global scale, with the consequence that they encounter different expectations and norms in different contexts. It is in order to handle this tension that they develop a transnational dimension which enables them to operate on a global scale through the transfer of capital, products and human resources between different state-based jurisdictions, functionally delineated spheres and cultural settings while maintaining internal coherency.

A variation of the tension between national and transnational frameworks can be observed in relation to public international organisations. Such organisations are *inter*-national organisations that are founded and funded by states. At the same time, to varying degrees, they tend to develop an additional transnational dimension which escapes the kind of control which can be ensured through delegation. This is especially apparent in relation to the European Union, which, in most instances, is described as a structure which is composed of an intergovernmental and a supranational dimension. The former dimension remains, at least ideally, under the control of the Member States while the latter operates beyond the exclusive control of the Member States. But even within less-developed international organisations, an additional transnational dimension tends to emerge. For example, the World Trade Organization has, within a very short time, developed an additional transnational dimension guided by an independent logic which cannot be captured by the concept of inter-governmentality, since it produces rules of ordering that cannot be directly traced back to its Member States. Consequently, international organisations must be understood as autonomous normative orders which internally rely on a hierarchical nucleus – albeit an often very weak one.

Within classical theories of delegation, the independent impact of transnational organisations and regimes are often regarded as rather limited because the founding states act as the 'masters of treaties'. The 'old European' (*alt-europäische*) concept of delegation, however, systematically downplays the fact that each act of delegation implies a certain degree of autonomy of the organisation to which delegation is made.[47] Comitology committees in the European Union are, at the same time, 'mini-councils' which rely on an inter-governmental set-up and extremely complex structures with a life of their own,[48] just as the impact of public and private international organisations, such as the International Monetary Fund and the World Trade Organization, cannot be reduced to reflections of the intentions of the founding and funding states. When viewed from a process-oriented perspective, classical concepts of delegation are inherently flawed, because such perspectives tend to ignore the immanent processes unfolding within the 'black box' in question.[49] Classical delegation theories and much mainstream political science and dogmatic legal theory fail to understand that, logically speaking, an 'output' cannot be traced back to an 'input' in a one-to-one manner. More generally, attempts to understand international organisations as effectively being under state control because states, formally speaking, remain the 'masters of the treaties', fail to acknowledge the structural drift which characterises such processes. Thus, independently of whether states pursue narrow 'national interests'[50] or larger normative endeavours,[51] when they engage in transnational processes, profound structural dynamics invariably tend to operate beneath the surface.

A metamorphosis similar to the one which could be observed when modern states grew out of the old feudal order can be observed. The French monarchs, for example, were formally in control during the century-long processes leading to modernity and the establishment of the modern French state. Nonetheless, the structural drift towards modernity forced them, step-by-step, to delegate more and more discretionary competences to the emerging modern state bureaucracy. But the modern state structures turned out to be parasitoids (parasites which eventually end up killing their hosts) since the modern state structures prevailed and the monarchy disappeared.[52]

To sum up, what public and private structures have in common is that they tend to be national *and* transnational at the same time, thereby highlighting the fact that transnationality must be understood as a specific *social practice* which is different from national practices. What entities developing a trans-national dimension have in common is that some of the activities in which they engage might be effectively controlled by states capable of imposing legal constraints at the same time as they – at least partly – are capable of escaping national control when operating in a transnational capacity.[53]

3.6 Multiple lines of conflict

It follows from the above that major entities of ordering, such as states, international organisations and multinational companies, are faced with a dual challenge. They are faced with the need to establish internal coherency and order, and, at the same time, to establish frameworks which will enable them to operate within a multi-contextual environment characterised by a diversity of social structures and forms of conflict. This is the functional reason for the emergence of normative orders. Organisations, regimes and states are faced with a functional need to develop a 'higher order' which comprises the entity in question and the different contexts they operate within. Or, to put it more precisely, such entities are forced to construct a context of their own, through the institutional stabilisation of expectations vis-à-vis a limited segment of world society, thereby making exchanges and transfers between the entity in question and its environment possible.

Transnational organisations and regimes, first of all, operate within a whole range of state-based legal orders, and the majority of social conflicts with which they are confronted are handled through their adherence to, or the establish-ment of, compatibility with state law. However, state law is characterised by massive differences in standards, regulatory philosophies and legal traditions. For public and private international organisations, the problem of ensuring adequate and simultaneous 'transplantation' of legal acts into several national legal orders remains, therefore, a central problem.[54]

Second, apart from the compliance demands which emerge from state-based legal orders, transnationally operating entities are confronted with a plurality of 'cultural values',[55] and are thus also confronted with a need to ensure compatibility between their operations and local norms. In the limited areas of a world characterised by century-long state-building processes and strong states, social practices have often been subject to a 'Hegelian codification' by national legal systems, thereby making this a less-pressing problem. But, as previously highlighted, the Hegelian state has only fully materialised itself in a small section of the world. In the vast parts of the world where the totality of the state is less profound, large segments of society continue to operate 'beneath' the state, upon the basis of a different set of norms than those upheld by the state. The numerous conflicts between multinational companies and indigenous people, especially within the natural resources business, illus-trate this very well.[56] But even within areas of the world with strong states, the successful social acceptance of the outcome of transnational processes remains, to a high extent, dependent on the establishment of compatibility in relation to culturally embedded and relatively intangible local values and traditions. For example, in a European context, the production and regulation of foodstuffs in general, and genetically modified organisms (GMOs) in particular, tend to encounter massive obstacles due to the lack of responsivity on the part of producers and regulators towards 'traditional ways of life'.[57]

Third, in addition to state-based and cultural barriers, transnational operating entities are confronted with a need to ensure compatibility between other functional spheres than their own. It is not only multinational companies that are faced with the need to handle, for example, the environmental and health effects of economic reproduction.[58] Similar lines of conflict can be observed at the other end of the private/public continuum in relation to organisations such as the European Union, understood as a conglomerate of functional regimes, and the World Trade Organization. Such organisations are based upon an international-law framework, and state actors are clearly the dominant group of actors within such organisations. But, as already indicated, such organisations do not only adhere to an interstate logic. For example, the complex risk-regulating structures that have emerged within both organisations are also directly aimed at handling functionally differentiated conflicts between the economy and, for example, the environment and health.[59] Another illustrative example of functionally delineated conflicts can be observed within the research and development policy in the European Union where scientific and economic perspectives collide. Different professions and epistemic communities approach the world from different perspectives and upon the basis of different kinds of normativity. Individuals with a science background partaking in the formulation of research and development policy tend to be aligned with a specific social role which orients them towards a focus on 'increased innovation'. Individuals from the economic sphere, in contrast, tend to be aligned with a role oriented towards 'increasing competitiveness'. The consequence is that individuals taking up specific social roles which are linked to different functionally delineated spheres are likely to go on doing what they always have done while they systematically talk past one another in a deliberately non-deliberative manner.[60] Moreover, as we will return to in the following chapter, such functionally delineated conflicts are being mirrored and reproduced within the legal system, thereby providing the constitutive basis for a plurality of functionally delineated legal discourses. If a matter related to economic reproduction is approached from an environmental law, health law or human-rights law perspective, rather than from the perspective of economic law, it is likely to make a world of difference.[61] In the absence of legal safeguards capable of ensuring a stabilisation of mutual orientation and symmetric interaction between different functionally delineated dimensions, the result is likely to be cognitive closure in which regulatory processes become inherently one-sided and dysfunctional.[62]

Thus, what is common for public and private transnational structures alike is that they *simultaneously* operate within a multiplicity of territorial, segmentary and functionally delineated contextual settings. They are confronted with a vast variety of conflict lines which forces them to adhere to a multiplicity of often contradictory demands and expectations at the same time.[63] The successful operationability of transnational entities is therefore dependent on their ability to develop stabilisation and translation mechanisms capable of ensuring their simultaneous embeddedness within a whole range of settings while maintaining internal coherency.

3.7 Establishing compatibility

Fulfilling the dual demand for establishing embeddedness and internal coherency is the essential function of governance structures.[64] Governance has become a central concept within both law and the social sciences in recent decades, but tends to be used in an all-embracing manner, thereby radically reducing its precision.[65] The concept can, however, gain precision if it is defined as referring to institutional frameworks which are located in between normative orders, and which serve the function of enabling the transfer of condensed social components between such orders. Accordingly, governance frameworks are, in contrast to governing frameworks, characterised by organisational and legal heterarchy just as networks tend to be their central organisational feature.

In the European Union context, Comitology and the Open Method of Co-ordination are examples of such structures, in that they are simultaneously oriented towards the channelling of condensed social components between: 1) the hierarchically organised governing dimension of the European Union, most notably the Commission, and the Member States; 2) between different Member State settings; and 3) performing a balancing of functionally differentiated conflicts.[66] The successfulness of such governance structures are, moreover, highly dependent on the degree that they themselves become epistemic communities which are structured around a shared objective. Such communities are only likely to emerge, however, if they are capable of developing a sense of 'cultural sensibility' which enables them to take account of more or less intangible cultural differences within the different settings that they bring together.

Within the World Trade Organization, a similar multi-dimensional structure can be observed within the framework of the Technical Barriers to Trade (TBT) and the Sanitary and Phytosanitary (SPS) committees (although the governing dimension of the World Trade Organization is far weaker than within the European Union). Moreover, as emphasised by Anne-Marie Slaughter, governance frameworks have emerged directly between national bureaucracies (without necessarily relying on international organisations) as well as between nationally organised jurisdictions.[67] The multitude of corporate social responsibility partnerships between, on the one hand, multinationals, and, on the other, state bureaucracies, public and private international organisations, research institutes and non-governmental organisations fulfil a similar function for multinational companies.[68]

Governance frameworks are reflexivity-increasing instruments that increase the capacity of observation and thereby the potential level of adaptability vis-à-vis developments unfolding in the social environments of these entities. But, at the same time, they also serve as channels of diffusion through which the social components, such as products, capital, legal acts, political decisions and human resources, produced by these entities are diffused into the wider society. They are double-edged structures which simultaneously serve as adaptation mechanisms and as 'tools of colonisation'. One of the many consequences is that the 'ownership' of governance frameworks is characterised by systematic uncertainty. They function as the 'neutral ground' where different orders engage, and this means that the ownership question tends to be a taboo. As epistemic ramification is a structural condition for operationability, and because most governance structures are characterised by an asymmetric distribution of resources and capabilities among those participating, discursive hegemony is a permanent threat. In many cases, a limited section of participants will tend to dominate, thereby making governance structures into one-way streets. Making this explicit through a declaration of hegemony is, however, likely to undermine such set-ups. Governance structures tend to be characterised by organised hypocrisy since the illusion of equality, for example, between the US Environmental Protection Agency and their Mexican counterparts,[69] has to be maintained. In particular, governance structures within the field of developing aid and corporate social responsibility processes tend to be characterised by such asymmetries because the role distribution between the donors and the receivers makes it virtually impossible to avoid such asymmetries.[70] In less-asymmetric settings – for example, due to existence of an elaborated set of legal safeguards aimed at reducing the impact of asymmetric relations – self-delusion tends to reign, in the sense that everyone involved tends to believe that he or she is in control. Or, as expressed by Joseph H.H. Weiler, commenting on Comitology and making a reference to John Le Carré: 'One gets the impression, by the cosy convenience between Commission and Council that each think Comitology is their own Smiley or Karla.'[71]

Another commonality of governance structures is that they are heterarchical structures which rely on the network form. A network is 'more than a variously densified grouping of negotiated relations among stable subjects'.[72] This does not mean that subjects are irrelevant, only that a network cannot be reduced to a mere expression of co-operation and bargaining between subjects. Subject relations are, therefore, only one of many components of a network in which the multiplicity of interdependent and complementary components provides a basis for continued re-combination. This creates synergy effects and produces new options which are only accessible through the network in question. Synergy effects are, therefore, conditioned by an acceptance of the logic regulating the evolution and functioning of the network itself. This is also the case for the results of bargaining, deliberation or co-operation between subjects within a given network. Their results can only be externalised through the network structure and not by the included subjects themselves, because any successful action needs to adhere to the overall logic and the norms guiding the network. Governance structures are channels of diffusion through which the 'content' of hierarchical governing processes are diffused. On the other hand, the kind of 'framing' and 'translation' which governance structures produce when carrying out diffusion processes tend to transform the content.

An additional feature of governance networks is their 'fluid' character. This fluidity makes the outcome of network operations radically open-ended, as the number of possible re-combinations among the elements of a given network is almost infinite. A network cannot, therefore, be seen as a stable unity, even though it can briefly become denser and easier to distinguish in the case of collisions with other decisional structures.[73] In many instances, governance networks are, moreover, oriented towards a deliberate erosion of the distinction between the public and private spheres. The function of many networks is to combine public and private elements in order to establish convergence between private- and public-policy objectives, and to stabilise relations between, for example, economic and political-bureaucratic structures. This tends either to undermine the old Hegelian distinction between state and society or to necessitate the development of legal frameworks capable handling public/private exchanges without such exchanges leading to dissolution of the distinction between the two dimensions.[74]

Another set of features of governance networks is the existence of reciprocal trust, repeated interaction and observation by third parties. Networks are, however, different from purely informal relations between subjects, as a minimum of institutionalisation is needed. Furthermore, they have the character of 'parasites', in the sense that, in most cases, they are attached to an organisation with hierarchical features. In most cases, they will indeed operate 'in between' such organisations, although, in some instances – for example, in relation to corporate social responsibility structures and developing aid – they might also act as channels between organisations and a more loosely delineated local community.[75]

Moreover, a special – but increasingly important – variant occurs through the developments of hybrids between hierarchal organisations and heterarchical networks. (Quasi-)regulatory agencies in the European Union context, which tend to combine classical Weberian features and 'reflexive approaches' are the most obvious example.[76] Such hybrids are likely to emerge as a result of increases in social complexity, which makes the 'processing capacity' of a fluid network structure an insufficient basis for handling the subject matter in question. That this sort of hybridity remains a particularly strong feature within the European context is hardly surprising. On the contrary, it reflects the status and position of the European Union which is itself a hybrid operating 'in between' national and global structures. The European Union is partly characterised by state-like features and partly by the kind of radically heterarchical structures which characterise global-governance structures. That said, a specific variant of the amalgamations between governing and governance can also be observed within the private sector, where it takes the form of a hybridity between 'market and hierarchy'.[77]

To sum up, great variations can be observed, in the sense that the institutional set-up and the 'strength' of governance structures vary a great deal. However, it is common for them that they are *Zwischenwelten* ('in-between worlds'),[78] in the sense that they are inter-contextual structures which rely on the network form, and which are aimed at achieving an increase in the reflexivity and thus the adaptability of the entities which they simultaneously link at the same time as they serve as dissemination channels for these entities. They are complex matrixes in which components derived from a multiplicity of societal structures and contexts are combined. In this sense, they can also be understood as co-ordinating structures which stand transversal to the forms of differentiation and conflict which characterise contemporary society. They produce a web of couplings which transcend the horizontal and vertical conflict lines of world society. They produce social integration, and, as such, they can be understood as the functional equivalents to the kind of (neo-)corporatist structures which fulfil(-led) a similar function within the context of (European) nation states in the age of classical modernity.[79]

3.8 Conclusion

A central argument of this chapter has been that the concept of world society is a useful but insufficient starting-point for a theory of constitutionalism in the global realm. It is useful because it highlights that there is far more to the world than states, and that states – when seen from a global perspective – are particularistic entities. But the concept of world society is also insufficient because the world in its entirety does not possess a key trademark of a society since it lacks a singular form of ordering. Furthermore, the Luhmannian idea concerning a relative reduction in the centrality of normative-based social processes and a concordant expansion in the centrality of cognitive-based social processes within the increasingly globalised structures of world society is seen as problematical. Instead, a re-configuration of the relationship between the normative and cognitive dimensions of social processes is observed. Within the functionally delineated segments of world society, moral communication tends to assume a more focused strategic function at the same time that 'lower level' processes are subject to increased cognitivisation. Against this background, the concept of normative orders was introduced in order to complement the concept of world society. The concept of normative orders is a meso-level concept and capable of taking account of the multitude of different social structures which are located at the local, national and transnational levels of world society. The existence of a multitude of normative orders in world society also implies the existence of a multitude of conflict lines of both a vertical and a horizontal nature. It is against this background that the governance phenomenon has emerged as the institutional form through which the compatibility between different normative orders is established.

Notes

1 Niklas Luhmann, 'Die Weltgesellschaft', *Archiv für Rechts-und Sozialphilosophie*, 1971, 57, pp. 1–35, reprinted in *Soziologische Aufklärung 2: Aufsätze zur Theorie der Gesellschaft*, Opladen: Westdeutsche Verlag, [1975] 2009, pp. 51–71.
2 This perspective is also being advanced by the world polity approach developed by the Stanford School. See John W. Meyer, John Boli, George M. Thomas and Francisco O. Ramirez, 'World Society and the Nation-State', *American Journal of Sociology*, 1997, 103, pp. 144–81.
3 Niklas Luhmann, *Die Gesellschaft der Gesellschaft*, Frankfurt am Main: Suhrkamp Verlag, 1997, p. 145 *et seq.*
4 Niklas Luhmann, 'Sinn als Grundbegriff der Soziologie', in Jürgen Habermas and Niklas Luhmann, *Theorie der Gesellschaft oder Sozialtechnologie: Was leistet die Systemforschung?*, Frankfurt am Main: Suhrkamp Verlag, 1971, pp. 25–100.
5 Daniel Chernilo, *A Social Theory of the Nation-state: The Political Forms of Modernity beyond Methodological Nationalism*, London: Routledge, 2007.
6 Niklas Luhmann, *Soziologische Aufklärung 2: Aufsätze zur Theorie der Gesellschaft*, Opladen: Westdeutsche Verlag, [1975] 2009, pp. 51–71, at 68.
7 Ibid., pp. 51–71.
8 Ino Augsberg, 'Observing (the) Law: The "Epistemological Turn" in Public Law and the Evolution of Global Administrative Law', in Paulius Jurčys, Poul F. Kjaer and Ren Yurakami (eds), *Regulatory Hybridization in the Transnational Sphere*, Leiden: Brill Publishing, 2013, pp. 11–27.
9 Moritz Renner, 'Death by Complexity – The Crisis of Law in World Society', in Poul F. Kjaer, Gunther Teubner and Alberto Febbrajo (eds), *The Financial Crisis in Constitutional Perspective: The Dark Side of Functional Differentiation*, Oxford: Hart Publishing, 2011, pp. 93–111, at 98.
10 Luhmann, *Die Gesellschaft der Gesellschaft*, p. 813.
11 Marc Amstutz, 'Eroding Boundaries: On Financial Crisis and an Evolutionary Concept of Regulatory Reform', in Poul F. Kjaer, Gunther Teubner and Alberto Febbrajo (eds), *The Financial Crisis in Constitutional Perspective: The Dark Side of Functional Differentiation*, Oxford: Hart Publishing, 2011, pp. 223–68.
12 Rudolf Stichweh, *Inklusion und Exklusion: Studien zur Gesellschaftstheorie*, Bielefeld: Transcript Verlag, 2005, p. 13
13 See, for example, Thomas Pogge, *World Poverty and Human Rights: Cosmopolitan Responsibilities and Reforms*, 2nd edition, Cambridge: Polity Press 2008.
14 Martti Koskenniemi, 'Constitutionalism, Managerialism and the Ethos of Legal Education', *European Journal of Legal Studies*, 2007, 1, pp. 1–18.
15 Robert M. Cover, 'Nomos and Narrative', *Harvard Law Review*, 1983, 97, pp. 4–68; Niklas Luhmann, 'Quod Omnes Tangit: Remarks on Jürgen Habermas' Legal Theory', *Cardozo Law Review*, 1996, 17, pp. 883–99, at 889
16 Luhmann, *Die Gesellschaft der Gesellschaft*, p. 145 *et seq.*
17 Marc Amstutz and Vaios Karavas, 'Weltrecht: Ein Derridasches Monster', in Gralf-Peter Calliess, Andreas Fischer-Lescano, Dan Wielsch and Peer Zumbansen (eds), *Soziologische Jurisprudenz: Festschrift für Gunther Teubner zum 65. Geburtstag*, Berlin, Walter de Gruyter, 2009, pp. 645–72, at 646 *et seq.*
18 Helmut Wilke, *Global Governance*, Bielefeld: Transcript Verlag, 2006, p. 34 *et seq.*
19 Talcott Parsons, *The System of Modern Societies*, Englewood Cliffs, NJ: Prentice-Hall 1971, p. 11; italics in original.
20 Rudolf Stichweh, 'Strukturbildung in der Weltgesellschaft – Die Eigenstrukturen der Weltgesellschaft und die Regionalkulturen der Welt', in Thomas Schwinn (ed.), *Die*

Vielfalt und Einheit der Moderne: Kultur-und strukturvergleichende Analysen, Wiesbaden: Verlag für Sozialwissenschaften, 2006, pp. 239–57, at 239 *et seq*; Rudolf Stichweh: 'Das Konzept der Weltgesellschaft: Genese und Strukturbildung eines globalen Gesellschaftssystems', *Rechtstheorie*, 2008, 39, pp. 329–55, at 329 *et seq*.
21 See Thomas Kuhn, *The Structure of Scientific Revolutions*, Chicago: University of Chicago Press [1962] 1996; Robert M. Cover, 'Nomos and Narrative', 4–68, *Harvard Law Review*, 1983, 97, pp. 4–68 at 6.
22 Martin Loughlin, 'In defence of Staatslehre', *Der Staat*, 2009, 48,1, pp. 1–28.
23 Cover, 'Nomos and Narrative'.
24 Carl Schmitt, *Der Nomos der Erde: Im Völkerrecht des Jus Publicum Europaeum*, Berlin: Duncker & Humblot [1950] 1997, p. 36 *et seq*.
25 Luhmann, 'Sinn als Grundbegriff der Soziologie', at 31; my translation.
26 Reinhart Koselleck, *Begriffsgeschichten: Studien zur Semantik und Pragmatik der politischen und sozialen Sprache*, Frankfurt am Main: Surhkamp Verlag, 2006, p. 77 et seq.
27 For a critical, Koselleck-inspired, reconstruction of the role of teleologies in relation to the European integration process, see Hagen Schulz-Forberg and Bo Stråth, *The Political History of European Integration: The Hypocracy of Democracy-Through-Market*, London: Routledge, 2010.
28 Jürgen Habermas, 'Geschichtsbewußtsein und posttraditionale Identität: Die Westorientierung der Bundesrepublik', in *Eine Art Schadensabwicklung. Kleine politische Schriften IV*, Frankfurt am Main: Suhrkamp Verlag, 1987, pp. 159–79.
29 Poul F. Kjaer, *Between Governing and Governance: On the Emergence, Form and Function of Europe's Post-National Constellation*, Oxford: Hart Publishing, 2010, p. 31 *et seq*.
30 Niklas Luhmann, 'Quod Omnes Tangit', *Cardozo Law Review*, 1996, 17, pp. 883–99.
31 Within normative theory similar insights have led to the development of a 'right to justification' which also has been stylised as the most fundamental basic right. See Rainer Forst, *Das Recht auf Rechtfertigung: Elemente einer konstruktivistischen Theorie der Gerechtigkeit*, Frankfurt am Main: Suhrkamp Verlag, 2007, p. 10.
32 In *praxis*, Luhmann, however, softens this position somewhat. In relation to the political system, for example, he identifies the primary code as *Machtüberlegenheit/Machtunterlegenheit*, but subsequently adds the codes government/opposition and progressive/conservative, thereby allowing for substantial changes to the system. Niklas Luhmann, *Politik der Gesellschaft*, Frankfurt am Main: Suhrkamp Verlag, 2000, p. 96 *et seq*; Niklas Luhmann, 'Der politische Code. "Konservativ" und "progressiv" in systemtheoretischer Sicht', *Zeitschrift für Politik*, 1974, 21, p. 253.
33 Shalini Randeria, 'Eisenstadt, Dumont and Foucault: The Challenge of Historical Entanglements for Comparative Civilization as Analysis', *Erwägen Wissen Ethik*, 2005, 17, pp. 59–62.
34 Niklas Luhmann, 'Die Soziologie und der Mensch', in Niklas Luhmann, *Soziologische Aufklärung Band 6: Die Soziologie und Mensch*, Opladen: Westdeutscher Verlag, 1995, p. 256.
35 The vertical dimension is, however, taken into account by Rudolf Stichweh; see Stichweh, 'Strukturbildung in der Weltgesellschaft – Die Eigenstrukturen der Weltgesellschaft und die Regionalkulturen der Welt'; Rudolf Stichweh: 'Das Konzept der Weltgesellschaft: Genese und Strukturbildung eines globalen Gesellschaftssystems', *Rechtstheorie*, 2008, 39, pp. 329–55.
36 Amstutz and Karavas, 'Weltrecht: Ein Derridasches Monster', p. 645, at 652.
37 Amstutz and Karavas, 'Weltrecht: Ein Derridasches Monster'.
38 Paul Schiff Berman, *Global Legal Pluralism: A Jurisprudence of Law Beyond Borders*, New York: Cambridge University Press, 2012.
39 Kjaer, *Between Governing and Governance*.
40 Nico Krisch, *Beyond Constitutionalism: The Pluralist Structure of Postnational Law*, Oxford: Oxford University Press, 2010.
41 Martti Koskenniemi, *The Gentle Civilizer of Nations: The Rise and Fall of International Law 1870–1960*, Cambridge: Cambridge University Press, 2001.
42 Saskia Sassen, *Territory, Authority, Rights: From Medieval to Global Assemblages*, Princeton, NJ: Princeton University Press, 2006.

43 Marc Amstutz, *Evolutorisches Wirtschaftsrecht: Vorstudien zum Recht und seiner Methode in den Diskurskollissionen der Marktgesellschaft*, Baden-Baden: Nomos Verlag, 2001, p. 101 *et seq.*

44 Anne-Marie Slaughter, *A New World Order*, Princeton, NJ: Princeton University Press, 2004, p. 65 *et seq.*

45 Armin Schäfer, *Die neue Unverbindlichkeit: Wirtschaftspolitische Koordinierung in Europa*, Frankfurt am Main: Campus Verlag, 2005.

46 Slaughter, *A New World Order*.

47 Charles Sabel and Joshua Cohen, 'Global Democracy?', *NYU Journal of International Law and Politics*, 2005, 37, pp. 763–97.

48 Christian Joerges and Florian Rödl, 'Zum Funktionswandel des Kollisionsrechts II. Die kollisionsrechtliche Form einer legitimen Verfassung der post-nationalen Konstellation', in Gralf-Peter Callies, Andreas Fischer-Lescano, Dan Wielsch and Peer Zumbansen (eds), *Soziologische Jurisprudenz: Festschrift für Gunther Teubner zum 65. Geburtstag*, Berlin: Walter de Gruyter, 2009, pp. 765–78.

49 Niklas Luhmann, *Zweckbegriff und Systemrationalität: Über die Funktion von Zwecken in sozialen Systemen*, Frankfurt am Main: Suhrkamp Verlag, [1968] 1999, p. 248 *et seq.*

50 Andrew Moravcsik, *The Choice for Europe: Social Purpose and State Power from Messina to Maastricht*, Ithaca, NY: Cornell University Press, 1999.

51 Nicole Deitelhoff, *Überzeugung in der Politik: Grundzüge einer Diskurstheorie internationalen Regierens*, Frankfurt am Main: Suhrkamp Verlag, 2006.

52 Norbert Elias, *Über den Prozeß der Zivilisation, Band 2*, Frankfurt am Main: Suhrkamp Verlag, [1938] 1976. For an analysis of similar crisis tendencies for modern states, see Jürgen Habermas, *Legitimationsprobleme im Spätkapitalismus*, Frankfurt am Main: Suhrkamp Verlag, 1973.

53 An insistence on states as the sole bearers of authority will, therefore, leave a 'gap' since substantial societal processes will then unfold outside constitutional frameworks, thereby providing a normative motivation for an engagement with transnational constitutionalism. For such a perspective, see Anne Peters, 'Are we Moving towards Constitutionalization of the World Community?', in Antonio Cassese (ed.), *Realizing Utopia: The Future of International Law*, Oxford: Oxford University Press, 2012, pp. 118–35.

54 For a sceptical view, see Pierre Legrand, 'The Impossibility of Legal Transplants', *Maastricht Journal of Comparative Law*, 1997, vol. 4, pp. 111–24.

55 Antje Wiener, *The Invisible Constitution of Politics: Contested Norms and International Encounters*, Cambridge: Cambridge University Press, 2008.

56 Donald N. Zillman, Alistair Lucas and George Pring (eds), *Human Rights in Natural Resource Development: Public Participation in the Sustainable Development of Mining and Energy Resources*, New York: Oxford University Press, 2002.

57 Damian Chalmers, 'Food for Thought: Reconciling European Risks and Traditional Ways of Life', *Modern Law Review*, 2003, 66, pp. 532–62; Donald Slater: 'Would Chocolate by Any Other Name Taste as Sweet? A Brief History of the Naming of Generic Foodstuffs in the EC with Regard to the Recent Chocolate Cases' (Case C-12/00, Commission *v* Spain and Case C-[14/00], Commission *v* Italy)', *German Law Journal*, 4, 2003, 4, pp. 571–87.

58 Oren Perez, 'The Many Faces of the Trade-Environment Conflict: Some Lessons for the Constitutionalization Project', in Christian Joerges, Inger-Johanne Sand and Gunther Teubner (eds), *Constitutionalism and Transnational Governance*, Oxford: Hart Publishing, 2004, pp. 233–55.

59 Poul. F. Kjaer, 'A Hybrid within a Hybrid: Contextualizing REACH in the Process of European Integration and Constitutionalization', *European Journal of Risk Regulation*, 2010, 4, pp. 383–96.

60 For an empirical analysis, see Poul F. Kjaer, 'Formalization or De-formalization through Governance?', in Rainer Nickel (ed.), *Conflict of Laws and Laws of Conflict in Europe and Beyond: Patterns of Supranational and Transnational Juridification*, Antwerp: Intersentia Publishing, 2010, pp. 189–200.

61 Martti Koskenniemi, 'Legal Fragmentation(s) – An Essay on Fluidity and Form', in Gralf-Peter Calliess, Andreas Fischer-Lescano, Dan Wielsch and Peer Zumbansen (eds), *Soziologische*

Jurisrudenz: Festschrift für Gunther Teubner zum 65. Geburtstag, Berlin: Walter de Gruyter, 2009, pp. 795–810; Andreas Fischer-Lescano and Gunther Teubner, *Regime-Kollisionen: Zur Fragmentierung des globalen Rechts*, Frankfurt am Main: Suhrkamp Verlag, 2006.

62 Kjaer, *Between Governing and Governance.*

63 For theoretical considerations on the concepts of 'context' and 'simultaneousness', see Poul F. Kjaer, 'Systems in Context: On the Outcome of the Habermas/Luhmann-debate', *Ancilla Iuris*, 2006, pp. 66–77.

64 This section not only builds a link to, but also expands upon my previous work on the concept of governance. See, most notably, Kjaer, *Between Governing and Governance.*

65 R.A.W. Rhodes, 'Understanding Governance: Ten Years On', *Organization Studies*, 2007, pp. 1243–64.

66 Poul F. Kjaer, 'Constitutionalizing Governing and Governance in Europe', *Comparative Sociology*, 2010, 9, pp. 86–119; Kjaer, 'A Hybrid within a Hybrid'.

67 Slaughter, *A New World Order.*

68 Poul F. Kjaer, 'Post-Hegelian Networks: Comments on the Chapter by Simon Deakin', in Marc Amstutz and Gunther Teubner (eds), *Networks: Legal Issues of Multilateral Cooperation*, Oxford: Hart Publishing, 2009, pp. 75–85.

69 An illusion which Anne-Marie Slaughter seems to share; see Slaughter, *A New World Order*, p. 58.

70 For the complexity of giving gifts, see Marcel Mauss, *Essai sur le don: Forme et raison de l'échange dans les sociétés archaïques*, Paris: Presses universitaires de France, [1925] 2007.

71 Joseph H.H. Weiler, 'Epilogue, "Comitology" as Revolution – Infranationalism, Constitutionalism and Democracy', in Christian Joerges and Ellen Vos (eds), *EU Committees: Social Regulation, Law and Politics*, Oxford: Hart Publishing, 1999, pp. 337–50, at 342.

72 Karl-Heinz Ladeur, 'Towards a Legal Theory of Supranationality – the Viability of the Network Concept', *European Law Journal*, 1997, 3, pp. 33–54, at 47.

73 Karl-Heinz Ladeur, 'Towards a Legal Theory of Supranationality', pp. 33–54.

74 For the history of public/private relations, see Charles Donahue, 'Private Law Without the State and During its Formation', *American Journal of Comparative Law*, 2008, 56, pp. 541–66; Duncan Kennedy, 'The Stages of the Decline of the Public/Private Distinction', *University of Pennsylvania Law Review*, 1982, 130, pp. 1349–57.

75 For further elaboration on the concept of network governance, see Poul. F. Kjaer, 'Embeddedness through Networks – a Critical appraisal of the Network Concept in the Oeuvre of Karl-Heinz Ladeur', *German Law Journal*, 2009, 10, pp. 483–99.

76 David M. Trubek and Patrick Cottrell, 'Robert Hudec and the Theory of International Economic Law: The Law of the Global Space', *Society of International Economic Law, Working Paper*, No. 02, 2008, p. 47.

77 Gunther Teubner, 'Das Recht hybrider Netzwerke', *Zeitschrift für das gesamte Handelsrecht und Wirtschaftsrecht*, 2001, 165, pp. 550–75.

78 Marc Amstutz, 'In-between Worlds: Marleasing and the Emergence of Interlegality in Legal Reasoning', *European Law Journal*, 2005, 11, pp. 766–84.

79 Poul F. Kjaer, 'The Structural Transformation of Embeddedness', in Christian Joerges and Josef Falke (eds), *Karl Polan, Globalisation and the Potential of Law in Transnational Markets*, Oxford: Hart Publishing, 2011, pp. 85–104.

Part II

Re-configurations of law and the political

4 The law within and in between normative orders

4.1 Introduction

The multiple worlds which can be observed in the global realm gain the status of normative orders to the extent that they are legally framed and stabilised. They become normative orders when they are condensed and given form through a coherent arrangement of rules, reflecting specific structures of expectations (*Erwartungsstrukturen*),[1] which are linked to the deployment of legal sanctions as a means of establishing compliance with these expectations upon the basis of a hierarchy of norms. The function and set-up of law is, however, different within different types of normative order which again reflect the different location and function of normative orders within world society. Nonetheless, certain general features of law common to all types of normative order in world society can be pinned down. In the following, these features are reconstructed through reference to the concepts of hybridity, fragmentation, heterarchy and inter-contextuality. Against this background, a key distinction is introduced between the internal and external dimensions of the law of normative orders. The former is oriented towards the internal stabilisation and condensation of such orders, while the latter is oriented towards the establishment of compatibility between a given normative order and other normative orders. The different function of the internal and external dimensions of law implies that the relative weight of normative and cognitive structures of expectations differs within the two dimensions. The orientation towards internal condensation is closely linked to the upholding of normative expectations, whereas the orientation towards external compatibility constitutes a structural setting in which adaptability through the reliance on cognitive approaches tends to dominate.

4.2 Hybrid law

The activation of legal instruments is the central mechanism through which the condensation of inner worlds into normative orders is achieved. But the law is not external to such worlds, but, instead, emerges through re-combinations in which immanent elements of social processes are combined with already existing legal set-ups. Hybrids, consisting of given social structures and the legal frameworks which stabilise such structures, emerge.[2] The law becomes distinct from the social processes towards which it is oriented when three interconnected and simultaneously unfolding dimensions can be identified. First, reflexive processes which stabilise the law's own reproduction by reference to a general symbol of validity (*Geltungssymbol*) in the form of the code lawful/unlawful (*Recht/Unrecht*). Second, a specific prestation of law is made vis-à-vis other partial segments of society which enables the law to serve as a medium for the stabilisation of conflicts between such partial structures. Third, as indicated earlier, there is the reproduction of a function (*Funktion*) for society as a whole through the upholding of normative expectations.[3] Through the upholding of normative expectations, law becomes the central category through which the factual unfolding of the social processes of a given world and the imaginary normative vision upon which this world relies are reconciled. As such, the function of law can also be understood as bridging the time gap between the changes in the actual composition of a specific world and the changes in the immanently unfolding vision of that world.

A particularly clear example of the hybridity of focal social processes and law can be detected in relation to the state-building processes which lead to the establishment of modern statehood and the relation between law and the political within these processes. A continuum of positions can be observed: Chris Thornhill argues that modern law and politics are deeply interwoven and, in fact, emerged in a fusioned manner. From this perspective, the modern form of the political is based upon the distinction of rights/non-rights, thereby making the legal form the form of the political. Or to put it more precisely, according to Thornhill, the distinction of rights/non-rights emerges as a 'meta-code' forging a unity of law and politics, since the code of lawful/unlawful for law and the government/opposition distinction of politics only unfolds within the larger frame constituted by the rights/non-rights distinction. Thus, from this perspective, no operational distinction exists between law and politics.[4] A less-radical, but, in practice, closely linked perspective is advanced by Jürgen Habermas, who advances the thesis of an 'internal connection between law and political power',[5] in which the law's stabilisation of normative expectations and political will formation is seen as emerging under a condition of simultaneousness.[6] For Luhmann, the internal link between law and political power is replaced with a 'certain functional synthesis between politics and law'.[7] But, at the same time, Luhmann continuously emphasises the difference between law and politics, since he underlines that the synthesis between them emerged upon the basis of two different functions: the stabilisation of normative expectations by the legal system, and collectively binding decision-making by the political system. But, in spite of this principle difference between the positions of Habermas and Luhmann, the practical difference remains more gradual than fundamental since the transfer of social components from one sphere to the other is addressed from a procedural perspective by both scholars. This is also reinforced by Luhmann's acknowledgement that the functional synthesis tends to lead to considerable overlaps in the modes of the self-description of the legal and the political systems, for example in relation to the concepts of legitimacy and justice.[8] This gradualism was, furthermore, anticipated and underlined by the early works of Gunther Teubner, who, upon the basis of his concept of reflexive law,[9] purposefully steered in between Habermas and Luhmann.[10] Finally, Marc Amstutz, while maintaining the idea of functional synthesis, emphasises a different kind of hybridity through his emphasis on the embeddedness of law in the broader cultural settings within which it operates.[11]

Amsutz's emphasis on the cultural dimension, which can also be found in the works of the late Gunther Teubner, means that hybridity is not only central in relation to law and politics. Instead, the figure of hybridity represents a far more general category which is apparent in essentially all relations between law and non-legal social structures. The law is a 'living law' which is derived from all sorts of social processes. The question of how law simultaneously handles both its attachment and its separation from non-legal social processes and thus the question of when a given communication actually 'becomes law' therefore become central. In national settings characterised by a high level of institutional stability certain stabilisation of expectations between legal and non-legal forms of communication can be observed, thereby making this question less pertinent. But at the transnational level of world society, the question is far more pressing because the boundaries between law and non-law tend to be systematically unclear. Legal and non-legal social structures tend to melt together in an impalpable manner which makes it difficult to establish clear-cut criteria concerning 'where the law ends' and where something else begins.[12] This can be observed in relation to a vast host of transnational regimes dealing with issues as different as product standards,[13] sport,[14] the Internet[15] and investment arbitration.[16] Although considerable variation exists in terms of maturity and denseness, processes of differentiation (*Ausdifferenzierung*) which lead to the establishment of increasingly elaborated legally framed regulatory regimes have emerged from within these social processes.[17] But this development has so far not led to the emergence of clear-cut boundaries, but has, instead, resulted in a state of 'permanent indeterminacy' between law and non-law as also reflected in the discourse on 'hard' *versus* 'soft' law. Corporate social responsibility frameworks and the kind of benchmarking frameworks deployed by the European Union, the International Monetary Fund, and the Organisation for Economic Co-operation and Development are examples of this in that the merger of legal and non-legal features has led to the emergence of social practices which resemble legal modes without these practices having a basis in formalised law.[18] The consequence is a gradualisation, taking the form of a continuum between 'hard' and 'soft' law, in which the 'shadow of hierarchy' and thus the capability to invoke negative sanctions gradually diminishes the more 'soft' the law becomes.[19]

Returning to the relationship between law and political-administrative frameworks, the functional synthesis between law and politics seems to be far weaker in transnational settings when compared with nation-state settings. Transnational legal regimes often rely upon 'judge-made law' to a far higher extent than is the case within nation-state structures, since it is developed without or only with very weak references to formal legislation produced within the political system.[20] One of the many signs which indicate a move towards increased juridification is the emergence of some 125 transnational courts or court-like structures.[21] The existence of such structures makes it plausible to speak of a distinct category of transnational law which compromises all-law regulating actions and events that transcend national frontiers.[22] A kind of law in which traditional (public and private) international law clearly provides a strong component at the same time as the category cannot be reduced to international law. Instead, international law merely fulfils the (important) function of structuring the embedment of states in world society in that it enables a transfer of the social components produced by states to the transnational layer or – via the transnational layer – from one state to another.[23] In addition, transnational political-administrative structures often expand their operations without relying upon a formal legal basis. In many instances, law is mainly activated *ex-post* in order to formalise the already existing structures.[24] In their internal organisation, transnational political-administrative structures are, moreover, characterised by an absence of democracy, in the sense that none of them operate upon the basis of hierarchy 'with a divided peak',[25] or in a manner which corresponds to more traditional concepts of parliamentary democracy.[26]

As already indicated, the conglomerate of transnational structures is, however, far from representing a group of homogeneous structures. Instead, we are dealing with a *continuum of concretisation* (Kelsen) in which some organisations and regimes are relatively closely tied to nation states within the framework of classical international law, whereas others operate in a more autonomous manner.[27] This is irrespective of the fact that none of them can be understood as mere 'extensions' of the nation-state universe, since all of them, albeit to different degrees, possess an autonomous element and operate upon the basis of internal dynamics. As mentioned previously, this is also the case in relation to transnational organisations which rely on formal delegation from nation states, since the delegation of competences implies recognition of the autonomy of the structure to which delegation is made, just as delegation implies a transfer of discretionary capacities which enable a choice between several possible operations. In practice, the distinction between national and transnational law is, therefore, not clear-cut. As a phenomenon such as the European Union, operating as a hybrid in between nation-state and global regulatory structures, testifies, it is possible to observe a certain gradualisation between national and transnational law operating upon a public law basis. The same is the case in relation to private-law structures in so far as the possibility of 'forum shopping' between state-based legal orders is an essential dimension of transnational private law. Thus, transnational private law is also closely linked to national legal orders. This again makes it difficult to subsume a given legal structure exclusively under one category. Instead, national courts, in the same manner as other nationally based organisations such as firms and non-governmental organisations, tend to develop an additional transnational dimension at the same time as the operationability of transnational legal structures remains conditioned by their ability to establish compatibility with nation-state law. For example, the co-operation between (especially lower level) national courts and the Court of Justice of the European Union (CJEU) testifies to the fact that transnational legal components are also being produced by structures that otherwise operate in a national context and vice versa. Thus, transnationality is, as previously noted, a specific social practice which relies upon a particular logic which is distinct, but nonetheless deeply intertwined with nation-state practices.

4.3 Fragmented law

In a similar manner to the way in which hybridity is a central element of law throughout world society, and a particular strong feature of transnational processes, the fragmentation of law along functionally differentiated lines is also particularly prominent within the transnational level of contemporary world society. As pointed out by Martti Koskenniemi, fragmentation is not a new thing but is instead a phenomenon which has emerged time and again at points in history at which the world was 'in flow'. The social world is, of course, always in flow, albeit as the evolutionary scheme of variation, selection and retention indicates different phases of social evolution are marked by different problem constellations. From this perspective, fragmentation tends to occur in moments with a high level of variation. Moments which are characterised by high levels of uncertainty in which well-known categories have broken down at the same time as new frameworks have not yet been established. This was the case when Roman law was re-formulated within the emerging European space in the eleventh and twelfth centuries, during the move towards natural law in the sixteenth and seventeenth centuries, and at the time of the move towards positivist law in the eighteenth and nineteenth centuries.[28] All of these transformations were closely linked to deeper structural transformations through changes in the forms of differentiation which characterised society as a whole. This can also be observed in relation to ongoing developments in which functional differentiation is expanding at a rapid pace, leading to the emergence and increased densification of functionally differentiated types of law such as economic law, environmental law and human-rights law. These different areas of law are characterised by different institutional structures, for example, in the form of the function of specific courts and arbitration frameworks, praxis of co-ordination through the reliance on specific conceptual frameworks and principles, such as the precautionary principle within environmental law and the efficiency criteria within economic law, and particular narratives concerning their respective 'missions' in the world. Thus, each legal regime tends to gain the form of epistemic communities, each of which promotes different and quite specific understandings of a given legal issue. For example, the legal problem concerning the regulation of genetically modified organisms can be approached from an economic law perspective, an environmental law perspective, or be seen as a human-rights law issue. Each of these perspectives will, furthermore, provide radically different solutions to the issue in question.[29] It follows that the existence of multiple legal perspectives on the same issue lead to battles of competences with all the legal fields involved claiming their unique capability to handle a given problem upon the basis of claims to supremacy. In practice, these battles of delineation of legal fields serve as the way through which the boundaries between different legal fields are continuously re-affirmed. This development is being further enhanced by the hybridity of law and the orientation of specific legal regimes towards specific focal social processes. This is the case because the different legal regimes distil a specific legal version of the world-view which these different social processes reproduce, thereby making the way in which law approaches a specific social problem into a question of the choice of concepts and categories. Economic law, for example, seeks to translate insights of economic theory into legal language and to provide economic interests and expectations a legal form, while environmental law derives it insights and distils a particular legal version of scientific insights concerning the state of the environment and the perspectives of environmental policy-makers.[30]

4.4 Heterarchical law

The notion of state sovereignty implies that national legal orders are, at least ideally, 'definite' legal orders, in the sense that there is 'nothing above them' at the same time as they internally are characterised by a hierarchy of norms. As stated in Chapter 2, the ideal of state-based legal orders possessing out-right supremacy within their respective territories remains, from a factual perspective, a fiction in the majority of the world, due to the persistent vibrancy of localistic forms of social ordering operating 'beneath' the state. Thus, sovereignty is a mere *claim* which can be more or less realised in different contexts. When the existence of extensive forms of legally framed transnational orders is added to the picture, it becomes immediately clear that states are just one, albeit extremely important, type of legal ordering. If one ranks the 193 states which are currently members of the United Nations according to the impact which they have on world society and subsequently plot in transnationally operating organisations such as the Church of Rome, the European Union, the World Bank, Google Inc., Wal-Mart, Amnesty International and the International Red Cross, according to their independent impact on the world, these orders would appear more powerful than many states, and, in some cases, even more powerful than the majority of states existing in the world. In world society, a multiplicity of legally condensed normative orders makes claims to their own sovereignty and legal autonomy, while seeking to fend off claims of superiority from competing legal orders. This is also not being changed by the normative objective of the United Nations legal order to install itself as the superior and unifying legal order of the world.[31] Not only does this intention remain a claim which is similar to other claims which have not factually materialised themselves, but with the increased reliance on functional differentiation as the organisational principle of transnational processes, the core United Nations activities centred around the security council have, furthermore, been reduced to one limited regime among others, which orients itself towards the handling of security issues in relation to the organised use of violence in the form of war and terrorism.[32]

It follows from the above that the structural reality of law is a reflection of the multiplicity of conflict lines which characterise world society. Whereas classical conflict of laws perspectives have concerned themselves with the relation between different state-based legal orders and the question of in which order a given legal problem should be addressed, we are, instead, dealing with a far broader constellation of conflict lines in which 'traditional and pre-modern' forms of social organisation operating beneath the nation-state layer, national state legal orders themselves as well as legally condensed transnational regimes collide. For example, the extraction of oil, gas and other mineral resources tends to provide a set-up in which the transnational legal regimes for energy, environmental protection, human rights, investment protection, security and transport are linked up with nation-state legal orders as well as the forms of normative ordering which characterise the ethnic and religious communities located within the states in question.[33] A new multi-dimensional conflict of laws has emerged which is not only oriented towards the horizontal conflict between state-based legal orders, but also towards the vertical conflicts between organisational principles linked to localistic, national and transnational forms of law,[34] and the horizontal conflicts between different functionally differentiated transnational legal regimes, as well as 'diagonal' conflicts between legal orders which belong to different categories.[35] Complex assemblages in which the different conflict lines intersect emerge and become the central *locos* of conflict.[36] This is also the case in the European setting. The advanced state of European integration has led to the emergence of a three-dimensional conflict of laws constellation in which the European Union legal order, the legal orders of the Member States and a multitude of private regimes intersect within specific functional areas, such as agriculture, business, environmental protection and health at the same time as an assemblage of assemblages has emerged loosely co-ordinating the different processes.[37] An assemblage of assemblages which itself is part of other assemblages through its intersection with non-Member State legal orders and globally operating regimes.[38] Thus, in spite of the existence of localistic meta-orders, such as the European conglomerate centred on the European Union, the world, as a whole, remains without a legally condensed unifying centre and without a meta-language capable of establishing a unified perspective on the world.

4.5 Intra- and inter-contextual law

The lack of a singular legal order in the global realm is the basis for the classical realist perspective within international relations studies, which sees the international world as characterised by anarchy and power politics.[39] From a sociological perspective, this is a deeply implausible perspective. The most puzzling factor is rather the high level of order and stability characterising the world. Not only do the vast majority of states comply with international norms almost all of the time, but also the level of open conflict between states remains surprisingly limited. Armed violent conflict is today, in the form of civil wars, mainly an inner-state phenomenon, while inter-state war is a very limited and particularistic phenomenon occurring within rather small segments of the globe. But also when one goes beyond inter-state relations the intensity of conflict in the global realm seems to be radically overstated. In spite of financial upheaval, recurrent ecological catastrophes and violent clashes, the social processes of, for example, the economy, science and the mass media possess an infrastructure which enables them to operate globally, and, in doing so, they are characterised by a surprising stability when the absence of a unitary order is taken into account.

Deciphering the enigma of how global order is possible in a heterarchical world necessitates a co-evolutionary perspective which is capable of highlighting the interfaces between and mutual fixation of different social processes. In earlier theories of social evolution, the problem of evolution was ultimately reduced to a question of adaptation. Out of a pool of possible selections, a social structure gives preference to those elements which are most aligned with the social environment in which the social structure in question operates. In other words, earlier theories of social evolution assumed that a sort of 'direct causality' exists between external pressures and internal selections. From such a perspective, the autonomy of social processes can only be understood as being rather minimal.[40] In order to make the evolutionary perspective compatible with the theory of autopoiesis, Luhmann instead reconstructed the relationship between variation, selection and retention as a purely internal process based upon an internal model of the environment within a given social system. Thus, the idea of one-to-one causality was rejected. At the same time, however, he sees the core trigger of evolutionary processes as the attempt of social systems to handle increased complexity in their environments. As such, he gives a more sophisticated account than his predecessors, but, despite his argument that he turns evolutionary theory 'outside in', he ulti-mately ends up with a similar perspective: the core trigger of evolutionary developments remains exogenous in nature. In contrast to this perspective, Marc Amstutz emphasises that evolutionary processes must be understood as 'co-constructing' processes in which internal and external factors are co-fixated *over time* in the form of a reciprocity loop. Thus, a social system remains strongly influenced by its social environment at the same time that the system in question simultaneously produces elements which change the composition of its social environment.[41] As such, Amstutz *de facto* makes the concept of *co-evolution*, rather than the concept of evolution, the central concept from which he departs. Although co-evolution is also a central aspect of Luhmannian systems theory, Amstutz's position, nonetheless, implies a subtle and quite central change of perspective in that it is the *mutual* stabilisation of different evolutionary processes, rather than the internal processes themselves, that thereby becomes the central object of study. It follows that the clue to deciphering the enigma of world society is located *in between* systems rather than within systems.[42]

Following Luhmann, co-evolution only unfolds in the limited cases of structural coupling which occur when a system gains the awareness that the existence and continued reproduction of another system is pivotal for its own self-preservation, thereby leading to a stabilisation of expectations vis-à-vis that system. When addressing the fragmentation of global law, Amstutz has, in contrast, advanced the hypothesis that in order to understand the specificities of global law adequately one would have to understand it as being characterised by interpenetration, rather than by the kind of general system/environment relations to which the concept of structural coupling refers.[43] This seemingly innocent move has quite drastic consequences, however. Interpenetration, in contrast to structural coupling, implies that a system makes its own complexity available for the build-up of complexity within another system. Moreover, both systems involved have direct effect on the texturing of the other system.[44] Amstutz does not, however, develop the proposal that interpenetration should be regarded as the rule, and structural coupling as the exception, upon the basis of mere legal insights. Instead, as already indicated, he sees a close link to the kind of cultural interpenetrations which can be described with the concepts of *métissage*, creolisation, amalgamation and alloysation.[45] He is hereby implicitly arguing that the Luhmannian version of systems theory is reductive in nature, providing a simplified picture of society, in the sense that the systemic component is only one of several aspects of society. Systems are, to a certain extent, parasites which are conditioned by the existence of latent socio-cultural structures from which they can distil their components. It follows that autopoietic systems cannot be considered to be 'pure' processes merely reproducing themselves upon the basis of recursive operations. Instead, the socio-cultural universes in which social systems are embedded serve as the resource which allows interpenetration to take place because successful interpenetration is conditioned by the existence of a common world of meaning (*Sinnwelt*).[46]

Modernity is, however, a 'second nature' which is different from the socio-cultural universes from which it emerged. To use a Leninist expression, the second nature of modernity manifests itself in the transformation of society into an 'organisational society' (*Organisationsgesellschaft*). So, although the common frames of meaning in the form of the larger socio-cultural universes provide a structural backdrop for co-evolution, the actual realisation of co-evolution, within the segments of world society which have undergone a profound process of modernisation, tend to be conditioned by the existence of organisational sites which are located in between different normative orders. The heterarchical governance arrangements analysed in the previous chapter are such sites. In the case of the European Union, Comitology committees, for example, not only serve as the channels through which transfers between the European Union and the Member State legal orders take place, but also serve as the kind of reciprocity loops to which Amstutz refers. They are frameworks that are located in the 'no man's land' between different legally condensed normative orders and which *simultaneously* make the resources of Member State administrations available for the European Union apparatus and the resources of the European Union available for the Member State administrations, thereby allowing for mutually reinforcing co-evolutionary processes. From this perspective, a deepening of European integration is, therefore, not to be understood as a zero-sum game which necessarily implies a weakening of the Member States. On the contrary, the establishment of increased compatibility between the Member State legal orders via the European Union framework as well as compatibility with the European Union legal order itself provides the Member States with resources and increased operational freedom that underpins, rather than undermines, the further evolution of the Member State legal orders.[47] A similar logic can be detected within the area of corporate social responsibility which Amstutz himself has explored. Corporate social responsibility frameworks serve as the institutional network-based framework through which multinational companies seeks to embed their activities in the broader societal contexts within which they operate.[48] Networks which tend to rely on commonly agreed normative objectives and declarations of intent while, in practice, serving as formulae for the stabilisation of expectations and the transfer of social components between the participating organisations. In practice, corporate social responsibility measures thus serve a co-evolutionary purpose, to the extent that they allow for an exchange of symbolic resources between organisations or a mutual reliance on resources reproduced by other organisations. Multinationals companies have financial resources, research institutes possess a particular kind of knowledge, public administrations possess capabilities of both rule creation and enforcement, and non-governmental organisations possess a particular kind of legitimacy and often also a certain kind of rootedness within local communities. Thus, the 'additional value' produced by corporate social responsibility frameworks are that they are aimed at enabling co-evolutionary processes to unfold through the stabilisation of mutually reinforcing relationships.

The emergence and, not least, the centrality of such intermediate structures located in between different social processes have decisive consequences for the understanding of the operationability of society and the location of law creation within it. The one-dimensional system-theoretical attempt to reduce the world to operationally closed processes is insufficient, because the internal structuring of social processes is structurally dependent on the existence of an external dimension which is located in between such processes. Such external dimensions are not mere structural couplings. Instead, they serve as *autonomous* sites for the generation of meaning, which produces an *independent impact* on the world.[49] The hybrid emergence of law from within non-legal social processes implies that such intermediate structures, furthermore, become autonomous sources for the production of law.

Recalling that normative orders are hybrids which establish the unity between systemic structures and their respective contexts, the law emerging from within such orders is also of a hybrid nature, in that it is possible to distinguish between the internal and external law of normative orders.[50] Both dimensions of law refer to the same code in the form of law/non-law, which serve as the central propeller of reflexivity through which the self-preservation of law is ensured. In a similar vein, the prestation which the internal and external dimensions of the law of normative orders produces vis-à-vis other partial segments of world society remains the same in so far as they are oriented towards the handling of social conflicts which occur in other partial segments of society. The fundamental, and very decisive, difference between the internal and external law of normative orders can be found in relation to their respective functions vis-à-vis world society in its entirety. The primary function of the internal dimension is to ensure a positive condensation, accomplished through re-iteration,[51] of the normative order in question and the establishment of a general convergence of the time structures (*Gesamt-gesellschaftliche Zeitausgleich*) reproduced by that order.[52] The function of the external law of normative orders is the direct opposite. Instead of condensation, its function is to facilitate the transfer of social components, such as economic products and capital, scientific knowledge, religious beliefs, political decisions and educational competences between different legally condensed normative orders. As, for example, is also apparent in the conflict of laws approach developed by Christian Joerges within the context of European Union law,[53] and the world-law theory of Marc Amstutz,[54] the external law of normative orders is essentially oriented towards establishing compatibility between different legally condensed normative orders. Or to express it differently, although both the internal and the external dimensions of the law of normative orders produce elements of positive and negative integration, both forms are characterised by a fundamental structural asymmetry in that the inner law of normative orders has a built-in bias in favour of positive integration through condensation while the external law has a bias in favour of negative integration through the facilitation of transfer.[55]

Not surprisingly, ideologically inclined participants in the ongoing academic debate on the globalisation of law and constitutional ordering tend to analyse the implications of the distinction between the internal and external dimensions of normative orders as a difference between republican and liberal perspectives on law and the political.[56] Going beyond such indulgence in semantics, which merely scratches the surface of the social, the fundamentally different functions of the internal and external dimensions of the law of normative orders provides an explanation of the *mutual constitutiveness* between national and transnational forms of ordering in world society. As indicated, the increased internal condensation of a normative order implies the fortification of its boundaries through the activation of exclusion mechanisms. But far more decisive is the fact that the effective maintenance of boundaries always implies adaptation to the environment in which such boundaries are made. A central insight of systems theory is, therefore, that the increased closure of a social entity is the condition for increased openness and *vice versa*.[57] Or to express it differently, increased condensation is conditioned by increased possibility of transfer. For example, the conversion of early-modern England and the Netherlands into the first modern states was closely linked to their being comparatively open economies just as the gradual strengthening of these states was structurally related to their embeddedness in imperial frameworks which relied on extensive transnational legal frameworks with a mainly private law character.[58] In the same manner, the most modern states today, such as those located in North America and North-western Europe, remain the states with the most open economies and the highest level of embeddedness in transnational frameworks, such as the quasi-imperial alliance system of the United States and the European Union. Furthermore – and rather counter-intuitively – a strong correlation seems to exist between the (economic) openness of a state and the size of its public sector. The more open the economy is, the larger the public sector tends to be, because increased openness implies increased volatility, thereby creating a functional need for the introduction of stabilising mechanisms.[59]

4.6 The normative and cognitive dimensions of law

The internal and external dimensions of the law of normative orders are apparent at both the national and the transnational level of world society. But, due to the different location and function of national and transnational structures within world society, the relative importance of the external and internal dimensions is very different. When compared with the national level, only weak forms of internal hierarchisation exist within transnational orders, at the same time as the external dimension plays a far larger role. This has direct consequences for the mixture of normative and cognitive forms of expectations which tends to prevail within the two layers.

Whereas nation-state law primarily produces and stabilises normative expectations of the kind which are maintained even if they are not materialised,[60] the cognitive aspect plays a relatively larger role within the transnational layer of world society. One reason for this is that functionally differentiated processes, such as the economy and science, which are characterised by a strong reliance on cognition when compared, for example, to politics and intimacy, tend to be the most globalised dimensions of society, and this is reflected within the transnational space. This argument is, however, only partially valid, in that structures characterised by a strong normative component, such as religious structures, have always been important within the transnational dimension of world society. Thus, the pre-dominance of cognitive structures might only be true for some dimensions of the transnational space. Another, and more central, reason for the larger role of cognitive components, relative to normative components, within transnational processes is the inter-contextual function of transnational processes. The constitutive function of transnational processes for world society as a whole is the facilitation of the transfer of social components from one context to another. This was the case for colonialism as well as for contemporary global regulatory frameworks. Common for, otherwise, very different processes such as risk regulation within the World Trade Organization and the European Union, the Open Method of Co-ordination Processes within the Organisation for Economic Co-operation and Development and the European Union, as well as corporate social responsibility processes are their orientation towards the enablement of the transfer of social components from one context to another. Such transfers are, however, only possible if the condensed social components in question are made compatible with the context to which they are transferred. The kind of legal stabilisation mechanisms which have emerged within such structures tend to be oriented towards enabling embeddedness through adaptation upon the basis of reflexive processes. Thus, transnational processes and, with them, the specific type of law guiding such processes tend to be structurally oriented towards facilitating learning processes, and are, therefore, characterised by a higher reliance on cognitive, rather than normative, structures of expectations.

The inter-contextuality dimension combined with the stronger cognitive component means that the effects on society produced by the kind law which has been described as transnational, global or world law (which, in effect, merely refers to the external law of normative orders) is very different than the effects produced by national law. This becomes especially clear when the distinction between reflexivity, prestation and function of law is kept in mind.[61] In relation to the first dimension, the form of transnational legal processes is relatively similar to the form of nation-state-based legal processes, and the outcome produced might thus be relatively similar. In relation to the prestation and function of law vis-à-vis other social structures and society as such, the effect of nation-state law and transnational law is, however, substantially different. The central characteristic of nation-state law is the production of social integration through the upholding of norms which are maintained even when not (fully) materialised in society. Or to express it differently, nation-state law is, by definition, conservative. Transnational law also produces social integration, in the sense that it is oriented towards bridging contexts. The manner in which this is achieved is, however, the direct opposite of nation-state law. At least when observed from a continental European civil-law perspective, national law produces integration through – in terms of space – the construction of clearly delineated national contexts and – in terms of time – a reduction in the pace of societal development in the sense that the norms upheld by the legal system change at a slower pace than other societal norms, thereby introducing a kind of 'friction' which tends to reduce the contingency, volatility and speed of social change. Transnational law, instead, produces an acceleration of time and an expansion in space, in the sense that it is oriented towards reducing the 'friction' which societal processes, such as economic transactions, encounter due to the existence of the diversity of cultures, functional spheres and states. This might also explain why transnational law is characterised by a far higher level of judicial activism in the sense that courts tend to act as the catalysts – rather than as the enforcers – of already established norms.[62] Thus, the societal impact of law is turned upside down when one compares nation-state and transnational law.

It follows that, despite of the entangledness and mutual constitutiveness of transnational and national law, the relationship is potentially conflictual in nature, as, for example, is exemplified by the stand-off between Argentina and the International Monetary Fund at the beginning of the new millennium and imposition of 'austerity' by the *troika* composed of the European Commission, the European Central Bank and the International Monetary Fund in relation to a number of crisis-ridden Member States in the eurozone in the wake of the 2008 financial crisis. When transnational legal acts are transplanted into national configurations, they are often disruptive elements which can, potentially, undermine the kind of complex institutional set-ups which have emerged through long-term evolutionary processes. National configurations are constituted through a complex mutual fixation of a whole range of dimensions, such as political, economic, educational and social-security structures. If the attachment to the configuration of a single dimension, such as the economic, is undermined, the entire construction is, therefore, prone to disintegration.[63] The kind of limited intervention vis-à-vis a single dimension which typically occurs when radically fragmented transnational law structures seek to transfer legal components into national settings, therefore, potentially threatened to release far more fundamental distortions into the set-up of national configurations.[64] The collision between territorial and functional forms of ordering and rule-making tend to be of a far more fundamental nature than what can be read out of the kind of surgical interventions which tend to be the trigger or catalyst of such collisions.

4.7 Conclusion

Above, a number of core features of the law of normative orders were reconstructed through a reference to the concepts of hybridity, fragmentation, heterarchy and inter-contextuality. The emergence of these notions reflects a deeper endeavour, which has become apparent in recent decades, to re-conceptualise the function and prestation of law in society. Common to these attempts have been the desire to understand law as a framework for the facilitation of learning processes in society, rather than as a framework for upholding normative expectations, a desire which has, furthermore, been reflected in the attempt to understand law as being increasingly reconfigured away from a reliance on normative expectations and towards a reliance on cognitive expectations. The above reconstruction provides the basis for a somewhat alternative perspective on this development. Rather than a transformation of law as such, the move towards the facilitation of learning is linked to very specific inter-contextual processes and the function of facilitating transfers between contexts. The internal and external dimensions of the law of normative orders are, therefore, characterised by substantially different combinations of normative and cognitive expectations. Only in the external dimension do cognitive forms of expectations tend to gain a structurally dominant position. The different function of national and transnational processes in the wider context of world society, as expressed in the notions of condensation and transfer, combined with their respective reliance on territorial and functional differentiation, furthermore, implies that the relative weight of the internal and external dimension of law differs fundamentally when ones compare national and transnational structures.

Notes

1 Robert N. Ross, 'Ellipsis and the Structure of Expectation, *San José State Occasional Papers in Linguistics*, 1, November, 1975.

2 Inger-Johanne Sand, 'Hybrid Law – Law in a Global Society of Differentiation and Change', in Gralf-Peter Calliess, Andreas Fischer-Lescano, Dan Wielsch and Peer Zumbansen (eds), *Soziologische Jurisprudenz: Festschrift für Gunther Teubner zum 65. Geburtstag*, Berlin: Walter de Gruyter, 2009, pp. 871–86, at 871.

3 Gunther Teubner, 'Globale Bukowina: Zur Emergenz eines transnationalen Rechtspluralismus', *Rechtshistorisches Journal*, 1996, 15, pp. 255–90, at 273 *et seq.*

4 For this perspective, see Chris Thornhill, 'A Sociology of Constituent Power: The Political Code of Transnational Constitutions', *Indiana Journal of Global Legal Studies*, 2013, 20, issue 2, pp. 551–603.

5 Jürgen Habermas, *Faktizität und Geltung: Beiträge zur Diskurstheorie des Rechts und des demokratischen Rechtsstaats*, Frankfurt am Main: Suhrkamp Verlag, 1992, p. 167; my translation.

6 From a system-theoretical perspective, simultaneousness implies that a given distinction, in this case the distinction between law and politics, is dissolved. See also Poul F. Kjaer, 'Systems in Context: On the Outcome of the Habermas/Luhmann Debate', *Ancilla Iuris*, 2006, pp. 66–77.

7 Niklas Luhmann, *Das Recht der Gesellschaft*, Frankfurt am Main: Suhrkamp Verlag, 1993, p. 153; my translation.

8 Ibid., p. 407.

9 Gunther Teubner, 'Reflexives Recht: Entwicklungsmodelle des Rechts in vergleichender Perspektive', *Archiv für Rechts-und Sozialphilosophie*, 1982, 68, pp. 13–59.

10 This consensus-seeking endeavour triggered criticism from both sides. See Jürgen Habermas, *Faktizität und Geltung: Beiträge zur Diskurstheorie des Rechts und des demokratischen Rechtsstaats*, Frankfurt am Main: Suhrkamp Verlag, 1992, p. 73; Niklas Luhmann, 'Einige Probleme mit "reflexivem Recht"', *Zeitschrift für Rechtssoziologie*, 1985, 6, pp. 1–18.

11 Marc Amstutz and Vaios Karavas, 'Rechtsmutation Zu Genese und Evolution des Rechts im transnationalen Raum', *Rechtsgeschichte*, 2006, 8, pp. 14–32, at 16 *et seq.* For a somewhat similar perspective, see Antje Wiener, *The Invisible Constitution of Politics: Contested Norms and International Encounters*, Cambridge: Cambridge University Press, 2008.

12 Sand, 'Hybrid Law'.

13 Harm Schepel, *The Constitution of Private Governance: Product Standards in the Regulation of Integrating Markets*, Oxford: Hart Publishing, 2005.

14 Tobias Werron, *Der Weltsport und sein Publikum: Zur Autonomie und Entstehung des modernen Sports*, Weilerswist: Velbrück, 2010.
15 Vagias Karavas, *Digitale Grundrechte: Elemente einer Verfassung des Informationsflusses im Internet*, Baden-Baden: Nomos Verlag, 2007.
16 Moritz Renner, *Zwingendes transnationales Recht: Zur Struktur der Wirtschaftsverfassung jenseits des Staates*, Baden-Baden: Nomos Verlag, 2011.
17 Andreas Fischer-Lescano and Gunther Teubner, *Regime-Kollisionen: Zur Fragmentierung des Weltrechts*, Frankfurt am Main: Suhrkamp Verlag, 2006.
18 Armin Schäfer, *Die neue Unverbindlichkeit: Wirtschaftspolitische Koordinierung in Europa*, Frankfurt am Main: Campus Verlag, 2005.
19 For the EU context, see Joanne Scott and David M. Trubek, 'Mind the Gap: Law and New Approaches to Governance in the European Union', *European Law Journal*, 2002, 8, pp. 1–18; David M. Trubek and Louise G. Trubek, 'Hard and Soft Law in the Construction of Social Europe: the Role of the Open Method of Co-ordination', *European Law Journal*, 2005, 11, pp. 343–64.
20 Marc Amstutz and Vaios Karavas, 'Rechtsmutation'.
21 Andreas Fischer-Lescano and Gunther Teubner, 'Regime-Collisions: The Vain Search for Legal Unity in the Fragmentation of Global Law', *Michigan Journal of International Law*, 2004, 25, pp. 999–1046, at 1000.
22 Philip C. Jessup, *Transnational Law*, New Haven, CT: Yale University Press, 1956.
23 For similar insights, see David M. Trubek and Patrick Cottrell, 'Robert Hudec and the Theory of International Economic Law: The Law of Global Space', in Chantal Thomas and Joel P. Tractman (eds), *Developing Countries in the WTO Legal System*, Oxford: Oxford University Press, 2009, pp. 129–50.
24 Karl-Heinz Ladeur, 'Towards a Legal Theory of Supranationality – The Viability of the Network Concept', *European Law Journal*, 1997, 3, pp. 33–54.
25 Niklas Luhmann, 'Die Zukunft der Demokratie', in *Soziologische Aufklärung 4, Beiträge zur Funktionalen Differenzierung der Gesellschaft*, Opladen: Westdeutscher Verlag, 1994, pp. 126–32, at 127.
26 Jürgen Neyer, 'Justice, Not Democracy: Legitimacy in the European Union', *Journal of Common Market Studies*, 2010, 48, pp. 903–21.
27 Hauke Brunkhorst, 'Constitutionalism and Democracy in the World Society', in Petra Dobner and Martin Loughlin (eds), *The Twilight of Constitutionalism?*, Oxford: Oxford University Press, 2010, pp. 179–98.
28 Martti Koskenniemi, 'Legal Fragmentation(s). An Essay on Fluidity and Form', in Gralf-Peter Calliess, Andreas Fischer-Lescano, Dan Wielsch and Peer Zumbansen (eds), *Soziologische Jurisprudenz: Festschrift für Gunther Teubner zum 65. Geburtstag*, Berlin: Walter de Gruyter, 2009, pp. 795–810.
29 Koskenniemi, 'Legal Fragmentation(s)', at 796; Nico Krisch, 'Pluralism in Postnational Risk Regulation: The Dispute over GMOs and Trade', *Transnational Legal Theory*, 2010, 1, pp. 1–29. More generally, see Nico Krisch, *Beyond Constitutionalism: The Pluralist Structure of Postnational Law*, Oxford: Oxford University Press, 2009.
30 Koskenniemi: 'Legal Fragmentation(s)', at 797.
31 For such a view, see Pierre-Marie Dupuy, 'A Doctrinal Debate in the Globalisation Era: On the "Fragmentation" of International Law', *European Journal of Legal Studies*, 2007, 1, pp.1–19.
32 Nico Krisch, *Selbstverteidigung und kollektive Sicherheit*, Berlin, Heidelberg: Springer-Verlag, 2001.
33 For an overview, see the contributions in John-Andrew McNeish and Owen Logan (eds), *Flammable Societies: Studies on the Socio-economics of Oil and Gas*, London: Pluto Press, 2012.
34 Christoph B. Graber, 'Aboriginal Self-Determination vs. the Propertisation of Traditional Culture: The Case of Sacred Wanjina Sites', *Australian Indigenous Law Review*, 2009, 13, pp. 18–34.
35 For the concept of diagonal conflicts, see Christian Joerges, 'Re-Conceptualising European Law as Conflicts Law, the ECJ's Labour Law Jurisprudence and Germany's Federal

Constitutional Court', in Bea Verschraegen (ed.), *Interdisciplinary Studies of Comparative and Private International Law (Vol. I)*, Vienna: Jans Sramke Verlag 2010, pp. 7–18; Christoph Ulrich Schmid, 'Diagonal Competence Conflicts between European Competition Law and National Law: The Example of Book Price Fixing', *European Review of Private Law*, 2000, 8, pp. 155–72.

36 Robert Wai, 'The Interlegality of Transnational Private Law', 107 – 27, *Law and Contemporary Problems*, 2008, 71, pp. 107–27; Gunther Teubner and Andreas Fischer-Lescano, *Regime-Kollisionen: Zur Fragmentierung des globalen Rechts*, Frankfurt am Main: Suhrkamp Verlag, 2006; Andreas Fischer-Lescano and Gunther Teubner, 'Regime-Collisions: The Vain Search for Legal Unity in the Fragmentation of Global Law', *Michigan Journal of International Law*, 2004, 25, pp. 999–1046.

37 For a three-dimensional conflict of laws perspective on European integration, see Poul F. Kjaer, 'Three-dimensional Conflict of Laws in Europe', *ZERP – Discussion Papers*, 2, 2009.

38 For the example of the intersection between the EU environmental regime and global governance, see Elaine Fahey and Ester Herlin-Karnell (eds), 'Deciphering Regulatory and Constitutional Competence between EU Environmental Law and Global Governance', Special issue of German Law Journal, *German Law Journal*, 2012, 13, pp. 1147–1268.

39 Hans Morgenthau (revised by Kenneth Thompson), *Politics Among Nations: The Struggle for Power and Peace*, 7th edition, New York: McGraw-Hill, [1948] 2005.

40 Marc Amstutz, *Evolutorisches Wirtschaftsrecht: Vorstudien zum Recht und seiner Methode in den Diskurskollisionen der Marktgesellschaft*, Baden-Baden: Nomos Verlag, 2002, p. 101 et seq.

41 Ibid., 112 *et seq.*; Marc Amstutz, 'Rechtsgeschichte als Evolutionstheorie: Anmerkungen zum Theorierahmen von Marie Theres Fögens Forschungsprogramm', *Rechtgeschichte*, 2002, 1, pp. 26–31, at 26.

42 For more on this point see; Poul F. Kjaer, 'Law of the Worlds – Towards an Inter-Systemic Theory', in Stefan Keller and Stefan Wipraechtiger (eds), *Recht zwischen Dogmatik und Theorie: Marc Amstutz zum 50. Geburtstag*, Zürich: Dike Verlag, pp. 159–75.

43 Marc Amstutz, 'Métissage : Zur Rechtsform in der Weltgesellschaft', in Andreas Fischer-Lescano, Florian Rödl and Christoph U. Schmid (eds), *Europäische Gesellschaftsverfassung: Zur Konstitutionalisierung sozialer Demokratie in Europa*, Baden-Baden, Nomos Verlag, 2009, pp. 333–51, at 338.

44 Niklas Luhmann, *Soziale Systeme: Grundriß einer allgemeinen Theorie*, Frankfurt am Main: Suhrkamp Verlag, 1984, at. 290.

45 Marc Amstutz: 'Métissage', at 334 *et seq.*

46 The socio-cultural dimension Amstutz refers to resembles Habermas's concept of 'life-world'; to which Habermas ascribes a function similar to the one Amstutz sees fulfilled by socio-cultural in that the continued evolution of function systems is seen by Habermas as being conditioned by their ability to tap into the resources of the lifeworld. See Jürgen Habermas, *Theorie des kommunikativen Handelns, Band 2, Zur Kritik der funktionalistischen Vernunft*, Frankfurt am Main: Suhrkamp Verlag, 1981, p. 229 *et seq.*

47 For the same insight developed in the vocabulary of the historical discipline: Alan S. Milward, *The European Rescue of the Nation-State*, 2nd edition, London: Routledge, 2000.

48 For the relationship between corporate social responsibility and constitutionlisation processes, see Grahame F. Thompson, *The Constitutionalization of the Global Corporate Sphere?* Oxford: Oxford University Press, 2012, p. 53 *et seq.*

49 The re-configuration and, indeed expansion, of the existing systems-theoretical framework into a two-dimensional theory of society, capable of emphasising the relationship of mutual increase between intra- and inter-systemic processes, is the logical long-term consequence of this insight. See Poul F. Kjaer, 'Systems in Context'.

50 For more on this point, see Poul F. Kjaer, 'Law of the Worlds'; Poul F. Kjaer, 'The Political Foundations of Conflicts Law', *Transnational Legal Theory*, 2011, 2, pp. 227–41; Poul F. Kjaer, 'Transnational Normative Orders: The Constitutionalism of Intra- and Trans-Normative Law', *Indiana Journal of Global Legal Studies*, 2013, 20, issue 2, pp. 777–803.

51 Poul F. Kjaer, 'Systems in Context', at 70.

52 Niklas Luhmann, *Recht der Gesellschaft*, Frankfurt am Main: Suhrkamp Verlag, 1993, p. 427 *et seq.*

53 See, for example, Christian Joerges, Poul F. Kjaer and Tommi Ralli (eds), 'A New Type of Conflicts Law as Constitutional Form in the Postnational Constellation,' Special Issue of Transnational Legal Theory, 152 − 285, *Transnational Legal Theory*, 2011, 2, pp. 152–285.

54 Marc Amstutz and Vaios Karavas, 'Weltrecht: Ein Derridasches Monster', in Gralf-Peter Calliess, Andreas Fischer-Lescano, Dan Wielsch and Peer Zumbansen (eds), *Soziologische Jurisprudenz: Festschrift für Gunther Teubner zum 65. Geburtstag*, Berlin: Walter de Gruyter, 2009, pp. 645–72, at 657.

55 For an illustration of this in relation to 'Social Europe', see Christian Joerges, '*Rechtsstaat* and Social Europe: How a Classical Tension Resurfaces in the European Integration Process', *Comparative Sociology*, 2010, 9, pp. 65–85.

56 See, for example, Fritz W. Scharpf, 'Legitimacy in the Multi-level European Polity', in Petra Dobner and Martin Loughlin (eds), *The Twilight of Constitutionalism?* Oxford: Oxford University Press, 2010, pp. 89–119.

57 Niklas Luhmann, *Soziale Systeme: Grundriß einer allgemeinen Theorie*, Frankfurt am Main: Suhrkamp Verlag, 1984, p. 593.

58 Martti Koskenniemi, 'Empire and International Law: The Real Spanish Contribution', *University of Toronto Law Journal*, 2011, 61, pp. 1–36.

59 Torben M. Andersen and Thor T. Herbertsson, 'Measuring Globalization', *IZA Discussion Paper Series*, 807, 2003.

60 Niklas Luhmann, *Das Recht der Gesellschaft*, Frankfurt am Main: Suhrkamp Verlag, 1993, p. 131.

61 Niklas Luhmann, *Die Gesellschaft der Gesellschaft*, Frankfurt am Main: Suhrkamp Verlag, 1997, p. 757. See also Marc Amstutz and Vaios Karavas, 'Weltrecht: Ein Derridasches Monster' in Gralf-Peter Calliess, Andreas Fischer-Lescano, Dan Wielsch and Peer Zumbansen (eds), *Soziologische Jurisprudenz: Festschrift für Gunther Teubner zum 65. Geburtstag*, Berlin: Walter de Gruyter, 2009, pp. 645–72, at 652.

62 Joanne Scott and Susan P. Storm, 'Courts as Catalysts: Rethinking the Judicial Role in New Governance', *Columbia Journal of European Law*, 2007, 13, pp. 565–94.

63 For a pessimistic view on the future of continental European national configurations under the conditions of Europeanisation and globalisation, see Wolfgang Streeck, *Re-Forming Capitalism: Institutional Change in the German Political Economy*, Oxford: Oxford University Press, 2009.

64 Christian Joerges, '*Rechtsstaat* and Social Europe: How a Classical Tension Resurfaces in the European Integration Process', *Comparative Sociology*, 2010, 9, pp. 65–85.

5 The political within and in between normative orders

5.1 Introduction

A central point of the previous chapter was the apparent absence of the functional synthesis between law and politics within transnational frameworks. Quite a number of legal scholars have argued for a re-conceptualisation of law, which would enable an understanding of law as a progressively more globalised 'learning law' which increasingly relies on cognitive, instead of normative, expectations. Common for these scholars is, however, that, while they observe a transformation of law, they tend to assume that the nature of the political has remained unchanged. They continue to see politics as an essentially normative endeavour which is mainly unfolded at the nation-state level and which is oriented towards the production of collectively binding decisions. A central argument of this chapter is, however, that not only has a new type of law emerged in the wake of the progressive materialisation of functional differentiated transnational structures, but also a new type of transnational politics has emerged which operates in a complementary manner to nation-state politics. A new type of the political which also primarily relies on cognitive expectations and which is characterised by its reliance on a number of functional equivalents to the basic infrastructure of the political in the nation-state form, since, at the transnational level, the concepts of the nation, the public sphere and representation are being substituted by the concepts of stakeholders, transparency and self-representation.

Hence, the functional synthesis between law and politics might not have disappeared at all. Instead, it is only taking a different form within the transnational dimension of world society when compared to nation-state settings, a form which does, however, remain unobservable if one applies the kind of conceptual and methodological lenses which were developed in nation-state settings. Instead, an adequate description of the political dimension of transnational structures is only possible through the development of a context adequate concept of the political which is substantially different than the nation-state concept of the political.

5.2 Primary and secondary forms of the political

Three dimensions of the political can be observed in nation-state settings. First, there is the political system in the 'narrow' sense, which compromises the parliament, the government and the state bureaucracy. This dimension is constituted through a reference to the distinction between the state and the rest of society (*Staat und Gesellschaft*) and thus equates the political with the state; a state which, at its core, is oriented towards taking collectively binding decisions under the permanent reference to the threat of negative sanctions in cases of non-compliance, upon the basis of a claim to a legitimate monopoly of power.[1] In the European setting, as previously noted, the fundamental infrastructure of this dimension emerged in the early-modern period in which the emerging modern states, with different degrees of success, oriented the vast majority of their resources towards the establishment and maintenance of a legally ramified monopoly of violence.

The second dimension of the political is the broader private-based civil society structures which have always existed beside the state. A core element here is the various forms of (neo-)corporatist institutions which played, and continue to play, an essential role in many parts of the world. These institutions can be conceived of as either state-centric institutions which serve as frameworks for the stabilisation of relations between the state and the rest of society, most notably the economic system,[2] or as autonomous institutional frameworks which mainly serve the purpose of internally stabilising different social spheres such as the economy, science, education and religion.[3] Alternatively, they can be conceived of as simultaneously fulfilling the *dual function* of establishing internal stabilisation and external compatibility.[4] Irrespective of the perspective chosen, these institutional formations can be understood as hybrid negotiation systems (*Verhandlungssysteme*)[5] which rely upon specific combinations of legal and non-legal norms in that they combine norms produced by the focal social processes which they are oriented against with legal norms.[6]

In relation to their status as political entities, the core difference between the two dimensions is, however, that the state *primarily* is a political structure. Whatever non-political issues, in relation to, for example, the economy, the environment and education, the state is confronted with, these issues remain framed by a political perspective, since they are processed within the generalised medium of political power and framed by the function of taking collectively binding decisions.[7] Thus, non-political perspectives and interests remain subordinate to the political perspective. In the second dimension, this is not the case in that the sort of institutional formations, for example, in the form of professions, trade unions, trade associations, religious councils, and scientific and educational bodies, which emerge within a given social sphere derive their primary focus on the world from the focal perspective which is reproduced within the economy, science, religion and so forth. Institutional formations emerging within these social spheres only gain a political character in a secondary sense since the dual task of establishing internal stabilisation and external compatibility remains secondary to the production of economic value, scientific truths and religious beliefs. Thus, the economy, for example, might be considered to be a polity in its own right,[8] but this is only possible upon the basis of a 'weak' definition of the political.

The third dimension of the political is linked to the semantic – but none-theless real – and, indeed, very powerful *claim* of specific social systems concerning their ability to establish a unity of society in its entirety. In modernity this claim has mainly been unfolded within different ideological belief systems, such as those associated with socialism, Islamism, nationalism and ecological perspectives on society. Common to these belief systems is their orientation towards the future, in the sense that they are structured around specific ideas concerning which form the ideal society should take and the subsequent striving towards the realisation of this ideal.[9] In practice, the orientation towards the future serves as a way to pursue continuously a substantial unity of society through a Hegelian *Aufhebung* of the distinction between state and the private sphere. The function of such belief systems is to externalise the paradoxical and non-unitary constitution of society by pledging the realisation of substantial societal unity at a later date, due to the impossibility of achieving such unity in societal settings characterised by a strong reliance on functional differentiation.

In transnational settings, a similar, and yet different, three-dimensional set-up can be observed. Since the late nineteenth century, a specific conceptual universe has emerged in the form of public international law and politics, which are structured around a steadily increasing number of public international organisations dealing with issues as diverse as security, labour, the economy, telecommunications and health. Common to the United Nations and its specialised agencies, such as the International Labour Organization, the International Monetary Fund, the International Telecommunications Union and the World Health Organization, as well as other organisations such the World Trade Organization, is that they deal with substantial issues which are linked to specific social spheres at the same time as they remain primarily political organisations which frame and handle issues upon the basis of a political perspective.

In relation to the second 'private' dimension of the political, a key difference between the national and transnational segments of world society is that pri-vate ordering plays a substantially larger role at the transnational level of world society when compared with nation-state settings. Having said that, private transnational organisations as diverse as the International Organization for Standardization, dealing with product standards, the International Accounting Standards Board, occupied with financial-reporting standards, and Human Rights Watch, which monitors human-rights standards worldwide, share features with national private organisations in that they derive their substantial mission and meaning from the focal social processes which they are oriented against at the same time as they serve as secondary structures of ordering which are oriented towards a stabilisation of the self-same social processes. That is, furthermore, the case in relation to multinational companies, which are complex conglomerates that typically comprise a mother company and a multitude of subsidiaries. This structural set-up tends to make the question concerning the degree of (de-)centralisation of authority a recurrent issue. No multinational can operate without refined hierarchically controlled mechanisms in terms of decision-making procedures, evaluation schemes and auditing systems, which are closely linked to the ability to impose negative sanctions at lower levels and the production of a densely defined set of norms which guide or determine the deployment of these control mechanisms. Or to express it differently, the old Hobbesian question concerning order and stability is also a pivotal issue for private structures such as multinationals.

Public and private transnational organisations, including multinationals, are, furthermore, faced with the same trade-offs. On the one hand, the structural set-up of world society implies that the central function of transnational structures vis-à-vis the world in its entirety is to act as frameworks for the facilitation of the transfer of social components between different contexts. On the other hand, fulfilling this function implies a certain level of internal coherency. Thus, what is common to transnational organisations is that they are continuously confronted with a need to square the circle between developing standardised frameworks capable of ensuring internal coherency and allowing enough flexibility for local operations to be aligned with the specific societal contexts within which they are operating, since such alignment is the condition for successful transfers. In order to gain substance, such standardised frameworks are, furthermore, conditioned by the existence of a hierarchical nucleus in the form of – in the legal sense – a hierarchy of norms and – in the political sense – a distinction between those defining the norms, and those who are subject to the norms.[10]

As the previously outlined emergence of a vast variety of heterarchical governance structures located in between hierarchical orders testifies that both public and private structures of ordering are engaged in permanent endeavours to stabilise their relations to their respective social environments. Here, a distinction can be made between intra- and extra-systemic relations. When multinational companies engage with sub-contractors and supplier networks, this is a process which unfolds within the economic field. Relations with research institutions, public authorities and non-governmental organisations, by way of contrast, fall markedly outside the economic field. Despite the difference in the character of the relations, similar institutional forms, oriented towards the structuring of such interaction, are needed. By the same token, the establishment of norms are likely to be a stronger feature within the second dimension since bridging the gap between different spheres of society increases the need for negotiation or dialogue schemes in which common ground can be found. As a consequence of this, the most mature and most juridified governance structures tend to be in place in precisely those areas in which the entangledness and conflicts between different social spheres are most outspoken.[11] It follows from the above that, both within public and private forms of ordering, hybridity is a central characteristic. Both public and private forms of transnational ordering tend to become regimes, understood as the formalised legal-political infrastructure of normative orders, which are constituted through the establishment of unity between internal hierarchy and external heterarchy. A sort of unity that is paradoxical in nature because it is a 'unity of something different'.[12]

Just as the third dimension of the political in nation-state settings externalises the aspiration of achieving substantial unity in the future, functionally differentiated transnational structures, reflecting the counter-factual striving towards the 'complete inclusion' (*Vollinklusion*) of functional systems, tend to have an in-built 'totalising logic'. The international trade regime centred on the World Trade Organization implicitly seeks to include all states in the world as its members and to make all international trade subject to its norms just as multinational companies, in principle, strives towards making the world population in its entirety into consumers of their products. In a similar manner, human-rights organisations such as Amnesty International and Human Rights Watch seek both the formal and the factual inclusion of all humans into the still emerging global human-rights regime and the global climate-change regime seeks to subject the globe in its entirety to its standards. Whereas nation states are characterised by a built-in de-paradoxicalisation mechanism through the never-ending stride towards a future establishment of substantial unity for society as a whole within a given territory, functionally differentiated public and private transnational regimes transform the same need of de-paradoxicalisation into a striving towards the monopolisation of a given social function throughout the world in order to establish substantial global unity within the social sphere related to that function.

5.3 'Nations' and stakeholders as forms

A central medium of the political system in the nation-state form is the nation or 'the people', in the sense that the nation is the object against which the political system orients its operations. As already pointed out by Rousseau, the nation is not, however, to be understood as the sum of the individual wills of a given number of people.[13] Furthermore, as argued by Foucault, the nation is not the subject which constitutes the state. On the contrary, the nation is an object constructed by the state.[14] In concrete, the nation is a generalised and therefore abstract construction developed and stabilised by territorially delineated sub-systems of the global political system which fulfil three interconnected functions.[15]

First, the concept of the nation is deployed by political systems in the state form in order to delineate the reach of their power and thereby the segment of world society to which they claim supremacy. The inclusion/exclusion mechanism defining the belonging to a nation can take different forms: territorial delineations, citizenship or cultural claims in the form of claims of representativeness on behalf of all members of a specific cultural entity defined through language, ethnicity or religion, and that irrespectively of the geographical location of the members of the cultural entity in question.

Second, the nation is used as a form through which political systems in the state form transpose their power into other parts of society, while – at the same time – enabling them to extract resources from other segments of society. The deliberate construction of, for example, myths of origin (*Gründungsmythen*) and 'purified' languages and claims to solidarity within a nation are deployed in order to enhance the acceptability and thus the level of compliance with the collectively binding decisions produced by political systems in the state form.[16] In other words, it is the instrumental codification and systematication of pre-existing socio-cultural patterns or life-worlds by modern states that provides a source of legitimacy. A source which is particularly relevant in relation to the extraction and transposing of resources, for example, in the form of taxes and military recruits, from the rest of society and into the state.

Third, the nation is a conceptual form through which social complexity is reduced and the reflexivity of the state is increased at the same time, in the sense that the concept is deployed in order to delineate the part of the world which a political system in the nation-state form takes account of in its decision-making. The United States Congress, for example, is only obliged to take account of the impact that its decisions have on the people of the United States and not the impact on the peoples of Canada and Mexico, although the factual impact tends to be just as significant for the Canadians and the Mexicans. The function of delineating a specific segment of world society is closely associated with the concept of democracy. Democracy can be understood as a specific form through which the political system observes the segments of society which are external to the political system. A form that is characterised by a duality between stability and change in the sense that the people, through the conception of the nation as a single entity, is defined as a relatively stable entity at the same time as the 'nature of the people' in terms of preferences, interests and norms remain dynamic, thereby allowing the political system to increase its level of reflexivity and thereby its ability to adapt when changes occurs in its environment. Thus, the specificity of democracy, when compared to other forms of rule such as feudalism and totalitarianism, is that, within the framework of the nation, it remains open to the future, in the sense that it is not prescribed what counts as a politically relevant problem or how it should be dealt with.[17] In this specific sense, democracy is characterised by a high level of adaptability, and this is probably the reason why it has proved to be 'evolutionary superior' when measured against the other forms of political rule which have existed to date. Or to express it differently, the success of democracy, as the gradual expansion of state-based democracy throughout the globe over the past 200 years testifies, is intrinsically linked to its function as a reflexivity-increasing instrument.

In contrast to the national level, the transnational level of world society is, tentative attempts to democratise the European Union apart, not characterised by democracy. Internally, no transnational organisation relies on a 'hierarchy with a divided peak' in the form of the government/opposition distinction just as they, externally, do not engage in the act of universal suffrage. The reason for this absence can be traced back to the absence of territorially delineated polities at the transnational level of world society. The functionally delineated character of transnational organisations and regimes provides a structural set-up which is, in its turn, characterised by systematic uncertainty concerning what the collective actually is against which decision-making within transnational structures are oriented, just as it remains difficult to establish who exactly are affected by such decisions. Thus, when compared with nation states, it remains far more uncertain what segment of their social environment transnational structures should observe in order to be able to adapt to changes in their environments.

It is against this background that the concept of stakeholders has emerged as a central semantic category. Both public and private transnational organisations continuously engage in sustained efforts to define the set of stakeholders with whom they seek to engage and to develop platforms for the stabilisation of expectations vis-à-vis these stakeholders. In *praxis*, the concept of stakeholders acts as a functional equivalent to the concept of the nation under the condition of a high level of functional differentiation. Stakeholders can be defined as an institutionalised set of 'actors' who are granted the status of 'affected parties' and thereby acquire the right to 'feed into' decisional processes at the same time as they also serve as the addressees for such decisions. Thus, stakeholder status serves as a form through which the entity in question delineates the section of its social environment which it regards as relevant for its operationability. It is the form through which it transmits the social components that it produces at the same time as it serves as a frame through which changes in the social environment can be observed, thereby providing a basis for increased adaptability through increased reflexivity.

The concept of the nation is a deeply normative concept expressing an idea of substantial unity which, even though nations, from a historical and factual perspective rarely have been particularly stable in terms of their extent and composition, is upheld over time. In contrast, the concept of stakeholders is a strongly cognitivised concept. This is most clearly visible in relation to the dynamic composition of stakeholder frameworks, which is characterised by a high level of inter-changeability, since the composition of the group of stakeholders can be changed as the problem constellations with which the entity in question is faced changes. Thus, the dynamics of inclusion and exclusion operate with a far higher speed in relation to stakeholder frameworks, thereby making the borders of stakeholder regimes extremely contingent and fluid. This tends to make stakeholder frameworks more adaptive than the form of the nation and thereby potentially even more 'evolutionary superior' than democratic structures. In marked contrast, and bearing in mind that the production of social meaning (*Sinn*) relies, to a high extent, upon reiteration,[18] the price paid for such fluidity might be a 'loss of depth'. The impact which can be achieved through the stakeholder form might, therefore, turn out to be relatively limited.

5.4 The public sphere and transparency

Original dating back to the seventeenth century, the concept of the public sphere, understood as an intermediary framework in which normative visions are developed and subsequently transposed into the political system, and, as such, the site where the will formation of the people is taking place, has gained a distinct relevance for democratic theory and *praxis* in the decades following Habermas's reconstruction in the early 1960s.[19] In the wake of Habermas, several perspectives have emerged each of which has emphasised different aspects. Bo Stråth and Hagen Schulz-Forberg distinguish between a late-modern, a post-modern and a relational perspective.[20] The first, building directly on Habermas's work, emphasises a unitary concept in which a singular public sphere acts as mediator between an institutionalised political system in the state form and the rest of society. The post-modern approach, associated with the work of Nancy Fraser, instead emphasises the existence of a plurality of discursive arenas which operates in a parallel manner and which serves as a basis for the development of counter-discourses, challenging the hegemonic narratives of institutionalised power structures.[21] The relational approach, in contrast, uses the concept of the public sphere as an umbrella concept which emphasises the social *praxis* of articulating values, norms and symbolic codes in social settings characterised by complex network-based interactions between individuals, groups and formal institutions. Thus, the relational approach is weakening the link to nation-state institutional set-ups, and, instead, sees the public sphere as a phenomenon which tends to emerge in a wide variety of contexts.[22] Whereas the late-modern approach emphasises dialogue and the possibility of rational consensus, and the post-modern emphasises the possibility of developing alternative, more confrontational, visions of society which are capable of challenging the existing hegemonic structures, the relational approach further tends to be more open-ended concerning the exact normative orientation of communicative praxis.

When factual developments are observed, the public sphere seems to be an increasingly marginalised institution. The mass media system has increasingly overtaken and monopolised the functions of the civic public sphere,[23] just as the concept of public opinion, understood as a formalised instrument which is deployed by states and other centres of power in order to measure interests and preferences cognitively, has gained in centrality.[24] The tendency towards a marginalisation of the public sphere, which can be observed in nation-state contexts is being further exacerbated by increased Europeanisation and globalisation. For normatively driven proponents and defenders of the concept, the central question today is, therefore, whether the concept can be or already has been transposed to the European and global settings.[25] This undertaking has, furthermore, been underpinned by descriptive analyses of the tentative emergence of a global public sphere.[26]

However, the academic attempts to transnationalise the concept of the public sphere are carried out upon the basis of the assumption that the fundamental normative function of the public sphere remains unaltered. Also in transnational settings, the public sphere is considered a social institution which enables the formulation of normative visions and the subsequent transposition of these visions into political entities. Thus, the attempts to transpose the concept into the transnational realm tend to underestimate the structural differences between territorially delineated national contexts and functionally differentiated transnational contexts. But, as already indicated in relation to the concept of stakeholders, the problem of defining the 'audience' in terms of the segment of the social environment which can be considered to be relevant components of will-formation processes, however, tend to be systematically unclear within the transnational segment of world society. As a reaction to this structural deficit, it is possible to observe that transnational regimes increasingly rely on a less-normatively demanding concept, namely, the concept of transparency. In recent decades, the concept of transparency and clear-cut commitments to transparency have become a part of the standard framework of multinational firms, public and private international organisations and other transnational bodies. The concept implies that these entities, upon the basis of self-reflexive processes, develop principles and policies of transparency which are aimed at increasing their *observability* by other structures through the disclosure of intentions, actions and the general state of affairs. Central examples of this include the rules guiding or determining access to documents within public international organisations,[27] the development of public registers for lobbyists and their activities[28] and the steps towards the development of a global regime of financial accounting standards.[29]

In contrast to the demanding objective of common will-formation associated with the concept of the public sphere, the concept of transparency does not primarily aim at establishing positive normative concordance. Instead, the very notion of observability is essentially cognitive in nature. Strategies of transparency enable social entities to observe developments within other social entities and to adapt accordingly without necessarily engaging in the demanding task of common will-formation.

5.5 Representation and self-representation

Another central concept of liberal political theory, in particular, which continues to dominate nation-state images of political ordering, is the concept of representation. Serving as a concretisation of the concept of the nation and as a concept which is complementary to the concept of the public sphere, representation establishes a formalised reflexivity loop, in the form of a legitimacy chain, between the political system and the rest of society. Modern political systems distinguish themselves from pre-modern transcendental forms of representation, as, for example, advocated by the Church of Rome, wherein the notion of representation is, instead, linked to the establishment of a holistic entity. In contrast, modern forms of representation unfold within the tension between formal legal representation, which seeks to depict the population or the geographical area which the population inhabits upon the basis of generalised criteria, and substantial representation, which is aimed at achieving the highest possible concordance between the population and their elected representatives upon the basis of criteria such as language, ethnicity, gender, social class, educational level and religion.

Within continental philosophy, in particular, the liberal notion of representation was deconstructed long ago upon the basis of the insight that a one-to-one causality between those represented and their representatives is impossible to achieve. Instead, representation is conceived of as a mere symbolic figure.[30] In systems-theoretical language, this insight leads to the idea that representation serves as a form through which the political system *internally* establishes a copy or a mirror image of the rest of society which is concretised through a formal legal set-up. Thus, systems theory, just like Foucault, turns classical liberal perspectives on the state and society on its head. Instead of an 'outside-in' perspective in which the main focus is on the transposition of societal preferences *from* society and *into* the state, the 'inside-out' perspective of systems theory emphasises that the depicting of the rest of society *within* the state does, indeed, increase the reflexivity of the state, but that this is a process which unfolds upon the basis of an infrastructure and criteria which are internal to the state. But here, too, a 'middle way' is possible to the extent that the tension between the external and the internal perspective can be reduced through an emphasis on the dialectical tension between the two dimensions and the possibility of achieving a stabilisation of expectations through learning processes that unfold over longer time-spans.[31]

The central, though not the only, operational form of representation in its modern form is universal suffrage through elections. As such, the modern form of representation is inherently bound to the concept of the nation and to the concept of territoriality. Transnational structures are, however, structurally barred from relying on these concepts, thereby making the question of how they construct internal images of their environments a central issue. In the search of a substitute, entities which operate within the transnational space have been forced to develop strategies of self-representation upon the basis of – to use a Habermasian term – dramaturgical rationality. As reconstructed by Martin Herberg in relation to the environmental protection measures of multinationals,[32] transnational structures re-*present* themselves towards their social environments in a particular manner. Similar frameworks can be observed within public internal organisations. A common feature of both public and private transnational organisations is that they develop policy programmes and establish targets for their achievement just as they develop ethical charters and accountability instruments through which their activities can be observed and evaluated.[33] Thus, in contrast to the 'passive' concept of transparency, the concept of self-representation implies an 'activist' approach. Public and private entities of ordering declare their intentions publicly. With such conscious acts, these entities present themselves to the world in a manner which aims at actively *co-constructing* the expectations of the rest of world vis-à-vis these entities. But, at the same time, these acts tend to become self-binding in that their repeated non-fulfilment leads to an erosion of their credibility. Thus, acts of self-representation are illocutionary acts which are structurally linked to an intention of actual realisation.

In practice, the move towards self-representation points towards a substitution of democracy with justification.[34] A form of justification which, in contrast to mainstream ideas of democracy, relies upon a specific kind of *ex post* rather than *ex ante* logic, in that social entities which produce effects on other segments of the world are inextricably bound to the demands for the justification of these effects. Thus, the striving towards establishing a reflexive mode of self-representation is intrinsically linked to the stabilisation of the dialectical relation between power-producing entities and those subjected to the consequences of this power within an institutional form, such as the stakeholder form, in which specific structures of justification can unfold.

Closely related to the concept of representation, the concept of delegation plays an important role in the institutional set-up of states as well as in their interaction with the transnational layer, through the delegation of competences to international organisations. However, as previously noted, a delegation is always more than just a delegation. Each delegation of legal competencies implies a *de facto* recognition of the autonomy of the structures to which competencies are delegated. Structures which operate upon the basis of delegation tend to exercise significant discretionary powers and to frame policy areas in a manner which produces a limited number of options for further policy development. They also tend to develop specific norms and become policy actors in their own right.[35] The delegation of competencies always implies a step into the unknown and into the uncontrollable. Thus, a 'gap' exists between what can be controlled through delegation and the structures which are actually in place. It is this gap which is filled through the emergence of different forms of self-representation measures.

5.6 The status of the political in the transnational space

The institutional forms of the different dimensions of the transnational form of the political are radically different from the democratic structures in the nation-state form. If one remains committed to the framework provided by classical theories of democracy, the transnational forms of the political are not non-democratic structures but are, instead, a-democratic structures. Any adequate conceptualisation of these structures will thus necessitate a deliberate conceptual move aimed at 'getting past democracy'[36] or, at least, beyond democracy in the forms that we have known to date.

Although, at a first glance, they produce societal effects similar to those of democratic structures, transnational forms of the political have a fundamentally different status and position in society when compared with the nation-state form of the political. The societal function of the political in the heyday of the nation state was 'to take society forward'. Ideologies such as liberalism and socialism were aimed at achieving emancipation through a break with tradition. They were engines of social change, which were aimed at accelerating social time through processes of modernisation. Historically speaking, nation-state universes – and with them modern capitalist economies – were, therefore, to a high extent, deliberately constructed by the state.[37] Transnational structures are, in contrast, far more spontaneous orders which have emerged incrementally as a result of functional needs. The explicit political dimensions of these structures tend to emerge *ex post*. Neither multi-nationals nor non-governmental organisations are inclined to have an explicit political project as their starting-point. Instead, they are interested in exploiting uncovered market demands and solve concrete social problems. The 'political consciousnesses' of such structures tend to emerge as they grow, since they – by their very existence – are likely to produce substantial unintended effects vis-à-vis their social environments thereby triggering a functional need for developing ways of handling such effects.

The same applies to public international organisations. The predecessors of what is now the European Union[38] were founded as 'legal communities', which, in many ways, were deliberately constructed as technocratic entities which had the avoidance of the high-level politicisation of their respective functional areas as a central objective. Only as it has kept expanding its reach has the European Union been increasingly forced to develop genuine political features. As Martti Koskenniemi's reconstruction of the centrality of private rights within early modern colonialism illustrates, pursuing political objectives is not the primary purpose of transnational entities.[39] Transnational forms of the political are forms of communication which mainly are oriented towards the handling of externalities. As such, transnational forms of the political tend to be compensatory forms which fall far short of the nation-state ideals of the concept of a political community as an end in itself. Or to express it differently, the transnational form of the political is structurally prone to advance a negative, rather than a positive, idea of freedom,[40] as also expressed in its tendency to rely on cognitive, rather than normative, structures of expectations.

5.7 The transnational form of the functional synthesis

It seems as though the role and relatively importance of law and politics is turned upside down when one compares the transnational and national dimension of world society. When societal processes encounter obstacles to their globalisation, they activate the law as an instrument through which such obstacles can be removed or minimised, since it is primarily through the activation of legal instruments that the frameworks of transfer are both established and stabilised in the transnational realm. In contrast, transnational forms of political communication primarily emerge as a reaction to the existence of negative externalities. In praxis, they thereby gain the function of brakes aimed at reducing the impact of negative externalities.

It follows from the above that the development of a theory of constitutionalism in the global realm as a framework for understanding the quest of legitimacy in the transnational sphere, necessitates a two-dimensional perspective in that the already existing legal perspectives, as developed by, for example, Marc Amstutz, Christian Joerges, Martti Koskenniemi, Karl-Heinz Ladeur and Gunther Teubner, would have to be complemented with a corresponding theory of transnational political processes. Martti Koskenniemi's characterisation of international organisations as structures of managerialism, which are characterised by a strong focus on technical realisation and which are also indebted to a strong rationalist belief in the blessings of technique, very much captures the essence of the transnational form of the political.[41] But the drive towards managerialism is, first of all, not a simple matter of belief, but, instead, a form of the political which relies upon specific institutional forms, as expressed in the stakeholder, transparency and self-presentation frameworks. These frameworks are, of course, also present in national settings, but they have gained a far more central position within transnational set-ups due to the structural impossibility of transnational processes to rely on the sort of institutional set-ups which are dominant at the nation-state level. Thus, the ideology of managerialism is very much a reflection of a specific structural set-up.

The dual perspective on law and politics implies a co-evolutionary perspective. To the extent that an understanding of constitutional structures which emphasises that they are legal structures which ensure a simultaneous constitutive and limitative framing of societal processes over time upon the basis of a reference to an external source of authority is advanced,[42] the clarification of the question of what precisely the structural conditions are which enable constitutions to emerge becomes central. Here, the reference to an external source of authority seems to necessitate that the focal social processes against which a constitution is oriented develop either a primary or a secondary form of the political, which is capable of internally establishing sufficient stability within the focal processes in question and of establishing an institutional *locus*, through the condensation of authority, thereby providing a fixed point to which simultaneously running legal processes can attach themselves.[43] Thus, the structural condition for the emergence of constitutions is that, within the framework of focal social processes, institutional forms emerge which are capable of reproducing political forms of communication. The emergence of a globalised form of sports law is conditioned by the emergence of an institution such as the Olympic Committee, which provides the functional equivalents to parliamentary legislation from which the global sports law can derive the components from which it produces law, just as the emergence of a specific type of law within the framework of the regime of the World Trade Organization is conditioned by a reference to the political deliberations emerging within the framework of its governing council. Thus, the structural coupling between law and a given focal non-political social process is not just a coupling between law and sports, law and the economy, and law and science, but is, instead, a coupling between law and the institutionalised forms of the secondary form of the political emerging within these social processes. Thus, in this specific sense, the emergence of a social constitution outside the classical constitution between law and politics is always a specific and targeted constitution which is primarily oriented towards the institutional set-up of social processes, rather than the processes themselves.

Moreover, from the very outset, transnational political organisations relied on an ideology which aimed at achieving an increased cognitivisation of the political. The founding of organisations, such as the League of Nations in the wake of the First World War and the European Communities and the United Nations in the wake of the Second World War, were directly tied to a vision of a fundamentally different form of the political, freed from the 'irrationalism' of nation-state politics. Jean Monnet, Robert Schuman, Aldo Spinelli and colleagues directly aimed at establishing a technified and rationalised form of the political based upon expert knowledge and neutral decision-making as an alternative to the normative-driven form of nation-state politics.[44] The 'technocratisation' of everything from risk regulation to central banking through the progressive expansion of the European integration process all serve to indicate that this is not just a result of 'rationalistic semantics', but instead represents a far more profound structural transformation, in the sense that it is possible to observe a move towards an increased reliance upon cognitive-based administrative, rather than normatively driven political, rationality.[45] The transnational form of the political is thus fundamentally different in nature from the national form of the political, in the sense that the cognitive component is far higher than it is within national politics. In contrast to the Luhmannian argument concerning the reduced centrality of law and politics in the transnational realm, we are instead observing a transformation of the very nature of law and politics within the transnational layer of world society, in the sense that, because of their accommodating function, they, too, are also undergoing a profound cognitivisation, without necessarily losing their centrality. This development has led to a cascade of criticism of the inherent technocratic character of transnational structures.[46] When viewed from the conceptual frameworks developed within nation states, such criticism is almost evidently true. On the other hand, such criticism tends to be based upon a category error, in the sense that it relies on an un-reflexive transfer of standards from one universe to another, in the form of the assumption that transnational forms of law and politics are simply the same at nation-state forms of law and politics. Furthermore, the more adequate comparison, in terms of normative quality, would be between colonialism and contemporary global regimes. This is the case since contemporary global regimes – at the deeper structural level – serve as the functional equivalents of the colonial form of transnationality, due to their common focus on the enabling of transfer of social components between contexts. At the same time, the norms and values inherent to colonialism and contemporary global governance are fundamentally different. Taking such a perspective, global structures are bound to emerge in a far more positive light than the comparison with nation-state set-up renders.[47]

5.8 Conclusion

The core insight of this chapter is that the emergence of a specific form of functionally differentiated structures possessing a transnational reach has led to the emergence of a specific transnational type of the political which, in its orientation, self-understanding and institutional set-up, is substantially different from the form of the political which tends to dominate in national contexts. This orientation differs due the relative pre-dominance of cognitive – as opposed to normative – structures within the transnational version of the political, just as the tendency to understand the political as a 'technical task' has gained a far more ingrained status in transnational, when compared to national, contexts. The *praxis* of politics is furthermore being framed by the reliance on a different institutional infrastructure due to the need to develop functional equivalents to the concepts of the nation, the public sphere and representation, three essential elements of national political systems.

Notes

1 Niklas Luhmann, *Politik der Gesellschaft*, Frankfurt am Main: Suhrkamp Verlag, 2000.
2 Philippe C. Schmitter, 'Still the Century of Corporatism?', in Philippe C. Schmitter and Gerhard Lehmbruch (eds), *Trends Toward Corporatist Intermediation*, London, Beverly Hills, CA: Sage Publications, 1981, pp. 7–52.
3 Gunther Teubner, *Organisationsdemokratie und Verbandsverfassung: Rechtsmodelle für politisch relevante Verbände*. Tübinger Habilitationsschrift, Tübinger Rechtswissenschaftliche Abhandlungen, Band 47, Tübingen: Mohr/Siebeck, 1978.
4 Poul F. Kjaer, 'The Structural Transformation of Embeddedness', in Christian Joerges and Josef Falke (eds), *Karl Polanyi: Globalisation and the Potential of Law in Transnational Markets*, Oxford: Hart Publishing, 2011, pp. 85–104.
5 Helmut Wilke, *Systemtheorie III: Steuerungstheorie*, Stuttgart: Lucius & Lucius, 1998, p. 109.
6 Gunther Teubner, *Constitutional Fragments: Societal Constitutionalism and Globalization*, Oxford: Oxford University Press, 2012, p. 114 *et seq.*
7 Jean Clam, 'What is Modern Power?', in Michael King and Chris Thornhill (eds), *Luhmann on Law and Politics: Critical Appraisals and Applications*, Oxford: Hart Publishing, 2006, pp. 145–62.
8 For this perspective, see Christian Joerges, Bo Stråth and Peter Wagner (eds), *The Economy as Polity: The Political Constitution of Contemporary Capitalism*, London: UCL Press, 2005.
9 Reinhart Koselleck, *Kritik und Krise: Eine Studie zur Pathogenese der bürgerlichen Welt*, Frankfurt am Main: Suhrkamp Verlag, [1959] 1973.
10 Not surprisingly, the existence of forceful compliance mechanisms thus seems to be a central condition for the emergence of vibrant transnational organisations. For an operationalisation

of the compliance *problématique*, see Michael Zürn and Christian Joerges (eds), *Law and Governance in Postnational Europe: Compliance Beyond the Nation-State*, Cambridge: Cambridge University Press, 2005.

11 For an example of this in relation to European chemicals regulation, see Poul F. Kjaer, *Between Governing and Governance: On the Emergence, Function and Form of Europe's Post-national Constellation*, Oxford: Hart Publishing, 2010, p. 138 *et seq.*

12 Niklas Luhmann, 'The Paradoxy of Observing Systems', *Cultural Critique*, 1995, 31, pp. 37–55.

13 Jean-Jacques Rousseau, *Du Contract Social ou Principes du Droit Politique*, Paris: Hachette Littératures, [1762] 2005.

14 Michel Foucault, *Il faut défendre la Société. Cours au Collége de France*, 1975–76, Paris: Gallimard, 1997, especially p. 21 *et seq.*

15 Étienne Balibar, *Nous, citoyens d'Europe? Les frontières, l'État, le peuple*, Paris: La Découverte, 2001, p. 31 *et seq.*

16 Ernst Cassirer, *The Myth of the State*, New Haven, CT: Yale University Press, [1946] 1977.

17 Michel Foucault, *Il faut défendre la Société: Cours au Collége de France*, 1975–76, Paris: Gallimard, 1997, p. 24 *et seq.*; Niklas Luhmann, 'Die Zukunft der Demokratie', in Niklas Luhmann, *Soziologische Aufklärung, Band 4: Beiträge zur Funktionalen Differenzierung der Gesellschaft*, Opladen: Westdeutscher Verlag, 1994, pp. 131–38.

18 Poul F. Kjaer, 'Systems in Context: On the Outcome of the Habermas/Luhmann Debate', *Ancilla Iuris*, 2006, pp. 66–77, at 70.

19 Jürgen Habermas, *Strukturwandel der Öffentlichkeit: Untersuchungen zu einer Kategorie der bürgerlichen Gesellschaft*, Frankfurt am Main: Suhrkamp Verlag, [1962] 1990.

20 Hagen Schulz-Forberg and Bo Stråth, *The Political History of European Integration: The Hypocrisy of Democracy-Through-Market*, London: Routledge, 2010, p. 88.

21 Nancy Fraser, 'Rethinking the Public Sphere: A Contribution to the Critique of Actually Existing Democracy', in Craig Calhoun, *Habermas and the Public Sphere*, Cambridge MA: MIT Press, 1992, pp. 109–42.

22 Margaret R. Somers, 'What's Political or Cultural about Political Culture and the Public Sphere? Toward an Historical Sociology of Concept Formation', *Sociological Theory*, 1995, 13, pp. 113–44.

23 Jürgen Habermas, *Ach, Europa*, Frankfurt am Main: Suhrkamp Verlag, 2008, p. 131 *et seq.*

24 Niklas Luhmann, 'Die Beobachtung der Beobachter im politischen System: Zur Theorie der Öffentlichen Meinung', in Jürgen Wilke (ed.), *Öffentliche Meinung, Theorie, Methoden, Befunde: Beiträge zu Ehren von Elisabeth Noelle-Neumann*, Freiburg: Verlag Karl Alber, 1992, pp. 77–86.

25 Hartmut Kaelble, 'The Historical Rise of a European Public Sphere?', *Journal of European Integration History*, 2002, 8, pp. 9–22; Hans-Jörg Trenz and Klaus Eder, 'The Democratizing Dynamics of a European Public Sphere: Towards a Theory of Democratic Functionalism', *European Journal of Social Theory*, 2005, 7, pp. 5–25.

26 Rudolf Stichweh, 'Die Entstehung einer Weltöffentlichkeit', in Hartmut Kaelble, Martin Kirsch and Alexander Schmidt-Gernig (eds), *Transnationale Öffentlichkeiten und Identitäten im 20: Jahrhundert*, Frankfurt am Main: Campus Verlag, 2002, pp. 57–66.

27 Rainer Nickel, 'Participatory Transnational Governance', in Christian Joerges and Ernst-Ulrich Petersmann (eds), *Constitutionalism, Multilevel Trade Governance, and Social Regulation*, Oxford: Hart Publishing, 2010, pp. 209–50.

28 Linda Jellum, 'Lessons to be Learned: Public Participation and Transparency in Norm Creation within the European Union and United States', *FSU College of Law, Public Law Research Paper No. 562.* 2011.

29 Moritz Renner, *Zwingendes transnationales Recht. Zur Struktur der Wirtschaftsverfassung jenseits des Staates*, Baden-Baden: Nomos Verlag, 2011.

30 Hauke Brunkhorst, 'Constitutionalism and Democracy in the World Society', in Petra Dobner and Martin Loughlin (eds), *The Twilight of Constitutionalism?*, Oxford: Oxford University Press, 2010, pp. 179–98.

31 Klaus Eder, *Geschichte als Lernprozeß? Zur Pathogenese politischer Modernität in Deutschland*, Frankfurt am Main: Suhrkamp Verlag, 1992.

32 Martin Herberg, *Globalisierung und private Selbstregulierung: Umweltschutz in multinationalen Unternehmen*, Frankfurt am Main: Campus Verlag, 2007; Martin Herberg, 'Global Legal Pluralism and Interlegality: Environmental Self-Regulation in Multinational Enterprises as Global Law-Making', in Olaf Dilling, Martin Herberg and Gerd Winter (eds), *Responsible Business: Self-Governance and Law in Transnational Economic Transactions*, Oxford: Hart Publishing, 2008, pp. 17–40.

33 See, for example, the International Non Governmental Organizations Accountability Charter. Available at: www.realizingrights.org/pdf/INGO_Accountability_Charter.pdf.

34 Within normative political theory, this development is being reflected in attempts to establish a 'right to justification', in the sense that the external actors which are (negatively) affected by a given activity are granted the right to demand justifications. See, especially, Jürgen Neyer, 'Justice, Not Democracy: Legitimacy in the European Union', *Journal of Common Market Studies*, 2010, 48, pp. 903–21; Jürgen Neyer, *The Justification of Europe: A Political Theory of Supranational Integration*, Oxford: Oxford University Press, 2012; more generally, see Rainer Forst, *Das Recht auf Rechtfertigung – Elemente einer konstruktivistischen Theorie der Gerechtigkeit*, Frankfurt am Main: Suhrkamp Verlag, 2007.

35 Joshua Cohen and Charles F. Sabel, 'Global Democracy?', *New York University Journal of International Law and Politics*, 2005, 37, pp. 763–97.

36 Edward L. Rubin, 'Getting Past Democracy', *University of Pennsylvania Law Review*, 2001, 149, pp. 711–92.

37 Poul F. Kjaer, 'Post-Hegelian Networks: Comments on the Chapter by Simon Deakin', in Marc Amstutz and Gunther Teubner (eds), *Networks: Legal Issues of Multilateral Co-operation*, Oxford: Hart Publishing, 2009, pp. 75–85.

38 The European Coal and Steel Community, the European Economic Community and the European Atomic Energy Community.

39 Martti Koskenniemi, 'Empire and International Law: The Real Spanish Contribution', *University of Toronto Law Journal*, 2011, 61, pp. 1–36.

40 Fritz W. Scharpf, 'Legitimacy in the Multi-level European Polity', in Petra Dobner and Martin Loughlin (eds), *The Twilight of Constitutionalism?* Oxford: Oxford University Press, 2010, pp. 89–119.

41 Martti Koskenniemi, *The Politics of International Law*, Oxford: Hart Publishing, 2011, p. 71 *et seq.*

42 Mattias Kumm, 'The Best of Times and the Worst of Times: Between Constitutional Triumphalism and Nostalgia', in Petra Dobner and Martin Loughlin (eds), *The Twilight of Constitutionalism?* Oxford: Oxford University Press, 2010, pp. 201–20, at 214 *et seq.*

43 As we will return to in Chapter 8, such processes are described by Gunther Teubner with the concept of 'double reflexivity'.

44 Jens Steffek, 'Tales of Function and Form: The Discursive Legitimation of International Technocracy', *Normative Orders Working Paper*, 02, 2011.

45 Alexander Somek, 'Administration without Sovereignty', in Petra Dobner and Martin Loughlin (eds), *The Twilight of Constitutionalism?* Oxford: Oxford University Press, 2010, pp. 267–78.

46 Christian Joerges, 'Bureaucratic Nightmare, Technocratic Regime and the Dream of Good Transnational Governance', in Christian Joerges and Ellen Vos (eds), *EU Committees: Social Regulation, Law and Politics*, Oxford: Hart Publishing, 1999, pp. 3–17; Martti Koskenniemi, 'Constitutionalism, Managerialism and the Ethos of Legal Education', *European Journal of Legal Studies*, 2007, 1, pp. 1–18; Rainer Schmalz-Bruns, 'Deliberativer Supranationalismus: Demokratisches Regieren jenseits des Nationalstaates', *Zeitschrift für Internationale Beziehungen*, 1999, 6, pp. 185–244.

47 Poul F. Kjaer, 'The Political Foundations of Conflicts Law', *Transnational Legal Theory*, 2011, 2, pp. 227–41.

Part III

Constitutional stabilisation

6 The breakdown of constitutional ordering through globalisation-induced crises

6.1 Introduction

This chapter and the following two explore the consequences of the emergence of novel forms of law and politics, due to the dual move towards a globalisation of statehood and the re-configuration of transnational structures away from their reliance on the centre/periphery differentiation and towards a reliance on functional differentiation, for the evolution and sustainability of constitutional ordering. The overall question pursued is to what extent constitutions can continue to serve as the frameworks for the normative stabilisation of social processes when the altered structural conditions are accounted for, and, in connection with this, how the constitutional concept can be re-worked in order to correspond better to the current structural realities of world society. Thus, the three chapters respectively deal with why a specific modern concept of constitutions has emerged, how constitutional frameworks have been transposed into new sites and what a constitution actually is, with the last referring to the meaning and implications of the constitutional concept.

In order to arrive at an answer to the above questions, a better understanding of the evolution of constitutional frameworks as well as the capacity of constitutional frameworks to respond to societal transformations is needed. The point of departure of this chapter is, therefore, a reconstruction of the move from a pre-modern static to a dynamic modern constitutional concept. This move was a reflection of the deeper transformations which characterised the emergence of modern society, and, in particular, of the immanent contradictions inherent to modern society. These contradictions have, time and again, led to profound societal crises and, accordingly, a specific understanding of societal crises is advanced. Crises are seen as phenomena which imply a breakdown of the internal coherency of a multiplicity of social spheres due to increased and sustained levels of coalescence between these spheres. Against this background, the nature of constitutional arrangements in national contexts becomes clearer since the way is paved for an understanding of national contexts as being characterised by complex constitutional conglomerates made up of a multiplicity of constitutions, which, in their primary societal function, are oriented towards the simultaneous safeguarding of the internal integrity of different social spheres and the stabilisation of the exchanges between these spheres.

As illustrated by the widespread collapse in constitutional ordering in the context of the two world wars and the Great Depression in the first half of the twentieth century as well as the developments leading to the 2008 financial crisis, successful constitutional stabilisation has proven difficult to maintain. Both of these crises, it is argued, reflected breakdowns in re-stabilising constitutional mechanisms due to structural transformations caused by increased levels of globalisation.

6.2 From static to dynamic constitutions

Changes in societal structures are reflected in how society semantically describes itself.[1] This is also the case for the constitutional concept.[2] At the time of its emergence, the constitutional concept did not refer to state constitutions. In the absence of states, the pre-modern constitutional concept instead referred to a multiplicity of ways through which societal structures were stabilised and framed over time through law.[3] Pre-modern Europe was characterised by a multitude of constitutions in the form of constitutions of trade regimes, the church, cities and so forth.[4] As it was the institution of the 'household', which we will return to, that served as the generic form of organisation of these different structures, it is, moreover, possible to characterise pre-modern constitutions as 'household constitutions'.[5]

The key feature which distinguished pre-modern constitutional structures from other types of law was the time dimension. Pre-modern constitutional concepts of '*status*' and '*constitution*' were linked to a semantic of immutability which emphasised the static element of constitutions upon the basis of the claim that they were, in principle, unchangeable. As highlighted in Chapter 2, the foundational period of modernity was, however, characterised by a double movement, in the sense that the importance of functional – as well as territorial – differentiation was dramatically increased. In this process, territorial differentiation emerged as an internal form of stabilisation within territorially based political systems and territorially based legal systems, just as other functional systems, such as the economic and the scientific systems, increasingly developed internal forms of stabilisation which indirectly relied on the territorially defined frames of the modern states since they – at the organisational level – established close couplings with the political and legal systems in the nation-state form. This development gradually undermined the constitutional autonomy of the pre-modern household-based structures.[6]

As a result of these processes, the constitutional concept changed in that it increasingly became oriented towards the regulation of specifically political institutions, which relied on modern forms of organisation. A central function of constitutions was to establish the delineation of the competences and the internal set-up of such organisations.[7] In addition, the static element increasingly disappeared, thereby triggering an increased focus on the procedural elements of constitutional set-ups. Proceduralisation embodies another key character-istic of modernity, apart from functional differentiation, namely, the ability of social structures to increase their level of 'dynamic stability' radically. Proce-duralisation allows for a relatively stable legal-framing of continuously changing social structures. Whereas pre-modern constitutions described themselves as, in principle, unchangeable, modernity implied an increased awareness of the time element and a formalisation of what had always been the case: namely, that the difference between constitutional and secondary law is merely a difference in time, in that the pace of the introduction of changes is slower within constitutional law than within secondary law. Constitutions became 'living constitutions'[8] which are based upon the recognition that they tend to change their meaning over time and are oriented towards the establishment of a second-order dynamic stabilisation of other legal structures. In modernity, constitutions are not anchors mooring a ship to a stable seabed, but rather drift anchors which flow with the ship but, in doing so, stabilise the ship as it moves.

6.3 The Janus-face of modernity

The multitude of autonomous and geographically overlapping societal structures, in terms of principalities, trade regimes, the church and the cities which characterised pre-modern Europe, all had their distinct features and all repre-sented overlapping, but nonetheless distinct, normative orders. As indicated, a common feature of these structures was that they relied on the household institution, defined as an autonomous social organism which constitutes an integrated community of economic and other social *praxes* and which ensured the link between the different strata.[9] In this sense, the household institution was the single most important structure for the integration of society in pre-modern Europe.

A key feature of the household institution was that it did not allow for any clear-cut distinction between economic reproduction and other forms of soci-etal operations. Thus, only when the household institution ceased to be a central societal category, due to the emergence of a distinct property- and contract-based form of economic production, was it possible to understand the economic system as a distinct societal category.[10] The breakdown of the household institution was, therefore, the central development which enabled Karl Polanyi to claim that the social embeddedness of economic activities had broken down in the wake of the unleashing of a specific capitalist logic, thereby paving the way to a modern society marred by crises.[11] Polanyi's perspective is, however, somewhat narrow, since the end of embeddedness through the breakdown of the household institution was, by no means, a phenomenon which merely unfolded in relation to the *praxis* of economic reproduction. Instead, the differentiation of a specific economic logic was part of a broader process, leading to the breakthrough of modernity, which cannot be reduced to the question of the form of economic reproduction. This is also exemplified by the fact that the state, and not the economy, was the first dis-embedded sphere of society. The modern state is, in contrast to pre-modern forms of rule, a distinct and abstract legal person, which is separate from its members. The modern sovereign state is a structure of generalised and impersonal rule, in the sense that all rules apply to all persons within a given territory. It is a form of rule which only requires a minimum of communication with its subjects, and only in a form which refers to specific roles which are unfolded within specific settings.[12] The constitutional structures of modern states can, therefore, only be understood as dis-embedded structures.[13] Thus, not only the emergence of a modern economy, but also modern statehood implied a break with the household institution, as is most clearly exemplified through the introduction of a distinction between the possessions of the state and the possessions of the monarch in early-modern Europe.

As previously highlighted, the central mechanism which triggered the European state-building processes of early modernity was the military revolutions which unfolded from the sixteenth century onwards.[14] These revolutions increasingly made functionally delineated and hierarchically organised political, legal and bureaucratic structures a defining feature of society, in so far as the result was a mutually reinforcing configurative relationship between the bureaucratic organisation of military capabilities, the structuring of territory and increases in the available economic resources, thereby leading to a co-evolutionary differentiation of the functionally delineated spheres of society within areas such as law, politics and the economy. In addition, the mercan-tilist economies of the early-modern era were state economies, in the sense that the social construction of what later became the 'free market' was, to a large extent, a process initiated by the state, just as the central organisational feature of the emerging industrial economy was the adaptation of the modern model of bureaucratic organisation, which had been developed within the realm of the emerging states, as the key feature of modern firms.[15]

To sum up, not only is the economic sphere not the only societal sphere which has undergone a process of dis-embedment, but it also not the most central sphere if one seeks to understand the central driving forces leading to modernity. Or to express it differently, Marx was wrong when he sought to turn Hegel upside down through his emphasis of economic structures, rather than the state, as the central mechanism of societal evolution in modernity.[16]

This argument can, moreover, be extended, since it was not just politics, law and the economy that became distinct functionally delineated spheres of society in the process which led to modernity. Instead, a multiplicity of functionally delineated structures emerged, in that areas such as science, art, intimate relations, health, sports, the mass media and education also emerged as distinct spheres of meaning (*Sinnwelten*) characterised by distinctly different social codes and norms. As a consequence thereof, a multiplicity of roles emerged, since the inclusion of human subjects in a given societal context became conditioned by their alignment with context-specific social roles. Subjects became consumers, pupils, citizens, patients, employees, and so forth.

Thus, dis-embeddedness can also be understood as a reflection of a more fundamental fragmentation of meaning (*Sinn*) structures through which holistic universes, such as the household structure, are broken down and replaced with a multi-contextual setting, in which the form of meaning differs from context to context.

Not surprisingly, modernity therefore implied a problematisation of what human subjects are. The positive reply, often aligned with a Kantian tradition, was the specifically modern concept of the individual and the process of individualisation, a concept which served as a tool for *de-paradoxialisation*, since its central function is to 'cover up' the death of the subject as a unitary figure as brought about by the transformation of human subjects into carriers of a multiplicity of social roles.[17] The emergence of highly complex social codes, expectations and norms inherent to each role was, moreover, conditioned by a 'civilising process' which, through the deployment of disciplinary mechanisms, re-created the human subjects in a manner which made it possible to align them with the specific roles of modern society.[18] In this sense, the move from the concept of the human subject to the concept of the single individual must be understood as being inherently connected to the shift from 'nature' to 'culture' which Kant diagnosed as a central element of the modern world.[19]

By way of contrast, the shadow side of the fragmentation of meaning structures was already *problematised* by Rousseau, who sought to develop a concept capable of retaining the perceived qualities of the 'embedded' pre-modern *polis* under the condition of modernity,[20] and Hegel, who was the first to combine the concept of modernity with a concept of critique systematically.[21] From these two scholars, a multitude of links can be established to, for example, Kierkegaard (existential fear), Marx (alienation), Weber (rationalisation), Durkheim (*anomie*), Heidegger (technification), Adorno and Horkheimer (reification), Elias and Foucault (disciplination), and Habermas (colonialisation). Distilling the core insights of the various approaches, modernity appears as a deeply ambivalent phenomenon, which sets the individual free at the same time as it makes him or her into an object of 'social engineering' through which the human subject is purposefully re-created.[22]

6.4 Forms of societal crises

It follows from the above that societal crises are an immanent and recurrent element of modernity.[23] But instead of understanding societal crisis as a reflection of dis-embeddedness, as implicitly advanced by large segments of modern political thought, a societal crisis, in its immediate and very general form, represents a discrepancy between expectations and actual developments. In a more profound structural sense, a crisis, furthermore, represents a condition in which the scope of the meaning production (*Sinnproduktion*) of one or more social systems is being reduced over a considerable period of time. A fall in gross domestic product implies a shrinking in the meaning production of the economic system and a reduction in the number of believers spells a crisis for religions. Such reductions might lead to various degrees of *anomie*, in the sense that the internal order of a given system is put under pressure, or it can be fatal in the sense that it reduces the scope of meaning production to a degree which endangers the continued existence of the system(s) in question.

One set of reasons for reductions in meaning production which occur are internal in nature. For example, a crisis related to the economic system might simply be the result of fluctuations of a business cycle which reflect a form of 'systemic overstretch', in the sense that the expansion of meaning production reaches an unsustainable level, thereby creating a discrepancy between the scope of meaning production and the intra-systemic resources and material basis available for supporting the production of its social components. Pyramid schemes within financing and other forms of financial speculation which lead to economic bubbles might be interpreted as representing severe forms of such overstretching. Military commanders who go 'a bridge too far' and – in more general terms – the ancient phenomenon of imperial overstretch in relation to political and military structures are other examples.[24]

But a crisis might also be the result of a more profound structural process due to a weakening of a particular tight coupling between systems due to increased differentiation. For example, the central focus of crisis for the system of higher education might be traced back to an inability to adapt to the increased weakening of the institutionalised linking of the systems of science and education within the framework of the Humboldtian model. Scientific discoveries can, moreover, undermine established scientific facts, thereby potentially provoking a crisis in relation to an established scientific paradigm.[25] Another example can be found in the relative weakening of the position of the religious system in society due to the emergence of a whole range of functional systems in early modernity. This led to an internal crisis for the Church of Rome due to an increased undermining of the world-view upon which its coherency relied, and, subsequently, to an internal re-configuration of the religious system through the Reformation.

Another set of reasons which may cause a crisis to occur are external in nature, in the sense that negative externalities, crowding-out effects and asymmetries between systems lead to a reduction in the meaning production of one or more of the systems involved. From a purely analytical and somewhat 'formalistic' Kantian- and Spencer Brown-inspired perspective, the term external cannot be understood in a strict causal sense.[26] The crossing of system boundaries is a form of operation which requires time.[27] As the receiving system, like all other systems, operates – or indeed – produces time in its movement from operation to operation, it will never be quite the same system at the time in which the external components arrive as it was at the time when the social components in question were dispatched. The receiving system is always one step ahead. In addition, external influences only have an effect when they are internally conceived and processed within the receiving system. The sovereignty of interpretation (*Deutungshoheit*) always remains the prerogative of the receiving system. Except for cases in which a system is being entirely eradicated in the Carthaginian sense, even the most systematic and prolonged forms of external pressure should, therefore, leave a certain degree of autonomy for the system which is the subject of external pressure.[28] From a genuine sociological perspective, such autonomy is, however, often more a formal than a real prerogative, because asymmetries, in practice, tend to take the form of processes of impalpable coalescence (*Zusammenfließen*) which potentially leads to a slow but steady erosion of system boundaries. In most cases, such processes only create an atmosphere of continued dysfunctionality, but they are also capable of inflicting far more fundamental disturbances within the systems in question because the weakening of system boundaries potentially can lead to system dissolution.

Externally induced asymmetries can, at least in principle, occur between all social systems as issues such as doping (health vs. sports), evangelism in the school system (religion vs. education), sexual harassment in the workplace (intimacy vs. formal organisations), pollution (economy vs. the socially constructed ecological environment), Islamic financing (religion vs. economy), pornography and the phenomenon of *paparazzi* (mass media vs. intimacy) all illustrate. Such asymmetries, however, rarely lead to a profound crisis as long as they remain purely binary relations. Instead, they merely imply the existence of inter-systemic 'grey zones' which serve as causes of irritation for the systems involved which subsequently tend to trigger regulatory attempts of containment by the legal system. In most cases, a 'real' crisis first occurs when a complex constellation consisting of a whole range of mutually entangled and overlapping asymmetric relations between several systems manifest themselves over a considerable period of time, thereby generating a mutually reinforcing drift towards systems decay. The forms of crisis which they potentially provoke therefore differ from system constellation to system constellation.

6.5 The constitutional conglomerates of national configurations

Departing from the structural differences between the pre-modern and the modern setting, Luhmann argued that constitutions are an explicit modern phenomenon which merely acts as a structural coupling between law and politics.[29] According to Luhmann, the core function of constitutions is to allow for the transfer of social components, in the form of legislative texts and legal judgments, between the political and the legal systems.[30] In his late, post-structuralist-inspired writings, the state is, moreover, reduced to a purely metaphorical phenomenon, in the sense that he defines the state as the structural coupling between law and politics.[31] Thus, the late Luhmann *de facto* understands the state and the constitution as identical.

Luhmann's reduction of the constitutional concept to a pure state-based concept is, when seen from a historical perspective, implausible. Throughout their existence, the modern state constitutions, which Luhmann focuses upon, have been supplemented by societal constitutions. A clear example of this can be found in the corporatist regimes which, through a mutation of the pre-modern guilds, became a defining phenomenon in European settings from the mid-nineteenth century onwards. A central element of such regimes was labour constitutions, which institutionalised the representation of 'vested interests', defined exclusion and inclusion mechanisms, and the specification of procedures for conflict resolution and arbitration between employers and employees.[32] But since these constitutions reflected the larger reach of the corporatist conglomerates, they were not just labour constitutions. Instead they were economic and social constitutions in a broader sense in that the regulation of the labour market served as a platform which, directly or indirectly, enabled a legal stabilisation of almost all areas of life from work and education to health and leisure activities, in a manner which – at the organisational level – were aimed at ensuring concordance between different forms of rationality within the framework of the emerging welfare-state conglomerates.

It follows that the phenomenon, which in mainstream language is denoted as nation states, should instead, be understood as far more complex configurations, consisting of a whole range of functional sub-systems, regimes, organisations, networks, professions and more or less intangible cultural components, all of which relate to each order in a multitude of ways. Such configurations are characterised by a dense web of mutually reinforcing structural couplings within a limited section of world society, which establish a convergence of expectations between multiplicities of observers. As such, they produce a kind of localised 'higher order', which cannot be reduced to the sum of its components. Instead, they have the character of autonomous universes which, to a large extent, constitute the social reality of individuals.[33]

Legal and political sub-systems clearly enjoy an important position within such configurations because their central societal function is to ensure the compatibilisation of the time structures of such configurations (*gesamt-gesellschaftlichen Zeitausgleich*).[34] But this does not mean that such configurations merely represent the sum of the legal and the political systems, or that they can be understood as structures in which other societal structures are succumbed to the primacy of the political-legal complex. Thus, a configurational web does not constitute unity in a substantialist sense and no singular state-embedded national culture exists.[35] Instead, it is possible to observe a multitude of mutually reinforcing, overlapping and thus intertwined cultures in the form of, for example, national legal cultures, national political cultures, national science cultures and – within the economy – the specific social *praxis* of 'doing business'. Apart from serving as reservoirs of knowledge, and thus as a basis for learning, such cultures also act as a sort of internal environments of the respective functional systems, in the sense that they frame the horizons which are taken into account in the continued selection of operations, thereby serving as stabilisation mechanisms which reduce the volatility of societal reproduction. They rely on fictional semantics, in the form of, for example, foundational myths and the social constructions of languages, traditions and 'vested interests', which are specific to each sphere of society. They are abstract constructions, or, in Hegelian terms, 'second natures',[36] which, nonetheless, remain 'real', in the sense that they have real effects in terms of which forms of communications are being selected.[37] They serve as frames for the production of societal trust within their respective societal spheres, and, as such, provide a contribution to the internal stability of such structures, in the sense that they tend to reduce volatility. Whereas functional systems, in their core, operate upon the basis of clear-cut system boundaries and accordant internal density, system cultures are far more fluid and overlapping, and, as such, are far less dense, thereby establishing a high level of inter-systemic entangledness.[38]

Whether the socio-economic constitutions should be understood as societal constitutions or should, instead, be seen as annexes to the state and the state constitutions largely depends upon which concept of state one departs from. Hegel, a contemporary observer of the breakthrough of modernity, was the first to conceptualise modern society as predominantly a functionally differentiated society. Under the influence of the economic studies of David Ricardo and Adam Smith, he was also the first to problematise the socio-economic aspect of the end to embeddedness systematically.[39] Thus, the central question for Hegel was the question of how society could remain integrated under the condition of the (relative) primacy of functional differentiation and a capitalist economy. His answer was the all-encompassing rational and sovereign (welfare) state. This answer was derived from his conceptualisation of functional, stratificatory and territorial differentiation as three independent forms of differentiation which stand in an orthogonal relationship to each other, and which enabled him to develop a three-dimensional concept of the state. First, he understood the state as being composed of the legal and the political system in the 'narrow sense', that is of functionally delineated structures such as the government, the state bureaucracy and the courts. Second, he understood the state as an entity composing society as a whole. This concept of the 'larger state' relied upon corporatist structures (*Korporationen*), framed by socio-economic constitutions, which reflected the social classes of the emerging industrial society. Third, the state was conceptualised as a container constituting itself through the delineation of one state towards other states. Thus, Hegel did not open the path to a return to a pre-modern form of embedded social *praxis* upon the basis of pre-modern morality (*Sittlichkeit*), but, instead, emphasised the integrative force of the rational state as the appropriate functional equivalent under the condition of modernity.[40]

Hegel's concept of the state, in which the state is ultimately understood as the unity of the political-administrative system and the rest of society, is a concept with obvious shortcomings. This is the case because it remains unclear how this unity is being constituted. It is a non-determined concept, in that it remains unclear whether the state or society is the object to which it refers. With Luhmann, one is faced with the opposite problem in so far as his theory, from a conceptual perspective, might be deemed coherent but empirical implausible. His definition of the state is more or less identical to Hegel's definition of the political-administrative system. In order to defend this definition, Luhmann, however, ends up with an overly formalistic definition of the political in the sense that, upon the basis of the distinction between power and influence, he reduces the political to a phenomenon which merely is being unfolded within areas which are subject to formalised negative sanctions.[41]

Irrespective of whether one follows Hegel or Luhmann, it emerges from the above that, under the condition of modernity, the kind of embeddedness which Polanyi departs from cannot be re-established. In modernity, the functional equivalent is, instead, a balancing of different functionally delineated spheres of society, such as, but not exclusively, the market and the (welfare) state. In a multi-contextual society, the question of 'social justice' is thereby transformed from a question of class conflict to the task of defining the social roles emerging within different spheres of society as well as the entrance criteria which regulate access to these roles.[42]

This development can also be illustrated by the move from corporatism to neo-corporatism. In the mid-twentieth century, the early forms of corporatism evolved into neo-corporatist negotiation systems (*Verhandlungssysteme*) within Western European configurations. Neo-corporatist structures are hierarchically organised 'peak associations' which mediate between their specific sectors of the economy and the state. In this sense, they bridge the gap between 'state and society' or – to be more precise – between politics and economy, thereby producing mutual stabilisation of the two spheres.[43] These structures served as the central axis of co-ordination of national configurations, but were, at the same time, characterised by a move towards an ever-increasing reliance on functionally delineated professions, which gradually made the earlier reference to the distinction between capital and labour and the social classes less profound. Thus, neo-corporatism can also be understood as a transitional phenomenon which bridges the gap between the Hegelian state-embedded society and the radical poly-contextual society.[44]

The reality of configurational webs is mainly established at the level of organisations and regimes. Formal organisation is the form through which internal order is established within functionally delineated areas just as they serve as the 'contact points' for inter-systemic exchange. The consequence is, as outlined in Chapter 5, that a particular form of second order politics can be observed. The internal form of ordering within functional spheres becomes a question which is being channelled into formalised organisational arrangements which produce collectively binding decisions or the functional equivalents to collective decisions within their respective functional areas. It follows that successful configurations neither operate upon the basis of a total subordination of society to political rationality, nor in a form in which the political only resides in the state in the narrow sense. Rather, a certain gradualisation of the political can be observed, in the sense that some linkages between the state-based form of the political and secondary forms remain tighter than others just as the internal degree of hierarchy within the secondary forms differs from societal area to societal area.[45]

Against this overall background, it becomes possible to argue that the central institutional structure which configurational orders rely upon is the constitutional form. National configurations are characterised by very complex constitutional conglomerates, in which state constitutions provide only one (very important) element. The framing of social order is instead achieved through a *double movement*, where multiple constitutions simultaneously constitute internal order within their respective functional areas and establish the possibility of stabilised linkages with other fields. Internally, such constitutions are a particularly dense form of the structures that they are oriented against. This, as we will return to, is also expressed in their reliance on formal organisation. Thus, in *praxis*, they are *not* societal constitutions, in the sense that a political or an economic constitution constitutionalises political or economic forms of communication as such. Constitutions do not reach out to the extra-parliamentary opposition (*außerparlamentarische Opposition*) or the black economy. Instead, they merely constitutionalise the parts which rely on formal organisation, thereby introducing automatic limitations.

In their external function, constitutions respond to the double problem of ensuring linkages through the institutionalisation of inter-systemic transfers of social components while stabilising and safeguarding the autonomy and integrity of the structures in question. A labour constitution, for example, is simultaneously oriented towards the framing of exchanges between the economic system and other societal spheres, such as the political system and the internal stabilisation of the economic system through the handling of the relations between employers and employees. It is this double function which makes constitutions into evolutionary counter-measures (*Gegensteuerungsmechanismen*) against societal crises. Internally they are oriented towards reducing volatility. Externally they serve as forms which are aimed at curtailing structural drifts. Their function is to counter asymmetric relations and the entangledness of functional cultures through the formalisation of authority, competences and decisional procedures, just as they more generally consolidate the functionally differentiated character of society through their underpinning of the organisational set-up upon which the functionally delineated spheres of society rely.[46] Thus, successful constitutional configurations can be seen as evolutionary responses to the looming threat of social crisis, since they produce order, understood as social stability, through the reduction of internal volatility within the social processes they are oriented against at the same time as crowding-out effects and asymmetries are minimised.[47]

6.6 Constitutional breakdowns

The kind of constitutional conglomerates described above represent highly improbable and complex evolutionary outcomes, because they imply a mutual fixation of a whole range of systemic structures, while allowing for their continued expansion.[48] Not surprisingly, therefore, history is full of examples of how the constitutional infrastructure of national configurations have broken down or come under sustained pressure, thereby unleashing societal crises. This was particularly the case in the inter-war period, most notably, but not exclusively, in the Weimar Republic. The immediate reason for the breakdown of the Weimar Republic was the dissolution of the distinction between public and private power in a manner which eroded the constitutional infrastructure filtering exchanges between the state and the rest of society.[49] As previously indicated, this happened in the wake of the introduction of the 'war economy' (*Kriegsökonomie*) during the First World War, and the war itself, and inter-state competition, thus provided the immediate contextual setting for this development.

When viewed from a structural perspective, the war was, however, more a symptom than a cause in itself, in that it was a reflection of the progressive breakdown of the Eurocentric world order which, as previously argued, had begun several decades before. Taking a bird's eye view, the overriding structural reason for the European implosion and the subsequent collapse in constitutional ordering seems to have emerged from the failure of (trans)national configurational webs to adapt internally to the increases in the globalisation through adequate internal re-configurations. The changes brought about by the relative increase in the centrality of the United States for the economic system from the late nineteenth century onwards was, for example, not reflected in a concordant shift in the institutional set-up. The British pound remained the global anchor currency long after the basis for that role had disappeared. In a similar manner, the rising importance of the United States was not reflected in an increased role of the US political system within the global political system, thereby creating a discrepancy between the form and location of the economic and political reproduction processes and the institutional architecture aimed at stabilising these processes. This was the case before the First World War and also afterwards, which thereby created a basis for the even larger catastrophe in the form of the emergence of totalitarianism and the Second World War. Only after the second act of catastrophe did sufficient learning processes unfold through the establishment of the Bretton Woods system, the institutionalisation of the US dollar as the global anchor currency and the internal re-configuration of the global political system through the handover of the hegemonic credentials from the UK to the US.

As previously indicated, the re-stabilisation achieved through the constitutional architecture of the 'Westphalian–Keynesian frame'[50] outlined in the Bretton Woods system, however, only maintained itself for a few decades, just as it essentially remained a structure which had the North Atlantic space as its core.[51] As embodied by the collapse of the Bretton Woods arrangement, a gradual breakdown of the distinction between the 'West and the rest' started in the 1970s, with the increased (re-)inclusion of Japan and later on through the increased weight of other parts of the East Asian region in the world economy. The immediate manifestation of the breakdown of the distinction between the 'West and the rest' can be found in the financial crisis of 2008. This crisis can be seen as the culmination of the far bigger transformational shift in the composition of world society which has unfolded since the 1970s, a shift which was contemporarily concealed through the kind of super-bubble, compromising a whole range of sub-bubbles within financial markets, private consumption, housing, government spending and so forth,[52] which has characterised large parts of the Western economy in the last three decades.[53]

It follows form the above that the breakdown of the re-stabilising distinction between the 'West and the rest' has strong structural affinities with the previous breakdown of the distinction between 'Europe and the rest'. The breakdown of the European space implied a radical breakdown of the boundaries between functional spheres of society. The 'cheap money' regime, which the expansion of the global economy, with the US economy as its anchor, has relied upon in the last three decades can be described with a similar vocabulary. The introduction of a new financial regime upon the basis of monetarist ideology represented an unviable compensatory reaction to structural changes, which led to a partial breakdown of the functional separation between the political and the economic system. The relative weakening of the position of the United States as the 'engine' and institutional anchor of the world economy over the last four decades created immense pressure for increasing growth levels in order to maintain a dominant position. Although such processes are far too complex to be reduced to the outcome of formalised political decisions, the introduction of 'Reaganomics' as a vehicle for winning the Cold War and more general to maintain the standing of the United States in the world is a case in point.

The neo-liberal ideological framework which was developed in order to underpin this development was, in principle, based upon the idea of a retrenchment of the state in order to let the market reign upon the basis of self-correcting processes. The consequence was, however, not so much a cut-back of the state as a re-configuration of the state and the tax regime upon which it relied. The result of the latter was an increase in economic and social inequality. But from a long-term perspective, the re-configuration of the state was far more important in that it led to a capture of the *raison d'État* by privatistic interests, thereby undermining the distinction between political and economic rationality. This was not only the case in relation to the privatisation of natural monopolies (water supply, railways, etc.) which have always operated on the borderline between the private and the public. Instead, a far more profound capture took place through the introduction of new public management instruments throughout the state, thereby subsuming political operations to economic rationality.

In addition, the regulatory function of the political system in the state form vis-à-vis the economic system was broken down through the move towards the deregulation of financial markets, a move which was not, however, so much about the degree of public control as a move implying capture, in the sense that public regulators influenced by monetarist ideology were transformed from the guardians of the public interest into servants of the financial industry, with the result that the relationship between operators and regulators increasingly became characterised by coalescence. This effectively undermined the value of the structural coupling between the economic and the political system, in the sense that the form of stability and restraint imposed by public regulation vis-à-vis economic processes was increasingly weakened. This had subsequent effects internally in the financial system because the differentiation between the different functions, products and levels of risk collapsed, in the sense that the distinction between banks, investment banks and hedge funds became increasingly blurred.

Thus, apart from a general reinforcement of publicly sanctioned regulation, a basis for new forms of societal constitutionalism has emerged within finance.[54] A form of societal constitutionalism which has functional separation as it is core element, in the sense that it is oriented towards maintaining a separation between different segments of the finance industry, thereby reducing the risk of exposure which low-risk activities such as traditional banking are confronted with from high-risk activities such as hedge funding. A case can be made for a complex re-configuration of the overall logic guiding the financial system based upon a double movement of public measures and private self-regulation, measures which are internally aimed at maintaining firewalls between different sectors of the financial system and which are externally aimed at curtailing coalescence through the maintenance of functional separation between the economic system and other social spheres, such as the political system, at the same time as channels for the *simultaneous* back coupling (*Rückkopplung*) is established through constitutionalised – and thus limited – structural couplings which rely on formal organisation and a formalised legal framing.

It follows from the above that the real problem exposed by the financial crisis is not foremost a question of the size of the state. Although it remains a legitimate and important field of political contestation, the question of whether the state should occupy 30 per cent or 40 per cent or 50 per cent of GDP is not the real issue. At a deeper structural level, the real danger is, instead, the breakdown of the operative distinction between political and other forms of social rationality, such as economic rationality. Such a breakdown is being purposefully pursued by political fundamentalist ideologies, which, in their different variants, share the characteristic that they seek to overcome the 'original sin' (*Sündenfall*) of functional differentiation[55] through the submission of society in its entirety to a single form of rationality. Fundamentalist ideologies are ideologies of coalescence. As such, neo-liberalism is – in its logical composition – also to be understood as a fundamentalist ideology in so far as it seeks to impose a one-dimensional economistic logic on society in its entirety.

The difference, apart, of course, from the radically different degrees of societal 'damage' which different fundamentalist ideologies have actually caused, is that 'extreme cases' such as communism, fascism and National Socialism sought to submit society in its entirety to an immediate form of the political without relying on an external semantic universe as its medium. These totalitarian ideologies share the view that the political system should transpose itself into all others spheres of society upon the basis of an unmediated political logic. They advocate a naked form of power in which the ambition to achieve the submission of society in its entirety is not covered up but is, on the contrary, deliberately highlighted and reinforced as a purpose in itself. In contrast, neo-liberalism and fundamentalist forms of ecologism, nationalism, religious fundamentalism and socialism, share the feature that they paradoxically use a single universe which is external to the political system, such as economic, environmental, national or religious belief systems, as a vehicle for the attempt to make society submit to a totalising political ideology. In contrast to radical totalitarian ideologies, they rely on an 'inter-mediating variable' in their relation to other parts of society, and it is this single inter-mediating variable which they seek to transpose to society in its entirety. Thus, paradoxically, an ideology such as neo-liberalism which seemingly is aimed at reducing the reach of the political system as much as possible can only achieve this through political means and within the framework of a political universe. As such, neo-liberalism remains guided by political – rather than economic – rationality, in the sense that the intention to submit society in its entirety to an economistic logic remains, first and foremost, a political objective, and only secondarily, an economic, one.

The central insight emerging from the above is that what we have come to understand with the term 'globalisation' in the last decades is probably better understood as a transitional phase which implies a relative change in the weight and centrality of different national configurations.[56] Crude seventeenth-century-inspired perspectives which assume that states are holistic entities encompassing society as a whole are likely to see such transformations as merely reflecting a change in the balance of power between states. Both the relative weight and the importance of states are certainly being affected by such transformations, but, in practice, what we are dealing with are far more fundamental changes in the relative weight of *different* – but mutually dependent – dimensions of national configurations, which has been caused by a fundamental change in the deeper structures (*Tiefenstrukturen*) of society, through an increased reliance on functional differentiation. As such, the current transitional phase merely implies yet another expansion of the primacy of functional differentiation into ever larger parts of the globe, an expansion which has led to the breakdown of the existing stabilising regimes within different functional areas, and the urgent need to develop replacements which correspond to the new structural realities. As such, the financial crisis of 2008 reflects a discrepancy between the structural composition of world society and the (trans)national regulatory architecture aimed at stabilising it. In this sense, the current crisis, and also the crisis of the first half of the twentieth century, can be understood as a form of globalisation crisis. This does not mean that globalisation, as such, is the problem, but it does mean that a striking inability to respond to structural transformations can be observed since increased globalisation is not reflected in corresponding adaptations and re-configurations of the institutional and, indeed, constitutional framing of economic as well as other social processes.

6.7 Conclusion

A central trademark of modernity is the move towards a dynamic and linear concept of time. This was also reflected in the transformation of the constitutional concept away from a static to dynamic concept. A further trademark was the increased dissolution of the multiplicity of overlapping constitutional orders of pre-modern society, a development which did not, however, lead to the establishment of a singular state-based constitution, but, instead, to the emergence of complex national configurations in which a multiplicity of social spheres were constitutionally stabilised over time.

The breakdown of the distinction between 'Europe and the rest' and the ongoing breakdown of the distinction between 'the West and the rest' have both, however, led to circumstances in which the constitutional arrangements of national configurations have either broken down or come under intense pressure. In both cases, increased levels of globalisation have served to undermine important dimensions of the constitutional set-up of national configurations and this has, in turn, led to a fracturing of the equilibrium between the different social spheres.

Notes

1 Niklas Luhmann, 'Gesellschaftliche Struktur und semantische Tradition', in *Gesellschafts-struktur und Semantik: Studien zur Wissenssoziologie der modernen Gesellschaft, Band 1*, Frankfurt am Main: Suhrkamp Verlag, 1980, pp. 9–71. For a critical analysis of the argument concerning a linear relationship between social structure and semantics, see Urs Stäheli, 'Die Nachträglichkeit der Semantik: Zum Verhältnis von Sozialstruktur und Semantik', *Soziale Systeme: Zeitschrift für Soziologische Theorie*, 1998, 4, pp. 315–40.
2 Reinhart Koselleck, 'Begriffsgeschichtliche Probleme der Verfassungsgeschichtsschreibung', in *Begriffsgeschichten: Studien zur Semantik und Pragmatik der politischen und Sozialen Sprache*, Frankfurt am Main: Suhrkamp Verlag, 2006, pp. 365–82.
3 Ibid.
4 'Verfassung (I)', in Otto Brunner, Werner Conze and Reinhart Koselleck (eds), *Geschichtliche Grundbegriffe: Historisches Lexikon zur politisch-sozialen Sprache in Deutschland, Band 6*, Stuttgart: Klett-Cotta, 1990, pp. 831–62, at 837 *et seq.*
5 'Haus' and 'Haushalt', in *Historisches Wörterbuch der Philosophie, Band 3*, Basel-Stuttgart: Schwabe & Co. Verlag, 1974, pp. 1007–20, and pp. 1020–21 respectively.
6 Gianfranco Poggi, *The Development of the Modern State: A Sociological Perspective*, Stanford, CA: Stanford University Press, 1978.
7 'Verfassung (I)', at 839.
8 The term 'the living constitution' was originally developed in the American context referring to the constitution of the United States. See Howard Lee McBain, *The Living Constitution: A Consideration of the Realities and Legends of our Fundamental Law*, New York: Workers Education Bureau Press, 1927.
9 'Haus' and 'Haushalt'.

10 Niklas Luhmann, *Recht der Gesellschaft*, Frankfurt am Main: Suhrkamp Verlag, 1993, p. 446 *et seq*.

11 Karl Polanyi, *The Great Transformation: The Political and Economic Origins of Our Time*, Boston, MA: Beacon Press, [1944] 2001, p. 84.

12 Ulrich K. Preuß, 'Disconnecting Constitutions from Statehood: Is Global Constitutionalism a Promising Concept?', in Petra Dobner and Martin Loughlin (eds), *The Twilight of Constitutional Law: Demise of Transformation?*, Oxford: Oxford University Press, 2010, pp. 23–46.

13 James Tully, 'The Imperialism of Modern Constitutional Democracy', in Neil Walker and Martin Loughlin (eds), *The Paradox of Constitutionalism: Constituent Power and Constitutional Form* Oxford: Oxford University Press, 2007, pp. 315–38, at 318.

14 Michael Roberts, *The Military Revolution, 1560–1660*. Belfast: Boyd, 1956; Charles Tilly, *Coercion, Capital and European States*, AD 990–1990, Oxford, Malden, MA: Blackwell, 1990; Jeremy A. Black, *A Military Revolution? Military Change and European Society, 1550–1800*, Basingstoke: Macmillan, 1991.

15 Poul F. Kjaer, 'Post-Hegelian Networks: Comments on the Chapter by Simon Deakin', in Marc Amstutz and Gunther Teubner (eds), *Networks: Legal Issues of Multilateral Co-operation*, Oxford: Hart Publishing, 2009, pp. 75–85, at 80 *et seq*.

16 Karl Marx and Friedrich Engels, 'Ludwig Feuerbach und der Ausgang der Klassischen Deutschen Philosophie', in *Marx & Engels: Werke, band 21*, Berlin: Dietz Verlag, [1888] 1975, pp. 262–307, at 293.

17 Luhmann, *Die Gesellschaft der Gesellschaft*, Frankfurt am Main: Suhrkamp Verlag, 1997, p. 1024 *et seq* and 1066 *et seq*. For a paradigmatic overview of the discussion, see also Agnes Heller, 'Death of the Subject', 22–38, *Thesis Eleven*, 1990, 25, pp. 22–38.

18 Norbert Elias, *Über den Prozeß der Zivilisation, Band 1*, Frankfurt am Main: Suhrkamp Verlag, [1938] 1976, and Norbert Elias, *Die höfische Gesellschaft*, Frankfurt am Main: Suhrkamp Verlag, [1969] 2002.

19 Gorm Harste, 'Kant und Luhmann über Teleologie in politischer Kommunikation und Natur', in Gorm Harste, Thomas Mertens and Thomas Scheffer (eds), *Immanuel Kant über Natur und Gesellschaft*, Odense: Odense University Press, 1996, pp. 169–83.

20 Jean-Jacques Rousseau, *Du Contract Social ou Principes du Droit Politique*, Paris: Hachette Littératures, [1762] 2005.

21 Jürgen Habermas, *Der philosophische Diskurs der Moderne: Zwölf Vorlesungen*, Frankfurt am Main: Suhrkamp Verlag, 1985, p. 13ff.

22 For the relation of mutual increase between freedom and disciplination, see, in particular, Michel Foucault, 'The Subject and Power', in Hubert Dreyfus and Paul Rabinow (eds), *Michel Foucault: Beyond Structuralism and Hermeneutics*, Chicago: Chicago University Press, 1982, pp. 208–26.

23 Hauke Brunkhorst, 'The Return of Crisis', in Poul F. Kjaer, Gunther Teubner and Alberto Febbrajo (eds), *The Financial Crisis in Constitutional Perspective: The Dark Side of Functional Differentiation*, Oxford: Hart Publishing, 2011, pp. 131–71.

24 Stress-related mental breakdowns might reflect a similar form of discrepancy-induced crisis in relation to individuals. It might also be possible to understand internal crises – or at least the frequency of such crises – as a reflection of increased acceleration (*Beschleunigung*) of the reproduction of societal structures. For a German critical theory perspective on the time structures of modern society, see Hartmut Rosa, *Beschleunigung: Die Veränderung der Zeitstrukturen in der Moderne*, Frankfurt am Main: Suhrkamp Verlag, 2005; For a French poststructuralist perspective, see Paul Virilio, *Vitesse et Politique: Essai de Dromologie*, Paris: Galilée, 1977; for an American critical theory perspective, see William E. Scheuerman, *Liberal Democracy and the Social Acceleration of Time*, Baltimore, MD: Johns Hopkins University Press, 2004. For a systems theory perspective, see Luhmann, *Die Gesellschaft der Gesellschaft*, p. 997 *et seq*.

25 The consequence of the implosion of scientific paradigms, however, tends to be the emergence of an increased number of competing sub-discourses within a specific academic field. This, again, might have an increase in the scope of meaning production as a long-term

consequence. For the emergence and implosion of scientific paradigms, see Ludwig Fleck, *Entstehung und Entwicklung einer wissenschaftlichen Tatsache: Einführung in die Lehre vom Denkstil und Denkkollektiv*, Frankfurt am Main: Suhrkamp Verlag, [1935] 1980; Thomas S. Kuhn, *The Structure of Scientific Revolutions*, Chicago: Chicago University Press, [1962] 1996.

26 Early insights going in a similar direction can also be found in Luhmann: see Niklas Luhmann, *Zweckbegriff und Systemrationalität: Über die Funktion von Zwecken in sozialen Systemen*, Frankfurt am Main: Suhrkamp Verlag, [1968], 1973, p. 250.

27 Although this might not necessarily be the case if an operation is repeated. See also Poul F. Kjaer, 'Systems in Context. On the Outcome of the Habermas/Luhmann Debate', *Ancilla Iuris*, 2006, pp. 66–77, at 70 *et seq.*

28 An equivalent figure related to the subject is Hegel's point that the slave always has the possibility to die in freedom through revolution or suicide. See Georg W.F. Hegel, *Grundlinien der Philosophie des Rechts oder Naturrecht und Staatswissenschaft im Grundrisse, Werke Band 7*, Frankfurt am Main: Suhrkamp Verlag, [1821] 1970, § 57 Zusatz.

29 Niklas Luhmann, 'Verfassung als evolutionäre Errungenschaft', *Rechtshistorisches Journal*, 1990, 9, pp. 176–220, at 180 *et seq.* See also 'Verfassung (II)', in Otto Brunner, Werner Conze and Reinhart Koselleck (eds), *Geschichtliche Grundbegriffe: Historisches Lexikon zur politisch-sozialen Sprache in Deutschland, Band 6*, Stuttgart: Klett-Cotta Verlag, 1990, pp. 863–99, at 866 *et seq.*

30 Luhmann, *Das Recht der Gesellschaft*. See also Rudolf Stichweh, 'Transfer in Sozialsystemen: Theoretische Überlegungen'. Paper, 12, 2005. Available at: www.unilu.ch/deu/prof._dr._rudolf_stichwehpublikationen_38043.html.

31 Niklas Luhmann, *Die Politik der Gesellschaft*, Frankfurt am Main: Suhrkamp Verlag, 2000, p. 390.

32 See, for example, Hugo Sinzheimer, *Arbeitsrecht und Rechtssoziologie, vol. 1*, Frankfurt am Main: Europäische Verlagsanstalt, 1976.

33 This is also one of the central insights of the varieties of capitalism approach although this approach remains reductionist in nature to the extent that it only takes account of economy and politics but leaves out areas such as science and religion. See Peter A. Hall and David Soskice (eds), *Varieties of Capitalism: The Institutional Foundations of Comparative Advantage*, Oxford: Oxford University Press, 2001.

34 Niklas Luhmann, *Recht der Gesellschaft*, p. 429.

35 For the opposite perspective, see Ulrich Haltern, *Was bedeutet Souveränität?* Tübingen: Mohr Siebeck, 2007.

36 Georg W.F. Hegel, *Grundlinien der Philosophie des Rechts*, Frankfurt am Main: Suhrkamp Verlag, [1821] 1970, § 4.

37 Aldo Mascareño, 'La Cultura chilena como ficción real', in Maximiliano Figueroa and Manuel Vicuña (eds), *El Chile del Bicentenario*, Santiago de Chile: Ediciones Universidad Diego Portales, 2008, pp. 183–220.

38 Poul F. Kjaer, 'The Structural Transformation of Embeddedness', in Christian Joerges and Josef Falke (eds), *Karl Polanyi: Globalisation and the Potential of Law in Transnational Markets*, Oxford: Hart Publishing, 2011, pp. 85–104.

39 Georg W.F. Hegel, *Grundlinien der Philosophie des Rechts*, Frankfurt am Main: Suhrkamp Verlag, [1821] 1970, especially § 244.

40 Georg W.F. Hegel, *Grundlinien der Philosophie des Rechts*, Frankfurt am Main: Suhrkamp Verlag, [1821] 1970, pp. 241–42.

41 Christian Borch, 'Systemic Power: Luhmann, Foucault and Analytics of Power', *Acta Sociologica*, 2005, 48, pp. 155–67. The difficulties related to the reduction of the state to the reliance on negative sanctions are also acknowledged by Luhmann himself in relation to the emergence of the welfare state. See Niklas Luhmann, 'Der Wohlfahrtsstaat zwischen Evolution und Rationalität', in Peter Koslowski, Philipp Kreuzer and Reinhard Low (eds), *Chancen und Grenzen des Sozialstaats*, Tübingen: J.C.B. Mohr, 1983, pp. 26–40.

42 Rudolf Stichweh, *Inklusion und Eksklusion: Studien zur Gesellschaftstheorie*, Bielefeld: Transcript Verlag, 2005, pp. 163–77.

43 For a critique of the concept of neo-corporatism from an American critical theory perspective, see David Sciulli, *Theory of Societal Constitutionalism: Foundations of a Non-Marxist Critical Theory*, Cambridge: Cambridge University Press, 1992, p. 73 *et seq.*

44 Helmut Willke, *Ironie des Staates: Grundlinien einer Staatstheorie polyzentrischer Gesellschaft*, Frankfurt am Main: Suhrkamp Verlag, 1992; Helmut Wilke, *Systemtheorie III: Steuerungstheorie, 2: Auflage*, Stuttgart: Lucius & Lucius, 1998, especially p. 109 *et seq.*

45 For somewhat similar insights, see Gunther Teubner, 'The "State" of Private Networks: The Emerging Legal Regimes of Polycorporatism in Germany', *Brigham Young University Law Review*, 1993, 2, pp. 553–75, and Gunther Teubner, *Constitutional Fragments: Societal Constitutionalism and Globalization*, Oxford: Oxford University Press, 2012, p. 114 *et seq.*

46 For a similar view, see David Sciulli, *Theory of Societal Constitutionalism: Foundations of a Non-Marxist Critical Theory*, Cambridge: Cambridge University Press, 1992.

47 Poul F. Kjaer, 'Law and Order Within and Beyond National Configurations', in Poul F. Kjaer, Gunther Teubner and Alberto Febbrajo (eds), *The Financial Crisis in Constitutional Perspective: The Dark Side of Functional Differentiation*, Oxford: Hart Publishing, 2011, pp. 395–430.

48 Niklas Luhmann, 'Der Wohlfahrtsstaat zwischen Evolution und Rationalität', in *Chancen und Grenzen des Sozialstaats*, pp. 26–40.

49 Franz L. Neumann, *Behemoth: The Structure and Practice of National Socialism, 1933–1944*, Washington, DC: Octagon, [1944] 1983, p. 3 *et seq.*

50 Neil Walker, 'Beyond Boundary Disputes and Basic Grids: Mapping the Global Disorder of Normative Orders', *International Journal of Constitutional Law*, 2008, 6, pp. 373–96.

51 For the argument that the North Atlantic space remains the core of the global economy also today, see Paul Hirst and Grahame Thompson, *Globalization in Question: The International Economy and the Possibilities of Governance*, 2nd edition, Cambridge: Polity Press, 2001.

52 For the concept of bubbles, see Dirk Baecker, 'The Culture Form of a Crisis', in Poul F. Kjaer, Gunther Teubner and Alberto Febbrajo (eds), *The Financial Crisis in Constitutional Perspective: The Dark Side of Functional Differentiation*, Oxford, Hart Publishing, 2011, pp. 173–88.

53 George Soros, *The New Paradigm for Financial Markets: The Credit Crisis of 2008 and What it Means*, New York: Public Affairs, 2008, p. 81 *et seq.*

54 A new form which can rely on old experiences and institutional set-ups since the Glass–Steagall Act of 1933 exactly maintained such a system until it was repealed in 1999. For a general theory of societal constitutionalism in the national realm, see David Sciulli, *Theory of Societal Constitutionalism: Foundations of a Non-Marxist Critical Theory*, New York: Cambridge University Press, 1992.

55 Niklas Luhmann, *Die Wirtschaft der Gesellschaft*, Frankfurt am Main: Suhrkamp Verlag, 1989, p. 264.

56 For similar insights, albeit upon the basis of a reductionist view which reduces such transformation processes to a question of an expansion of a pure economic logic, see Immanuel Wallerstein, 'Globalization or the Age of Transition?', *International Sociology*, 2000, 2, pp. 249–65.

7 The transmutation of constitutional ordering

7.1 Introduction

Both the developments in the first half of the twentieth century and the still ongoing transformations – as empathically condensed in the financial crisis – have triggered constitutional transmutations which have led to a re-calibration of constitutional conceptuality to new structural realities. In relation to the developments in the early twentieth century, the clearest example of this can be observed in relation to the institutionalisation of economic constitutionalism in the context of the European integration process. This development was subsequently complemented with the embryonic emergence of a whole range of other sectorial constitutional frameworks in relation to other policy areas of the European Union.

In a similar manner, the global transformations which have unfolded in recent decades have led to the gradual emergence of a new type of sectorial constitutions with a global reach within a wide range of social spheres. Thus, the structural transformations outlined earlier on, and the kind of societal crises which they have caused, have led to the emergence of new types of constitutional ordering. That is especially the case in relation to the emergence of the conglomerate of organisations and regimes which subscribe to the Washington Consensus doctrine for the regulation of economic flows on a global scale. The one-dimensional economic focus of this conglomerate has, however, led to a counter-movement in the form of the emergence of new transnational structures which also rely on constitutional conceptuality and which are aimed at offsetting the negative externalities of global economic processes. This is illustrated through an analysis of the constitutional infrastructure of the global fair-trade certification scheme.

7.2 The emergence and mutation of the European economic constitution

The societal crises of the first half of the twentieth century deeply influenced constitutional thinking. One central strand of constitutional thinking which gained ground against the backdrop of the catastrophe was the idea of economic constitutions. Based upon ideas already developed in the inter-war period, this conceptual framework gained particular strength in the post-war German Federal Republic. Here, the concept of the economic constitution was seen as providing a possible guarantee against a repetition of the economic and social disaster of the 1930s and the even larger political disaster which followed. This was the case because the objective was to achieve a legal, and thereby normative, stabilisation of the economic system and its relations to the political system through the establishment of a coherent principle-based framework.[1]

The German debate is, to a high extent, linked to the ordo-liberalist school which advocated the existence of an economic constitution based upon the pillars of property, contract, competition and monetary institutions.[2] In the German post-war context, the concept of the economic constitution which, after intense debate, gained ground was, however, not merely referring to economic processes in the narrow sense, but rather to a concept which was explicitly aimed at establishing the legal foundations for a social-market economy (*soziale Marktwirtschaft*).[3] This framework combined liberal, religious and corporatist social-democratic ideas in a manner which made it substantially different from the type of order which the ordo-liberal school had advanced.[4] The objective was to develop generalised constitutional rules for the market through the guaranteeing of free competition upon the basis of the insight that power is not only exercised by states and public actors, but also by private actors.[5]

From the 1950s onwards, the idea of an economic constitution was transposed into a new framework in the form of the European integration process. This development implied that the transnational European setting – rather than national settings – gradually became the central *locus* for the stabilisation of economic processes in Europe. Hans Peter Ipsen identified four defining principles of the European economic constitution: 1) the rule of law; 2) supranationality; 3) the principle of established procedures of decision-making; and 4) the principle of democracy.[6] In substance, the European economic constitution, moreover, referred to the well-known principles of freedom and non-discrimination in relation to the free movement of capital, products, services and labour. Hence, at a first glance, the European economic constitution was, in contrast to the German socio-economic constitution, an explicit liberal order, in the sense that it only served as a market constitution in the narrow sense.[7]

The emergence of the phenomenon of European integration, with the European economic constitution as the central form of its legal framing, can be understood as reflecting a decrease in the internal reliance on territorial and stratificatory differentiation within the functionally differentiated structures of the economic system. The European Union operates within a territorial frame, but, due to its sheer size, the continued enlargement process and the strategy of binding neighbouring countries (for example, Norway and Switzerland) as close as possible to the Union, territorial differentiation plays a far less-important role in the European Union context when compared with the nation-state contexts. Even though it is, in principle, a territorially differentiated structure, the European Union does not, in many instances, refer to a concept of territoriality, but, instead, to a concept of space, thereby making it into an entity without well-defined boundaries. This is also expressed in the semantic labels of regimes such as *the European Space of Freedom, Security and Justice, the European Economic Area* and *the European Research Area*.[8]

When observed from an economic perspective, the turn to integration has, furthermore, proved to be 'evolutionary superior' because the integration process reduces the number of structural couplings in which economic operations are entangled, since the different legal and political demands towards the economic system produced by each Member State is being substituted with the demand to adhere to a single framework.[9] In this sense, integration produces 'economies of scale' in relation to the cognitive resources which firms and other market actors within the economic system need to deploy in order to sufficiently adjust to their social environments. Thus, integration reduces the 'friction' emerging from the social environment of the economic system and thereby facilitates the economic systems quest for re-production.[10] Similar advantages can, albeit to a lesser extent, be observed in relation to other social spheres, such as science, (higher) education, professionalised sports and the mass media. For this reason, the political and the legal system are faced with pressure from the wider society, and, in particular, from the economic system, to pursue further integration, a kind of pressure, which, moreover, is supplemented by structural changes which are internal to the political and legal systems, as expressed in the relative decline of the importance of European states in the global political system.[11] This decline provides the political sub-systems in the Member State form with an incentive to pool resources in order to remain relevant on the global scene. Thus, from this perspective, the emergence of the integration process must be understood as being intrinsically linked to increases in the level of globalisation.

The emergence of the European economic constitution implied a de-coupling of the economic sphere from the broader welfare conglomerates which economic processes were embedded in at national level. This, again, has led to the diagnosis that a permanent tension exists between the increased Europeanisation of economic policy and national welfare policies.[12] Following Polanyi, such a de-coupling is, however, unsustainable because the economic system is always embedded in a wider social context, since economic production processes can only unfold when they are aligned with broader social reproduction processes.[13] The establishment of the internal market in the 1980s seems to confirm this, since this development did not lead to de-regulation. Instead, this move triggered intensive re-regulation at European level within a whole range of policy areas such as the environment, gender equality and consumer safety, which cannot be understood as an expression of economic regulation in the narrow sense.[14] Thus, there seems to be no empirical foundation for the claim that the European Union is producing dis-embeddedness. Instead, the integration process proves that the liberalist quest for a free-flowing economic system capable of operating detached from the rest of society is a mirage.

Nonetheless, there is a widespread perception in broad sections of the European public space as well as within academia that European integration *does* lead to dis-embeddeddness. This view is, however, only plausible if one merely observes the world from the life-world of a labour unionist, in that the integration process has, indeed, contributed to the relative decline in the centrality of the organisational structures which characterised the nation-state configurations of the 1950s. This development is, however, to be understood as a reflection of the deeper structures (*Tiefenstrukturen*) of society, rather than as a result of the integration process itself. As described by Ulrich Beck, the transition towards a 'second modernity' implies a (gradual) change away from classical welfare policies and towards polices of risk regulation.[15] Going a step further than Beck, this development can also be understood as a reflection of increased societal complexity, which in turn has triggered an increase in the reliance on functional differentiation. Trade-offs, asymmetries and externalities is the result in that economic reproduction clashes with other societal spheres such as health and the environment, thereby creating new forms of societal problems.[16] These problems reflects a radicalisation of modernity to the extent that they can be understood as the side-effects of an increased reliance on functional differentiation, since they are problems and conflicts which are being reproduced along functionally delineated rather than stratificatory and territorial lines. Thus, the neo-corporatist structures are faced with a relative decrease in significance because the host of problems that they address are increasingly being reduced to one set of problems among many. From this perspective, the way in which the European Union frames economic interaction does not necessarily indicate a reduction in social embeddedness, but merely reflects a transformation in the very form of embeddedness, in so far as the European Union responds to a different set of problems than was the case for the neo-corporatist nation states in their founding period.[17]

However, a different take on the above is that the discrepancy between the *actual* developments and the *perception* of these developments indicates that the concept of embeddedness is an insufficient analytical tool under the present conditions. In its substantialist variant, the concept of embeddeness is essentially pre-modern in nature, since it does not take sufficient account of the organisational and legal move towards the reliance on the formalised structures which characterise modernity.[18] Hence, the modern variant of the constitutional concept might be considered a functional equivalent to the concept of embeddedness under the condition of functional differentiation, since it is a concept which is directly aimed at achieving a simultaneous internal stabilisation of functionally differentiated spheres and the establishment of compatibility with the rest of society.

This also seems to be confirmed by the evolution of the European Union in the last decades. Although the German Constitutional Court famously argued otherwise,[19] the entering into force of the Treaty of Maastricht in 1993 is generally considered to indicate formally the end of the European Community as a mere economic entity.[20] This was the case because the introduction of the Treaty of Maastricht meant that the economic constitution, which, until then, had served as the central legal framing of the Community, was no longer the sole pillar upon which the integration project rested.[21] This development can be understood in two ways: either the Treaty of Maastricht transformed the Community into an (embryonic) polity, with the consequence that the principles structuring economic interaction became subsumed under the political rationality guiding the operations of the newly established Union's emerging political system; or the Treaty of Maastricht can be understood as an evolutionary transmutation which meant that the existing economic constitution was merely supplemented by a number of other (embryonic) functionally delineated constitutions, in the form of a European environmental constitution, a European consumer constitution or a European science constitution.

The former perspective is only a potential option if one transfers the claim to substantialist unity embodied in nation-state mythology to the European setting. But it is not only the high level of cultural and linguistic diversity of the European setting which seems to render this impossible, an even more fundamental obstacle is the function of the European Union vis-à-vis the segment of world society against which it is oriented. The European Union, as previously mentioned, is a hybrid located in between nation states, in the form of the Member States and the rest of world society, and, consequently, it has features which partly resemble statehood and other features which resemble global structures of ordering such as the World Trade Organization.[22] In relation to the latter dimension, the central function of the European Union is therefore, just like other transnational regimes, to act as frameworks of transfer between different social contexts. This function is also embodied in functionally delineated frameworks such as the Internal Market, the European Research Area, and the Area of Freedom, Security and Justice. All of these regimes rely on legally condensed principle-based frameworks which are aimed at handling three issues: the question of internal stability of the processes against which they are oriented; the compatibility of these processes with the rest of society; and how future issues can be addressed. The European Research Area, for example, is based upon a copy of the principles which guide the internal market principles concerning freedom of establishment and the free movement of capital, products, services and labour, and non-discrimination. In the area of science and research, these objectives are transformed into 'negative integration' principles concerning non-discrimination, and 'positive integration' measures concerning the establishment of common frameworks in order to remove obstacles to the transfer of scientific knowledge between different national contexts. These principles have been condensed into objectives concerning the establishment of free movement of researchers, the free circulation of scientific knowledge, a European research-integrity code and open competition for research funding, thereby establishing an internal stabilising framework for science and research. At the same time, the European Research

Area, through its strong focus on innovation policy, is explicitly oriented towards the establishment of compatibility between scientific and non-scientific processes, most notably economic processes through a focus on innovation. The focus on innovation implies that the question of establishing frameworks of compatibility which enable transfers of social components, such as scientific knowledge, between different social spheres is brought to the forefront. Finally, the European Research Area is committed to a logic concerning increased integration and the potential fusion of the respective national research areas, thereby establishing a principle-based approach capable of guiding future actions.[23]

It follows that, instead of a move to statehood, the development formally initiated with the Treaty of Maastricht merely implied a transmutation which transformed the Community from a functional regime into a complex Byzantine matrix consisting of a plurality of partially overlapping functional regimes, engaging with each other in a multitude of ways, upon the basis of their respective (embryonic) constitutional frameworks which might or might not refer to the same legal texts and rely on the same legal structures in their separate attempts to stabilise and justify their respective operations. Thus, the fate of the economic constitution goes to the core of the European Union's *raison d'être*: a conglomerate of functionalist regimes or a state? No clear-cut answer can be given to this question at the present. Instead, the European Union continues to oscillate between the two forms on a more or less permanent basis, at the same time as the paradoxical tension between the two dimensions are externalised into the future through the adherence to the quest for 'ever closure Union'.[24]

Irrespectively of which direction the European Union will take, it is unlikely to happen upon the basis of a conscious decision but will probably occur in an evolutionary fashion reflecting deeper structural changes. If the globalisation wave continues, the European Union is likely to find itself facing a need of continuous enlargement, and a steady increase in its entanglement with other regional as well as global structures of ordering, thereby rendering the transformation of the European Union into a kind of 'true' polity impossible. Globalisation has, however, been with us for 500 years, and has always developed in a two-steps-forward and one-step-back manner.[25] Thus, it is possible that world society is currently about to enter a period of 're-stabilisation' through a (temporary) contraction in the degree of globalisation, a contraction which will potentially make a prolonged period of stabilisation of the European construction, within a well-defined territorial frame, a viable possibility, thereby providing a structural basis for the emergence of a European polity with a potential to establish a more coherent linking of the different functional regimes which currently make up the Union and to structure the embeddedness of the economy, but not the economy itself, upon the basis of the political priorities established by the polity. But, at the same time, the changed nature of economic reproduction, and thus the character of the societal problems with which contemporary society is confronted, means that such embeddedness is unlikely to take the same form or to have the same substance as the forms of embeddedness which characterised the European nation-state conglomerates in the post-war period.

7.3 Constitutional ordering in the global realm

The year after the Treaty of Maastricht formally became the foundation of the European integration project, agreement was reached on the treaty establishing the World Trade Organization, which entered into force in 1995. The world trade regime has since undergone a jurdification process which has triggered the question of whether we are seeing a move towards the establishment of a global economic constitution.[26] The World Trade Organization is, however, only one of several globally operating regimes which structure economic communication flows. Rather than a singular global economic constitution, it is possible to observe the existence of a conglomerate of overlapping, partly reinforcing and partly contradictory regimes, which has been subject to different degrees of constitutionalisation. Apart from the World Trade Organization, this conglomerate consists of public international organizations such as the International Monetary Fund and the World Bank and private public organisations such as the International Organization for Standardization. A conglomerate which effectively establishes a constitutional framework for the global economy upon the basis of specific principles for the organisation and status of the essential components of the global economic system, from monetary policy and investment protection, to trade and product standards. This conglomerate has developed gradually since the early post-war period but reached a different quality in the post-Cold War era due to the development of a specific 'constitutional consciousness' capable of giving it normative direction. From the late 1980s onwards, a doctrinal framework emerged which was condensed in the form of the 'ten commandments' of the so-called Washington Consensus. This framework, among other things, institutionalised principles concerning fiscal discipline, free trade, privatisation, de-regulation and, not least, the immunity of economic processes against their submission to non-economic social forces.[27] Not surprisingly, the Washington Consensus agenda has come to stand as the embodiment of the neo-liberal policy agenda of the past decades.[28] Indeed, the Washington Consensus framework seems, with the vocabulary advanced by Gunther Teubner, to be solely oriented towards unleashing and speeding up economic processes without taking the need of a self-limitation of economic production in order to curb the expansion of economic logics into other societal spheres into consideration.[29] It is a framework which has, only to a very limited extent, built-in reflexivity-increasing mechanisms which enable it to address the negative externalities emerging from economic production processes.

But the problems of the Washington Consensus framework are not only a reflection of a one-sided constitutional design and the ideological basis upon which it relies. It is also a reflection of the structural basis within which the global operating regimes associated with organisations such as the International Monetary Fund and the World Bank unfold their operations. The differences between the global conglomerate and the European Union are, for example, quite substantial. Whereas the European Union, albeit to a lesser extent than nation states, partially relies upon territorial differentiation, these regimes are global regimes which rely even less on territorial differentiation. Second, although the European Union is an independent and autonomous legal order which cannot be understood as merely representing the sum of the Member States, it is still deeply entangled with the Member States. In addition, the European Union benefits from the relative homogeneity of the European space in relation to social structures and the type of societal problems with which the Union finds itself confronted. In comparison, global regimes are confronted with an environment which is dramatically more varied, in the sense that they, at least in principle, refer to stakeholders residing in Switzerland as well as Swaziland. Thus, the ambition of establishing general principles for the internal stability and external compatibility of globally unfolding processes through legally structured frameworks is being hampered by the sheer difficulty of developing coherent strategies and legal principles capable of taking account of the fundamentally different nature of societal problems in the developed and the less-developed areas of the world. These differences largely reflect the different forms of societal differentiation upon which the developed and the less-developed parts of world society relies, in the sense that the move towards the primacy of functional differentiation has not prevailed as the dominating form of differentiation in the less-developed world. In other words, globally unfolding structures are faced with the problem of defining coherent policies since the relative weight and relation between functional, territorial and stratificatory differentiation are radically different within different segments of the world. Thus, irrespective of the type and quality of their constitutional framing, such frames are likely to have a substantially reduced ability to ensure a high level of compatibility across the board when compared with national- and regional-based frameworks.

7.4 Counter-movements through new sectorial constitutions: the example of fair trade

It follows from the above that only a low level of normative compatibility seems to be possible at global level.[30] But if, by the same token, one emphasises that the central function of transnationally unfolding social processes vis-à-vis world society in its entirety is to enable the transfer of social components from one social context to another, the conclusion need not to be so dramatic. Transnational structures do not frame social processes in their entirety, but only the *actual transposition* – that is, the concrete moment – in which the social components are transferred from one context to another. If one limits the focus to this quite specific task, a more plausible picture concerning the potential of constitutional structuring at the global level of world society emerges.[31]

A different reason for this alternative picture to emerge can, moreover, be found in the fact that constitutional frameworks oriented towards economic processes are, albeit the most developed, not the only type of frameworks which operate in the global realm. Non-economic concerns are, therefore, not so much *integrated* into economic processes as *handled* by complementary structures located *outside* economic-oriented frameworks. Thus, also at the global level of world society, the quest for substantialist embeddedness has been transformed into a question of non-substantialist compatibility.

The concrete example of the global fair-trade certification scheme might serve as an illustration of this. The scheme is organised and overseen by a private international organisation, the Fairtrade Labelling Organizations International (FLO).[32] The organisation was founded in 1997 as an international umbrella organisation for national fair-trade labelling organisations. Its core task is to develop and co-ordinate standards for fair trade and assist producers in gaining and maintaining certification of fair trade. The central focus is on agricultural products such as bananas and coffee, but the reach has also been expanded into areas such as textiles. What all the products have in common, however, is that they are part of global production, distribution and consumption chains, and typically imply a transfer between the developing and the developed parts of the global economy.[33]

The orientation is twofold to the extent that the standards are aimed at ensuring ecological sustainability as well as establishing social and labour standards in the production process. A key strategy of the Fairtrade Labelling Organizations International is further to establish transparent and long-term trade relations between producers, importers, processors and distributors through long-term contracts which, among other things, set minimum prices, thereby reducing the exposure of the producers to market volatility and the pressure brought to bear on them from large-scale companies. In addition, a 'social premium' is paid, which *de facto* serves as a sort of tax, which is allocated to the promotion of common goods which are of relevance to the producers and are typically invested in local development, such as education and health facilities for the producers. The producers who own the production sites themselves, typically agricultural land, are organised in co-operatives. Alternatively, work councils are established which represents the employees towards the landowners

In 2004, the organisation was split into two sub-units: FLO International and FLO-CERT. FLO International maintained the core task of developing fair-trade standards, while FLO-CERT ensures that producers and traders comply with the standards of FLO International. FLO-CERT has the competence to impose sanctions in cases of non-compliance. The ultimate sanction is de-certification and exclusion from the system. Both organisations are based in Bonn, Germany, and established under German law. FLO International is a non-profit organisation (*eingetragener Verein*) and operates in concordance with the German public benefit law. FLO-CERT is structured as a limited company (*GmbH*) under German law.[34]

Fairtrade Labelling Organizations International has developed a foundational text which it calls a constitution.[35] The constitutional text is an 11-page document with a preamble and 18 paragraphs which sets out the basic framework upon which the organisation operates, including a specification of its central organs and the purpose of its activities. The constitution may only be amended through a majority of 75 per cent of the members.[36] The constitution establishes the General Assembly as the central institutional organ. It comprises 50 per cent producer representatives and 50 per cent representatives from the national labelling organisations. The two groups are, furthermore, organised into two different sub-assemblies. The assembly has the character of a 'parliament' in that its core function is representation, the development of legislative-like rules and general oversight. As such, the assembly serves as the ultimate *locus* of authority for the organisation, at the same time as it remains coupled to law through the constitution, the internal procedural framework as well through the reliance on German law.

The General Assembly elects the board which consist of five representatives from the labelling organisations, four representatives from producer organisations (representing different geographical regions), two representatives from certified traders and three external independent experts. Both in relation to the assembly and the board, a key characteristic is the deliberate design of a multiple-stakeholder framework. The organisation, in this sense, reflects a balance of interest approach as known from classical state-based constitutional set-ups. At the same time, the 'external experts' are granted a privileged position, since they hold the key to establishing a majority. The mediation between different stakeholder groups is, in other words, assigned to representatives who are expected to represent a neutral and knowledge-based, and thus 'cognitivised', position. A similar framework exists in relation to the various sub-committees, most notably the standard-setting committee.

The multiple-stakeholder framework also serves as an internal mirror which reflects the organisation's external environment. By defining specific categories of producers, importers, processors and distributors in its constitution,[37] the organisation delineates the segment of world society which can *potentially* be included in the framework, and thereby establishes the boundaries of the normative order which it seeks to establish. This is then combined with specific procedures for actual inclusion through membership application and certification, thereby creating a dual framework based upon a distinction between potentiality and actuality. Actual inclusion is, furthermore, linked to a dense framework of rights, imposing a dual framework of obligations and standing, most notably through adherence to the standards and through access to review and decision-making processes. At the same time, the rights framework serves as the central infrastructure which enables the production of a specific prestation vis-à-vis other segments of world society, in that it is oriented towards the facilitation of the transfer of products and capital between the producers, importers, processors and distributors. Thus, a move towards constitutionalisation can be observed in so far as Fairtrade Labelling Organizations

International defines a constitutional subject via its multiple-stakeholder framework and subsequently seeks to minimise the distinction between potential and actual inclusion. The implementation of the rights dimension is outsourced to FLO-CERT, which, through inspections, certifies compliance and, in the case of non-compliance, imposes sanctions, such as demands for corrective measures and, ultimately, through expulsion. Thus, FLO-CERT serves as an independent 'judiciary' which combines an investigative function with the objective of applying the norms produced by FLO International.

Finally, the Fairtrade Labelling Organizations International has condensed its activities into a mission statement, namely, 'to connect disadvantaged producers and consumers, promote fairer trading conditions and empower producers to combat poverty, strengthen their position and take more control over their lives'.[38] This mission is deduced from a vision of 'a world in which *all* producers can enjoy secure and sustainable livelihoods, fulfil their potential and decide on their future'.[39] As such, the organisation remains strategically guided by a normative and thus counter-factual objective concerning full inclusion for the segment of world society against which it orients itself, thereby externalising the tension between potential and actual members in the future. Thus, Fairtrade Labelling Organizations International can be understood as a fully fledged normative order, which internally produces coherency between its different dimensions, as represented by producers, importers, processors and distributors, and externally demarcates itself through the double delineation of potential and actual members, through the establishment of a constitutional structure characterised by a dual political and legal hierarchy, and a normative vision granting it an articulated form of constitutional consciousness which points to the future.

The reconstruction above says little about the actual effect of the Fairtrade Labelling Organizations International on global trade flows, the environment and global health. However, the central point here is not to evaluate the effects of such schemes, but the far more specific one, which is to understand how they go about the dual task of establishing internal coherency and external compatibility within a specific segment of world society. In addition, to illustrate how this dual task can be adequately described within a constitutional vocabulary, thereby establishing a basis for a re-calibration of the constitutional concept.

7.5 Conclusion

The focus of this chapter was to trace the transmutation of constitutional ordering into new sites in the wake of the structural transformations which have characterised world society since the breakdown of the European world order. A direct result of the breakdown of this order was the emergence of an economic constitution within the framework of the European integration process. Subsequently, this constitution became supplemented by a range of other (embryonic) constitutional frameworks with a functionally delineated reach in the wake of the launch of the Internal Market in the 1980s, thereby transforming the European Union into a constitutional conglomerate which consists of a multiplicity of legally framed, partly overlapping, and partly contradictory, orders.

The European developments have, in particular, over the last decades been supplemented by global developments through the emergence of a conglomerate of transnational organisations and regimes which cover all areas of economic life, from monetary policy and investment protection to trade and product standards. This conglomerate has a history dating back to the early post-war period, but it was especially in the post-Cold War period that it gained a 'constitutional consciousness' due to its enshrinement of a specific doctrinal world-view as embodied in the Washington Consensus, a world-view which is one-dimensional given that it is based upon a narrow economistic logic. The limited ability of this conglomerate to establish compatibility with non-economic spheres of society has triggered a counter-movement through the emergence of frameworks which are aimed at offsetting the negative externalities of economic processes. This was illustrated through a reconstruction of the global fair-trade certification scheme which explicitly describes itself as a constitutional order.

Notes

1 Peter C. Caldwell and William E. Scheuerman (eds), *From Liberal Democracy to Fascism: Legal and Political Thought in the Weimar Republic*, Boston, MA, Leiden: Humanities Press, 2000, especially, Peter C. Caldwell, 'Is a Social *Rechtsstaat* Possible? The Weimar Roots of a Bonn Controversy', in Peter C. Caldwell and William E. Scheuerman (eds), *From Liberal Democracy to Fascism: Legal and Political Thought in the Weimar Republic*, Boston, MA, Leiden: Humanities Press, 2000, pp. 136–53.

2 Gunther Teubner, *Constitutional Fragments: Societal Constitutionalism and Globalization*, Oxford: Oxford University Press, 2012, p. 30 *et seq.*

3 Hans Carl Nipperday, *Soziale Marktwirtschaft und Grundgesetz*, Cologne: Heymann, 1961.

4 Christian Joerges, 'What is Left of the European Economic Constitution', *EUI Working Paper Law*, 13, 2004, p. 9 *et seq.*

5 Hans H. Rupp, *Grundgesetz und 'Wirtschaftverfassung'*, Tübingen: J.C.B. Mohr, 1974, p. 14 *et seq.*; Niklas Luhmann, *Macht*, Stuttgart: Ferdinand Enke Verlag, [1975] 1988, p. 81 *et seq.*

6 Hans Peter Ipsen, *Europäisches Gemeinschaftsrecht in Einzelstudien*, Baden-Baden: Nomos Verlag, 1984, p. 35 *et seq.*

7 See, for example, Jürgen Basedow, *Von der deutschen zur europäischen Wirtschaftsverfassung*, Tübingen: J.C.B. Mohr, 1992, p. 26 *et seq.*

8 For the distinction between territory and space, see Alain Supiot, 'The Territorial Inscription of Laws', in Gralf-Peter Calliess, Andreas Fischer-Lescano, Dan Wielsch and Peer Zumbansen (eds), *Soziologische Jurisprudenz: Festschrift für Gunther Teubner zum 65. Geburtstag am 30. April 2009*, Berlin: Walter de Gruyter, 2009, pp. 375–93. Supiot contrasts the concept of territory with the concept of air and sea space. This *problématique* is, moreover, having a history which is as long as modernity itself. For example, according to both Hegel and Schmitt, the distinction between 'land and ocean' (*Land und Meer*) can be understood as the constitutive distinction between pre-modern and modern forms of social organisation. See Georg W.F. Hegel, *Grundlinien der Philosophie des Rechts oder Naturrecht und Staatswissenschaft im Grundrisse, Werke Band 7*, Frankfurt am Main: Suhrkamp Verlag, [1821] 1970, § 247,

and Carl Schmitt, *Land und Meer: Eine weltgeschichtliche Betrachtung*, Stuttgart: Klett-Cotta, [1942] 2008.

9 Poul F. Kjaer, 'The Societal Function of European Integration in the Context of World Society', *Soziale Systeme: Zeitschrift für Soziologische Theorie*, 2007, 13, pp. 369–80, at 371.

10 This element is, moreover, supported by the internal change in the form of economic reproduction due to the relative decline of industrial production and the emergence of a service and knowledge economy. See also Karl-Heinz Ladeur, *Der Staat gegen die Gesellschaft: Zur Verteidigung der Rationalität der 'Privatrechtsgesellschaft'*, Tübingen: Mohr Siebeck, 2007.

11 Carl Schmitt, *Der Nomos der Erde im Völkerrecht des Jus Publicum Europaeum*, Berlin: Duncker & Humblot, 1950.

12 For example, Fritz W. Scharpf, 'The European Social Model: Coping with the Challenges of Diversity', *Journal of Common Market Studies*, 2002, 40, pp. 645–70.

13 Karl Polanyi, *The Great Transformation: The Political and Economic Origins of Our Time*, Boston MA: Beacon Press, [1944] 2001.

14 James Carporaso and Sidney Tarrow, 'Polanyi in Brussels: Supranational Institutions and the Transnational Embedding of Markets', International Organization, 2009, 64, pp. 593–620.

15 Ulrich Beck, *Risikogesellschaft: Auf dem Weg in eine andere Moderne*, Frankfurt am Main: Suhrkamp Verlag, 1986.

16 Oren Perez, 'Facing the Global Hydra: Ecological Transformation at the Global Financial Frontier: The Ambitious Case of the Global Reporting Initiative', in Christian Joerges and Ernst-Ulrich Petersmann (eds), *Constitutionalism: Multilevel Trade Governance and Social Regulation*, Oxford: Hart Publishing, 2006, pp. 459–87.

17 For an empirical example in relation to chemicals regulation, see Poul F. Kjaer, 'A Hybrid within a Hybrid: Contextualizing REACH in the Process of European Integration and Constitutionalization', *European Journal of Risk Regulation*, 2010, 1, pp. 383–96.

18 Poul F. Kjaer, 'The Structural Transformation of Embeddedness', in Christian Joerges and Josef Falke (eds), *Karl Polanyi: Globalisation and the Potential of Law in Transnational Markets*, Oxford: Hart Publishing, 2011, pp. 85–104.

19 See case BVerfGE 89, 155 vom 12. Oktober 1993. Available at: www.servat.unibe.ch/dfr/bv089155.html.

20 Joseph H.H. Weiler, *The Constitution of Europe: Do the New Clothes Have an Emperor?*, Cambridge: Cambridge University Press, 1999.

21 Christian Joerges, 'The Market without the State? The "Economic Constitution" of the European Community and the Rebirth of Regulatory Politics', *European Integration online Papers (EIoP)*, 1, 19, 1997; Christian Joerges, 'States Without a Market? Comments on the German Constitutional Court's Maastricht-Judgment and a Plea for Interdisciplinary Discourses', *European Integration online Papers (EIoP)*, 1, 20, 1997.

22 Poul F. Kjaer, *Between Governing and Governance: On the Emergence, Function and Form of Europe's Post-national Constellation*, Oxford: Hart Publishing, 2010.

23 Communication from the Commission to the European Parliament, the Council, The European Economic and Social Committee and the Committee of the Regions: A Re-inforced European Research Area Partnership for Excellence and Growth, Brussels, 17 July 2012, European Commission, COM(2012) 392 final.

24 For an analysis of the European hybridity, see Kjaer, *Between Governing and Governance*.

25 Rudolf Stichweh, *Die Weltgesellschaft. Soziologische Analysen*, Frankfurt am Main: Suhrkamp Verlag, 2000, especially pp. 248–267; Theresa Wobbe, *Weltgesellschaft*, Bielefeld; Transcript Verlag, 2000.

26 Joel P. Trachtman, 'The Constitutions of the WTO', *European Journal of International Law*, 2006, 17, pp. 623–46. For a critical perspective, see Robert Howse and Kalypso Nicolaidis, 'Legitimacy and Global Governance: Why Constitutionalizing the WTO is a Step to Far', in Roger B. Poter, Pierre Suave and Arvind Subramian (eds), *Efficiency, Equity, Legitimacy and Governance: The Multilateral Trading System at the Millennium*, Washington, DC: Brookings Institution, 2001, pp. 227–52.

27 Danny Nicol, *The Constitutional Protection of Capitalism*, Oxford: Hart Publishing, 2010.

28 David Held, *Global Covenant: The Social Democratic Alternative to the Washington Consensus*, Cambridge: Polity Press, 2004; Danny Nicol, *The Constitutional Protection of Capitalism*, Oxford: Hart Publishing, 2010.

29 Gunther Teubner, 'A Constitutional Moment? The Logics of "Hitting the Bottom"', in Poul F. Kjaer, Gunther Teubner and Alberto Febbrajo (eds), *The Financial Crisis in Constitutional Perspective: The Dark Side of Functional Differentiation*, Oxford: Hart Publishing, 2011, pp. 3–42; Gunther Teubner, *Constitutional Fragments: Societal Constitutionalism and Globalization*, Oxford: Oxford University Press, 2012.

30 Andreas Fischer-Lescano and Gunther Teubner, 'Regime-Collisions: "The Vain Search for Legal Unity in the Fragmentation of Global Law"', *Michigan Journal of International Law*, 2004, 25, pp. 999–1046.

31 A good example of the focus on the actual transposition is research on 'global value chains' in relation to economic processes. See, for example, Stefano Ponte and Timothy Sturgeon, 'Explaining Governance in Global Value Chains: A Modular Theory-Building Effort', *Review of International Political Economy*, published online 7 August 2013, pp. 2–29.

32 www.fairtrade.net.

33 For an overview of the framework, see Alex Nicholls and Charlotte Opal, *Fair Trade, Market-driven Ethical Consumption*, Thousand Oaks, CA: Sage, 2004. See also Valentin Beck, 'Theorizing Fairtrade from a Justice-related Standpoint', *Global Justice: Theory, Practice, Rhetoric*, 2010, 3, pp. 1–21; Daniel Jaffee, *Brewing Justice: Fair Trade Coffee, Sustainability and Survival*, Berkeley, CA: University of California Press, 2007; Loraine Ronchi, 'The Impact of Fairtrade on Producers and their Organisations: A Case Study with Coocafé in Costa Rica', 11, *PRUS Working Paper*, 2002.

34 'The Constitution of Fairtrade Labelling Organizations International', § 1.1. and 1.2. Available at: www.fairtrade.net/our_vision.html.

35 'The Constitution of Fairtrade Labelling Organizations International'.

36 'The Constitution of Fairtrade Labelling Organizations International', § 3.1.

37 'The Constitution of Fairtrade Labelling Organizations International', sub-section 'Definitions'.

38 http://www.fairtrade.net/our_vision.html.

39 Ibid.; italics added by the author.

8 Re-calibrating the constitutional concept

8.1 Introduction

The transmutation of constitutional conceptuality and the emergence of new sites of constitutional ordering profoundly challenge the world-view upon which constitutional theory has relied to date. This is also reflected in the nature of the academic debates on constitutionalism. From the relatively narrow confinement within national constitutional law discourses, constitutional conceptuality has, in the wake of increased globalisation, crept into almost all legal sub-disciplines as well as into political science, international relations and sociology. Essentially, the ongoing academic debate is centred on the question of whether the – still ongoing – transmutation of constitutionalism marks the triumph of constitutionalism or its demise. From the latter perspective, the attempt to re-invent the constitutional concept merely reflects the increasingly desperate attempts to maintain the constitutional outlook in the face of structural developments which have undermined the all-encompassing unity of state-based constitutional orders. As such, the debate goes to very core of the future of democracy and the rule of law.

Rejecting the fatalistic perspective of state-centric constitutional theory this chapter binds together the findings presented in the previous chapters through the advancement of a sociologically based re-calibration of the constitutional concept, capable of reconstructing the meaning and function of constitutions in a manner which corresponds to the structural realities of contemporary world society. To start out with the strong reliance on formal organisation in modern society is emphasised, thereby enabling an understanding of formal organisations, as such, and not states, understood as a specific type of formal organisation, as the object of constitutions under modern conditions. This is the case because a constitution establishes a hierarchy of legal norms and the possibility for doing so is structurally conditioned by their orientation towards formal organisation. But a constitution also institutionalises a specific form of double reflexivity through reference to an external source of authority which leads to the establishment of a clearly demarcated social entity which is *simultaneously* framed and condensed in a manner which corresponds with a legal, as well as a focal (political, economic, religious, scientific, etc.) perspective. Only when these two elements are in place, is it possible to claim that a constitution is in place.[1]

But apart from establishing internal order through double reflexivity, a constitution also structures exchanges between a constitutional order and the wider context within which it operates. This endeavour is described with the term 'constitutionalisation'. The concrete form of constitutionalisation processes is rights-based frameworks, and it is through these rights that a constitutional subject which is external to the constitutional object is established. Such frameworks serve as mechanisms for the establishment of a specific form of *double prestation*, in the sense that compatibility between a condensed internal order and its external context is constructed upon the basis of the dual legal and focal perspective which is oriented towards handling the exchanges between the constitutional order in question and a limited segment of world society.

This external orientation is, however, a quest which is continuously pursued but is unlikely to be factually realised, and is, therefore, externalised into the future. In this specific sense, constitutional orders develop principles aimed at establishing a *modus operandi* for approaching the future. Constitutional orders develop a constitutional consciousness in the form of an elaborated idea of their mission in the world. Such articulations, furthermore, serve as a basis for the construction of claims concerning a monopoly of ordering for a specific segment of world society upon the basis of either territorial or functional delineations, and, are thus, concerned with the monopolisation of a specific function with relevance for world society in its entirety. Such forms of constitutional consciousness can also be described with the term 'constitutionalism', and it is through this self-same constitutionalism that the paradoxical tension between internal condensation and external compatibility is externalised into the future.

8.2 The organisational society

The emergence of a functionally differentiated society went hand in hand with the emergence of formal organisation.[2] Today, essentially all major parts of an individual's life unfold within the framework of formal organisations – from the kindergarten to the nursing home. This development is a reflection of a century-long evolutionary development. As previously highlighted, it was the spiral of mutually reinforcing relationships between increased military capabilities, the expansion of territory and the increased need to extract financial resources from these territories in order to support further increases in military capabilities which led to the emergence of modern statehood. The military revolutions of the sixteenth and seventeenth centuries, however, triggered an equally important organisational revolution, which served as the foundational basis for the political and economic revolutions of the late eighteenth and nineteenth centuries. As such, it is the organisational revolution, rather than the American and French Revolutions, which represents the single most important transformation associated with modernity.[3]

In modern society, formal organisation not only plays an essential role within all functional areas, but the form of formal organisation is also surprisingly similar within organisations such as ministries, art museums, hospitals and firms, and this is irrespective of whether they are public or private, national or transnational. In all these cases, formalised exclusion and inclusion mechanisms are in place, an internal separation between public and private exists just as formal procedures of decision-making and hierarchical ordering are in place. In addition, all organisations are legal entities. Thus, the distinctions between the state and society and between the political and the social are, to a great extent, irrelevant at the organisational level of society.[4] Thus, the traditionally emphasised economy/politics and public/private dichotomies not only fail to capture but, indeed, also actively hide the fact that the core logic of the organisational structures upon which the economic and political structures of society rely remains to a large extent, identical. The organisational structure adopted by modern firms in the breakthrough of industrialisation, for example, had the state bureaucracy as its role model, just as the introduction of New Public Management instruments in recent decades relies upon the modern firm as its source of inspiration.[5]

The logic of displination and the systematic reduction of autonomy through subordination to hierarchy, as well as the 'alienation' occurring from the split between private and public, are just as dominant within public as within private organisations. It follows that, to the extent that one would want to identify an untapped potential for emancipation, as pursued by normative political and legal theory, in the late-modern society this can only be achieved through a break with the economy/politics and public/private dichotomies. Instead, the focus has to be oriented towards a lower level, in the sense that a transformation in the organisational forms 'on the ground' is the central issue. At least in the most functionally differentiated parts of world society, the introduction of progressive pedagogical instruments in the school system and enabling management techniques aimed at increasing the autonomy and self-organisation of employees is likely to have a far greater impact on the degree of autonomy of individuals than changes to the state constitution or random demonstrations in the streets. The master–apprentice relations of the chair-based (*Lehrstuhl*) continental European university, the equally semi-feudal structures of the family-owned small- and medium-sized enterprises (SMEs) (*Mittelstandsunternehmen*) and the hegemonic power of the legal profession (*Juristenstand*), operating within the framework of the political and legal systems in the form of the semi-authoritarian state (*Obrigkeitsstaat*), are the real issues upon which emancipative legal and social theory should focus. Or to express it differently, the very concrete question concerning what action a member of a formal organisation can take without obtaining a signature of his or her superior is the genuine question of emancipation in contemporary society.

This insight, however, tends to be ignored by emancipative strands of social theory,[6] just as this insight is not adequately reflected within the ideological formations of classical modernity, as, for example, reflected in the distinction between liberal and socialist perspectives. From the internal perspective of the political system, the question of the relation between the political system and the rest of society is essentially reduced to the question of whether we wish for more or less statehood. But even 'well-intended' ventures such as the political quest for the establishment of welfare-state regimes tend to produce negative side-effects in the form of reification and the transformation of citizens into clients, upon the basis of a rationalising logic, in the Weberian sense.[7] Thus, the market and the welfare-state bureaucracy must be understood as two sides of the same coin. *Staunch* defenders of the welfare state fail to acknowledge this.[8] Instead, they tend to conceptualise the state/economy and the public/private distinctions as reflections of the embeddedness/dis-embeddedness distinction. But, from the organisational perspective, the classical state/economy and public/private distinctions should, instead, be understood as reflecting the delineation of meaning spheres without any of the spheres in question possessing any particular substantialist superiority.[9]

Contemporary left- and right-Luhmannians have sought to circumvent this issue by taking a non-*étatist* stand. What is common to them is that they share a romanticist vision of a self-organising society. In so doing, the left-Luhmannians follow in the footsteps of Karl Marx, Antonio Gramsci, Karl Polanyi, Antonio Negri and Michael Hardt, who all developed somewhat different – but equally vague – visions of a democratic, but non-state-based organisation of the economy.[10] The right-Luhmannians, however, advocate the self-organising network-society upon the basis of von Hayekian insights.[11] The right-Luhmannian network-approach sees networks as the fundamental building-blocks of society, and might, thereby, overemphasise the importance of the network phenomenon to a degree which makes it difficult to identify the specific prestation and function of networks in society.[12] In relation to one central aspect, the approach does, however, possess an important theoretical advantage vis-à-vis the left-Luhmannian position because one of its central focus points is the concrete operational form of organisational structures. In contrast, the left-Luhmannians tend systematically to disregard the organisational aspect, with the consequence that the question concerning the concrete organisational model which they wish to advocate remains unanswered.[13] The left-Luhmannian approach is, therefore, not capable of illuminating the logics which drive societal developments, as, for example, is highlighted by the kind of hyper-complex meltdowns of organisations and regimes which can be observed in relation to the financial crisis which broke out in 2008. Instead, their central focus remains limited to various forms of civil-society-based 'street activism' as a strategy capable of mobilising pressure for change. They tend to ignore the fact that pressure for change needs to be transformed into generalised bureaucratic measures if pensions are to be paid, treatment to be carried out in hospitals and alphabets learned in the schools. But rendering it explicit that the realisation of political claims in modern society is impossible without relying upon complex forms of formal organisation automatically highlights the limited reach of the left-Luhmannian agenda, because it radically restricts the potential role which they can play in society. As long as they do not undertake a combined analysis of, and march through, the institutions (*Marsch durch die Institutionen*), they will confine themselves to a parasitic role in which they are merely capable of irritating the processes of social systems without profoundly interfering with the actual form of these processes. In practice, the function of the left-Luhmannians remains restricted to a recycling of the kind of supplementary partisan semantics originally cultivated by the left-Schmittians, with the predictable outcome that struggle (*Kampf*) is ultimately elevated into an end in itself (*Selbstzweck*).

8.3 Internal condensation through constitutions

In spite of the pivotal centrality of formal organisation in modern society, a one-dimensional organisational perspective on society, however, tends, as forcefully argued by Gunther Teubner, to ignore the creative tension between formal organisation and spontaneous ordering in modern society. This tension between hierarchy and heterarchy is, for example, expressed in the dualisms between the political system and its voters; between firms and the market, and between religious institutions and their believers.[14] Constitutions can be seen as a response to the handling of such dualisms to the extent that they are *internally* oriented towards condensing hierarchical ordering which relies on modern forms of formal organisation while they *externally* seek to stabilise exchanges and establish compatibility with the congregations surrounding such hierarchical orders.[15]

In classical constitutional vocabulary, the distinction between the internal and external dimensions of constitutional orders re-emerged in a revised form through the introduction of the distinction between a constitutional subject and a constitutional object. This distinction, originally formulated by Abbé Sieyès, through his distinction between the *pouvoir constituant* and the *pouvoir constitué*, serves as the foundational distinction of classical constitutional theory.[16] The claim of constitutional theory that constitutions establish a unity of the constitutional object and the constitutional subject, furthermore, allowed for an understanding of constitutions as frames which possess a quasi-transcendental character derived from the semantics of the body politics which characterised early modernity.[17]

Throughout modern history, the formal organisations of normative orders, rather than the normative orders themselves, have, however, been the object of constitutions. This very fundamental distinction has usually been disregarded within constitutional scholarship. For example, those who maintain that states are the only proper constitutional objects rely upon, sociologically speaking, an under-complex understanding of statehood, in which the state is equalled to a given normative order, or society, in its entirety. As has been clear ever since Hegel's introduction of the state/society distinction, a state is, however, a specific form of formal organisation among others, or more correctly, a loosely coupled conglomerate of several organisations, which only exists providing that it is formally and operationally separated from the other segments of society. The constitution of the state is, therefore, not the constitution of a normative order in its entirety, but of a specific organisational conglomerate. Thus, the reach of a constitution is more limited and more focused than what can be read out of constitutional semantics.

In the wake of Hegel[18] and Weber,[19] a number of core features of organisations can be pointed out:

1   Formalised exclusion and inclusion mechanisms upon the basis of membership which enables the establishment of boundaries between an organisation and its environment. Such membership is, moreover, divided between primary (*Leistungsrollen*) and secondary roles (*Publikumsrollen*).
2   Formalised competences and procedures of decision-making which enable a continued production of decisions, which are applicable to all members, with one decision recursively emerging from earlier decisions.
3   A reliance on dual organisational and legal hierarchies as the form through which decisions are taken and transposed to the members.
4   The existence of a formalised *locus* of authority which acts as a vehicle for producing acceptance of the decisions produced.

To the extent that all of these features are in place, it becomes possible to speak of organisations as specific forms of autonomous ordering, in the sense that they become self-contained structures which produce decisions in a recursive manner in which one decision refers to earlier decisions through reference to an internal source of authority. As such, organisations first exist in a mature form when they become self-reflexive, in the sense that the production of decisions becomes an internal process which unfolds over time.

A linking to an external dimension, however, remains in that it is only possible to speak of organisations as *formal* organisations if they are legally structured. Organisations only become formal organisations through a linking with a legal framework because concordance with a coherent legal framework is the form through which the four dimensions are structurally linked and through which coherency is established. As also argued by Gunther Teubner, formal organisation implies a specific form of *double reflexivity*, in the sense that the perspective of the organisation in question and a specific legal perspective are coupled together.[20] Thus, the social process reproduced by a given organisation is *simultaneously* mirrored in a concordant legal perspective or, to express it differently, organisational hierarchy is mirrored in a correspondent hierarchy of legal norms.

The structural condition for the emergence of double reflexivity is, however, as indicated under points 3 and 4 above, the internal existence of hierarchy and autonomous sources of authority which can serve as a basis for collectively binding decision-making. Thus, without the existence of a political infrastructure within a given social structure, there is no basis for a stable institutionalisation of double reflexivity. As previously argued, the Court of Arbitration for Sport can only engage in a mode of double reflexivity as long as a political counterpart exists in the form of the Olympic Committee, and the World Trade Organization's Panel and Appellate Bodies are only capable of establishing frameworks which possess the quality of double reflexivity through a linkage to the political dimension of the World Trade Organization in the form of the Ministerial Conference and the General Council. This form of double reflexivity can, as demonstrated by Moritz Renner, also be understood as a triangular structural coupling between the legal and political systems and given focal social process.[21] An alternative to the triangular perspective emerges through the distinction between primary and secondary forms of the political. A distinction between, on the one hand, couplings of law and processes which are primarily political, such as those unfolding within states and public transnational bodies such as the European Union, the United Nations and the World Trade Organization, and, on the other hand, couplings between the legal system and private social processes in which political decision-making structures have emerged internally.[22] The latter form can be observed within private entities such as trade associations, private regulatory bodies and non-governmental organisations, and can be described as a form of 'secondary politics' outlined in Chapter 5, because such structures primarily describe themselves in relation to the substantial function that they exercise in relation to, for example, the economy, sports, health or religion, at the same time as their strive towards a stabilisation of such processes gives them an additional political quality.

One implication which follows from the insight that the constitutional object is not the state, but instead formal organisations, is that the range of constitutional objects is far broader than is typically assumed. This is also underlined by the historical evolution of modern forms of formal organisation, since the basic organisational features of states were originally developed within the framework of the Roman Catholic Church, and only subsequently adopted by the emerging modern states. In a similar manner, the modern firm and other private organisations have relied on the modern state as the role model from which they adopted their basic organisational features.[23] Thus, the switch from a focus on the state to a focus on formal organisations opens up a conceptual horizon which makes it possible to imagine quite a radical expansion in the sort of organisations which can be observed through a constitutional lens. The attempt to maintain a distinction between 'big C' and 'small c' constitutions is thereby put under pressure to the extent that the principle dominance of state constitutions is called into question.[24]

A second implication of the importance of formal organisations is that the culturalist version of legal pluralism misses a fundamental point when it leaves out the organisational perspective.[25] Whereas the state-centrist argument, concerning constitutions being specific to modern states, falls too short, its insight concerning the specific modern character of constitutions remains fundamentally true. Indian tribes in Amazonia do not have constitutions in the modern sense. Instead, the modern form of dynamic constitutions is intrinsically linked to the phenomenon of modern formal organisation, because, as already highlighted by Kant, modern organisations are dynamic entities as is also expressed in their capability to pursue constant reform.[26] Thus, whereas modern statehood and transnational forms of ordering are co-evolutionary phenomena, because they rely upon the same form of modern formal organisation, they are both engaged in a zero-sum relation vis-à-vis the kind of 'pre-modern' and 'culturalist' entities, such as tribes, clans and nobility networks, which operate 'beneath' both the state and transnational orders, and which are gradually being marginalised as a result of the conversion of society into a modern organisational society.

To sum up, constitutions can, in their *internal function*, be understood as institutions which, in their *political function*, frame the body of rules and norms which establish the formal structure, decisional competences and a hierarchically based *locus of authority* within an organisational structure, at the same time as they, in their *legal function*, lay down principles for the structuring of conflicts between norms within such entities. Constitutions are, in this sense, laying down the enabling and the limitative rules guiding formal organisations. Thus, it is, *in principle*, possible to claim that constitutions exist in *all* cases in which a legal and a non-legal social structure are bound together within the framework of a formal organisation, thereby establishing a particular form of double self-constitution which ensures concordance between a legal and non-legal perspective. It is not just states, but, in principle, *all* formal organisations, including those which operate in the transnational sphere, that can be the object of a constitution.

8.4 External compatibility through constitutionalisation

In the above section, constitutions were treated as an internal feature of formal organisations, in the sense that a linking with law enables a condensation of authority through the establishment of legal and organisational hierarchy. But, as with all other types of social system, organisations only come into existence through a demarcation and maintenance of the boundaries to their respective social environments. The establishment of coherency through the development of a consistent set of internal norms is conditioned by the maintenance of such boundaries. At the same time, organisations, like all other types of social system, also intersect with other social structures in their social environment. Besides handling the functional need of internal coherency preservation, as outlined in the previous section, the establishment of external compatibility is the most central function of constitutions. Constitutions, in their external dimension, delineate the segment of their social environments of which organisations, or conglomerates of organisations, take account. Constitutions construct such external environments, in the sense that they establish an abstract medium which fulfils a dual role: first, the transposition of social components, such as political decisions, economic capital and products, scientific knowledge or religious promises of salvation, into the wider society; and second, the channelling and incorporation of the social components produced elsewhere in society into a given organisation. The *praxis* of fulfilling this dual function is what is described with the term 'constitutionalisation',[27] to the extent that this term denotes the process of stabilising the exchanges between a given formal organisation and a specific segment of world society. Returning to classical constitutional vocabulary, constitutionalisation can also be understood as the process through which a formal organisation delineates a constitutional subject, which at the same provides a mirror image of the organisation's social environment and serve as a medium for the transposition of social components to and from its social environment.

The external boundaries of constitutional orders established through constitutionalisation processes are faced with a need of constant validation. This is especially the case, since such boundaries are based upon internally developed *claims* which might or might not be taken account of by the rest of society, just as they might or might not be positively accepted by the rest of society. Thus, the external dimensions of constitutional orders are 'enacted environments' which are co-created through the constant unfolding of the orders themselves.[28] The immediate form of enactment processes within the political system in the state form is, as previously highlighted, embodied in the concept of the nation. The construction of a nation, understood as an abstract and generalised form which should not be understood as equal to the sum of the individuals within a given territory, is made in order delineate the segment of its social environment which a given political system observes and takes account of in its decision-making. Essentially, similar features can be observed when one observes the relation between, for example, economic or religious structures and the way in which they frame their relations to their social environments. Religious organisations or labour unions also delineate the section of their environments of which they take account through the establishment of a body of believers or a specific social class or a specific profession, which serve the dual role of transposing elements out in the environment and transferring elements back into the organisation in question upon the basis of specific social roles. As previously highlighted, at the transnational level of world society, the turn to network-based governance structures fulfils a similar role for organisations operating within functionally delineated normative orders. Here, the networks become the constitutional subject in that they serve as heterarchical frameworks through which transfer of social components are both framed and stabilised.

But also in relation to the external dimension, a dual form exists to the extent that the constitutional subject is always mirrored in a corresponding legal conceptuality in the form of rights. Rights are instruments which simultaneously safeguard the autonomy and impose obligations upon legal subjects in that they are the form through which liberties are secured *and* obligations imposed. Not surprisingly, the thrust of rights-based legal scholarship has, therefore, been characterised by a built-in tendency to focus upon the impact of rights on individuals, within an inclusion/exclusion schema. This perspective, however, underplays the more general and abstract contribution of rights regimes for the facilitation of exchanges between social spheres. From a societal perspective, rights can be understood as frameworks which establish the modalities through which social components are delineated and transposed between social spheres while simultaneously safeguarding the integrity and autonomy of the spheres involved. Taxation, for example, is a formalised and limited framework for the extraction of resources from the parts of society which are external to the receiving entity, most notably from the economic sphere and into the political system, a framework which is intrinsically linked to the safeguarding of private property and the right to influence the use of the resources extracted as also expressed in the 'no taxation without representation' slogan of the American Revolution. In a similar manner, freedom of religion is a right which safeguards the autonomy of religious congregations in exchange for their adherence to the secular legal framework of the guaranteeing state and thus the transposition of the state's claim to a legitimate monopoly of violence into the religious sphere. It follows that rights and rights-based frameworks are the single most important basis for the maintenance of the functionally differentiated society, to the extent that their built-in objective is *simultaneously* to safeguard the separation of societal spheres and to enable exchanges between these spheres.[29]

The centrality of rights for the stabilisation of societal exchanges is the basis for Chris Thornhill's argument that rights essentially are the *only* form through which inclusion/exclusion processes and therewith processes of transfer are handled.[30] The structural capability of both national- and transnational-based formal organisations to develop rights-regimes seems, however, to be conditioned by their attachment to generalised non-legal media. Such media represent a distilled version of the already existing socio-cultural substances as also expressed in the concepts of the nation and religious congregations as well as in the contemporary category of stakeholders. Even though rights regimes tend to emerge from *within* the social processes to which they are attached, rather than being externally imposed, they only become identifiable and operational when a distinction between the legal and the non-legal dimensions is established.[31] Or, to express it differently, rights are always rights for someone who is external to the legal form. Constitutionalisation processes are, therefore, based upon a specific form of *double prestation*, in the sense that such processes simultaneously handle the exchanges between a constitutional entity and a limited segment of world society upon the basis of a legal as well as a focal perspective, with the latter being derived from a continuously articulated idea concerning the appropriate delineation and meaning of a given nation, congregation or group of stakeholders.

It follows from the above that constitutionalisation does not just imply an increase in the self-reflexivity of a constitutional object. It is not just an exercise in negative self-binding which organisations pursue in order to reduce the risk of self-destruction through systemic overstretch. Instead, constitutionalisation processes also provide a more positive prestation towards other segments of society to the extent that they are aimed at reducing negative externalities, colonising tendencies and crowding out effects vis-à-vis the respective environments of constitutional orders.[32]

This is also confirmed by the contextual settings within which constitutional orders emerge. Constitutions never stand alone but always emerge in co-evolutionary settings in which several orders emerge simultaneously. As previously highlighted, nation states are not unitary structures, but, instead, take the form of constitutional conglomerates in which, for example, state constitutions, church constitutions and economic constitutions intersect, overlap and collide. This, again, converts the multiple intersections between them into the battlefields in which constitutional orders are delineated and in which justifying narratives emerge concerning the prestation which specific constitutional orders produce vis-à-vis other segments of society. Or to express it differently, the emergence of internal constitutions is structurally conditioned by external constitutionalisation processes capable of guaranteeing that mutually reinforcing co-evolutionary processes unfolds. The emergence of an autonomous constitutional order within the European Union is a perfect example of this, given that the internal establishment of legal *and* organisational hierarchy was conditioned by the co-evolutionary emergence of heterarchical legal *and* organisational frameworks, in the form of the governance structures associated with Comitology and the Open-Method of Co-ordination (OMC), capable of ensuring compatibility between the emerging constitutional order of the European Union and its environment, most notably the constitutional orders of the Member States.[33]

8.5 Approaching the future through constitutionalism

The distinction between internal condensation and external compatibility, which can also be described with the help of the distinction between hierarchically organised and spontaneously heterarchical processes,[34] constitutes a paradoxical tension. Furthermore, as previously argued, a normative order does not come into existence before a unity of these two dimensions is established. In relation to transnational structures, these two dimensions are condensed into a distinction between hierarchical organisations and heterarchical networks whose unity takes the form of regimes. The unity of such entities is paradoxical because they are unities of 'something different', and the quest for unity is therefore externalised into the future.[35] In the vocabulary of classical constitutional theory, this recourse in time is described with the concept of constitutionalism since the central thrust of constitutionalism is to dissolve the tension between republican politics and liberal rights through societal learning processes unfolded over time.[36]

It follows that constitutional set-ups do not just mirror existing structures but, instead, express a specific vision of the future upon the basis of a specific understanding of the past. Such visions can also be described as representing a form of 'constitutional consciousness' capable of providing a basis for *counter-factual* claims concerning a possible constitutional framing of a normative order in its entirety. At the operational level, the establishment of a constitutional consciousness in the form of a coherent principle-based framework for approaching the future can, therefore, be found in the central function of constitutionalism. Or to express it differently, the central function of constitutionalism is to establish the epistemic dimension which guide the never-ending quest towards the establishment of normative orders.

The counter-factual pre-positions of constitutionalism can also be described with the term 'double function'. Constitutionalism implies that, from a focal (for example, economic, political or scientific) perspective, as well as from a legal perspective, a vision of 'complete inclusion' is developed, which implies that, *in principle*, all humans can be subject to inclusion into the normative order in question. Originally developed within the Church of Rome, the counter-factual quest for complete inclusion – in this case through the transformation of all humans into members of the Catholic Church and the subordination of all worldly powers into subordinates of Rome – has become generalised. As previously mentioned, the French Republic, the historical role model for most continental states, has traditionally relied on a self-understanding which was closely linked to the counter-factual idea concerning a realisation of the ideals of the French Revolution throughout the world in its entirety, just as the World Trade Organization seeks to include all international trade-flows under its framework and the global human-rights regime seeks, both formally and factually, to include all human beings throughout the world. In other words, constitutionalism implies the institutionalisation of normative teleologies and a hierarchical relationship between such teleologies and increasingly cognitivised processes of juridification. First, when such logics are in place, it is possible to talk about constitutionalism in a deep and mature sense. Constitutional ordering is, therefore, not only about facilitative and limitative rules, but also reflects a move towards a particular kind of self-transcendence through the unfolding of a universalistic aspiration.

It follows that the difference between national and transnational constitutional orders is, at the same time, limited and very fundamental. Within both dimensions of world society, the triangular relationship between constitutions, constitutionalisation and constitutionalism is based upon the same fundamentally modern logic, just as formal organisations provide a central starting-point for both forms. Both in relation to national as well as transnational normative orders, constitutions, constitutionalisation and constitutionalism respectively reflect the three world dimensions (*Weltdimensionen*) or meaning dimensions (*Sinndimensionen*) of social systems – the material (*Sachdimension*), the social (*Sozialdimension*) and the time (*Zeitdimension*) dimensions[37] – since it is the unity of these three dimensions which establishes a comprehensive view on the world.

From a one-dimensional legal perspective, the principles and instruments which national and transnational constitutional orders rely upon are, moreover, fundamentally identical. The difference lies in the switch from a reliance on territorial to functional differentiation, and the consequent emergence of new categories and non-legal conceptuality as expressed in the terms stakeholders, transparency and self-representation. A switch which implies the emergence of a different kind of semantics and self-understanding, as is also expressed in the ethos of managerialism which dominates at transnational level and the resulting tendency to reduce constitutional ordering to a 'technical task'. This fundamentally different epistemic vocabulary, however, reflects the function of transnational structures within world society, in that they primarily act as frameworks of transfer and, as such, are only oriented towards very limited – and yet very essential – segments of the communicative processes unfolding in the world. A function which is also expressed in the strong reliance on cognitivised legal and political formats by transnational organisations and regimes.

But, in world society, also nation states are particularistic orders, in that their condensation implies the formal as well as the factual exclusion of other segments of the world. Although they respectively rely upon territorial and functional delineations, both national and transnational types of constitutional ordering are based upon a paradoxical tension between universalism and particularism. Thus, the constitutional infrastructure of such orders fulfils the same core function, namely, to reconcile internal condensation and external compatibility within a limited segment of world society. However, as a reflection of the strong emphasis on transfer, the external dimension tends to play a relatively larger role vis-à-vis the internal dimension in transnational settings when compared to national settings, thereby indicating that rights and rights-based frameworks are likely to – and, in fact, have already – gained an even higher level of importance at the transnational level of world society compared to what has been the case at national level.[38]

The true difference between national and transnational forms of constitutional ordering thus seems to lie in their different epistemic foundations. The managerialism of transnational constitutional orders gives them a technocratic touch, which one can either bemoan or regard as representing a step towards 'sociological enlightenment', as they are orders which are freed from the mythological foundations of the modern nation states. If taking the latter perspective, regarding this development as an act of emancipation, it is, however, important to bear in mind that also transnational forms of ordering are based upon mythological foundations in the form of the belief in religions with a universal aspiration, in the added value of free trade and the 'self-evident' value of universal human rights.

8.6 Conclusion

From the theoretical framework outlined above, three core dimensions of a mature constitutionalist order can be deduced. First, a constitutional order is characterised by double reflexivity through a coupling between a constitutional object, in the form of a hierarchical organisation which is capable of reproducing an autonomous source of authority, and a concordant legal framework. Second, constitutionalisation processes imply a specific form of double prestation through a coupling between, on the one hand, an internal reconstruction of an external constitutional subject within the constitutional object, and, on the other, a register of legal rights, establishing a framework for exchanges between the constitutional object and the wider world as represented by the constitutional subject. Third, constitutionalism, through the institutionalisation of a double function, in the form of a principle-based and legally fortified quests towards universal inclusion delineated along either territorial or functional lines, providing a sense of direction in time through an articulated form of constitutional consciousness.

Notes

1 Gunther Teubner, *Constitutional Fragments: Societal Constitutionalism and Globalization*, Oxford: Oxford University Press, 2012, p. 102 *et seq.*
2 Niklas Luhmann, *Organisation und Entscheidung*, Wiesbaden: Verlag für Sozialwissenschaften, 2011.
3 Gorm Harste, *Modernitet og Organisation*, Copenhagen: Politisk Revy, 1997.
4 Jürgen Habermas, 'Hannah Arendt's Communications Concept of Power', *Social Research*, 1977, 44, pp. 3–24.
5 Poul F. Kjaer, 'Post-Hegelian Networks: Comments on the Chapter by Simon Deakin', in Marc Amstutz and Gunther Teubner (eds), *Networks: Legal Issues of Multilateral Co-operation*, Oxford: Hart Publishing, 2009, pp. 75–85.
6 A clear illustration of this can be found the work of Jürgen Habermas, since the question of the concrete organisational form is essentially absent in his theory of deliberative democracy. See Jürgen Habermas, *Faktizität und Geltung: Beiträge zur Diskurstheorie des Rechts und des demokratischen Rechtsstaats*, Frankfurt am Main: Suhrkamp Verlag, 1992. For an important exception, see the work of David Sciulli, in particular, David Sciulli, *Theory of Societal Constitutionalism: Foundations of a Non-Marxist Critical Theory*, Cambridge: Cambridge University Press, 1992, and David Sciulli, *Corporate Power: An Application of Societal Constitutionalism*, New York: New York University Press, 2001.
7 This is also acknowledged by Habermas. In relation to his re-formulation of Adorno and Horkhheimer's reification thesis (*Verdinglichungsthese*), one, for example, finds the following statement: 'The Social worker is just *another* expert who does not liberate the clients of the welfare-state bureaucracy from their position as objects' (author's translation); Jürgen Habermas, *Theorie des kommunikativen Handelns, Band 2, Zur Kritik der funktionalistischen Vernunft*, Frankfurt am Main: Suhrkamp Verlag, 1981, p. 544; italics in original.
8 See, for example, Wolfgang Streeck, *Re-Forming Capitalism: Institutional Change in the German Political Economy*, Oxford: Oxford University Press, 2009.
9 Poul F. Kjaer, 'The Structural Transformation of Embeddedness', in Christian Joerges and Josef Falke (eds), *Karl Polanyi: Globalisation and the Potential of Law in Transnational Markets*, Oxford: Hart Publishing, 2011, pp 85–104.
10 For the left-Luhmannian programme announcement, see Andreas Fischer-Lescano, 'Kritische Systemtheorie Frankfurter Schule', in Gralf-Peter Calliess, Andreas Fischer-Lescano, Dan Wielsch and Peer Zumbansen (eds), *Soziologische Jurisprudenz: Festschrift für Gunther Teubner zum 65. Geburtstag*, Berlin: Walter de Gruyter, 2009, pp. 49–68; see also Sonja Buckel, *Subjektivierung und Kohäsion: Zur Rekonstruktion einer materialististischen Theorie des Rechts*, Weilerswist: Velbrück, 2007.

11 See, most notably, Karl-Heinz Ladeur, *Der Staat gegen die Gesellschaft: Zur Verteidigung der Rationalität der Privatrechtsgesellschaft*, Tübingen: Mohr Siebeck Verlag, 2006.

12 Poul. F. Kjaer, 'Embeddedness through Networks – a Critical appraisal of the Network Concept in the Oeuvre of Karl-Heinz Ladeur', *German Law Journal*, 2009, 10, pp. 483–99, at 483.

13 See, for example, Sonja Buckel, *Subjektivierung und Kohäsion: Zur Rekonstruktion einer materialististischen Theorie des Rechts*, Weilerswist: Velbrück, 2007, p. 316 *et seq.*

14 Teubner, *Constitutional Fragments*, p. 88 *et seq.*

15 The crucial importance of formal organisation as the starting-point for a theory of constitutions is also recognised by Gunther Teubner: 'Although these processes [of constitutionalization] are set in motion by functional differentiation, the constitutionalisation process is not directed toward the major function systems themselves. Finance and product markets are globalized, scientific communication takes place at a global level, the systems of communicative media, news agencies, tv, internet transmits news across the whole globe. Despite the operational closure of these world systems ... [they] lack the capacity to take action, to become organized and, therefore to be constitutionalized. The various attempts at global constitutionalism are directed rather at social processes "beneath" the function systems, at formal organizations and at formalized transactions that are not tied to the territorial borders of nation-states.' See Gunther Teubner, Hans Lindahl, Emilios Christodoulidis and Chris Thornhill, 'Debate and Dialogue: Constitutionalizing Polycontexturality', *Social and Legal Studies*,2011, 20, pp. 209–52, at 221–22.

16 A particular clear illustration of this can be found in the debate between Hans Kelsen and Carl Schmitt. See Hans Lindahl, 'Constituent Power and Reflexive Identity: Towards an Ontology of Collective Selfhood', 9–24 in Martin Loughlin and Neil Walker (eds), *The Paradox of Constitutionalism: Constituent Power and Constitutional Form*, Oxford: Oxford University Press, 2007, pp. 9–24.

17 Ernst Kantorowicz, *The King's Two Bodies: A Study in Mediaeval Political Theology*, Princeton, NJ, Princeton University Press, [1957] 1997.

18 Georg W.F. Hegel, *Grundlinien der Philosophie des Rechtsoder Naturrecht und Staatswissenschaft im Grundrisse, Werke Band 7*, Frankfurt am Main: Suhrkamp Verlag, [1821] 1970, § 277.

19 Max Weber, 'Bureaucracy', in Hans H. Gerth and Charles Wright Mills (eds), *From Max Weber*, London: Routledge [1946] 2007, pp. 196–244.

20 Gunther Teubner, 'A Constitutional Moment? The Logics of "Hitting the Bottom"', in Poul F. Kjaer, Gunther Teubner and Alberto Febbrajo (eds), *The Financial Crisis in Constitutional Perspective: The Dark Side of Functional Differentiation*, Oxford: Hart Publishing, 2011, pp. 3–42, at 25.

21 See Moritz Renner, 'Occupy the System! Societal Constitutionalism and Transnational Corporate Accounting', *Indiana Journal of Global Legal Studies*, 2013, 20, issue 2, pp. 941–964; Moritz Renner, *Zwingendes transnationales Recht: Zur Struktur der Wirtschaftsverfassung jenseits des Staates*, Baden-Baden: Nomos Verlag, 2010.

22 For more on this point, see Poul F. Kjaer, 'Law and Order within and Beyond National Configurations', in Poul F. Kjaer, Gunther Teubner and Alberto Febbrajo (eds), *The Financial Crisis in Constitutional Perspective: The Dark Side of Functional Differentiation*, Oxford: Hart Publishing, 2011, pp. 395–430.

23 Kjaer, 'Post-Hegelian Networks'.

24 Mattias Kumm, 'The Best of Times and the Worst of Times: Between Constitutional Triumphalism and Nostalgia', in Petra Dobner and Martin Loughlin (eds), *The Twilight of Constitutionalism?*, Oxford: Oxford University Press, 2010, pp. 201–19, at 205; Cormac Mac Amhlaigh: 'The European Union's Constitutional Mosaic: big "C" or small "c", is that the question?', in Neil Walker, Jo Shaw and Stephen Tierney (eds), *Europe's Constitutional Mosaic*, Oxford: Hart Publishing, 2011, pp. 21–48.

25 Paul Schiff Berman, *Global Legal Pluralism: A Jurisprudence of Law Beyond Borders*, Cambridge: Cambridge University Press, 2012.

26 Immanuel Kant, *Kritik der Urteilskraft: Werkausgabe Band X*, Frankfurt am Main: Suhrkamp Verlag, [1790] 1996, p. 323.

27 Martin Loughlin, 'What is Constitutionalisation?', in Petra Dobner and Martin Loughlin (eds), *The Twilight of Constitutionalism?* Oxford: Oxford University Press, 2010, pp. 47–69, at 59.

28 Francisco J. Varela, *The Embodied Mind: Cognitive Experience and Human Experience*, Cambridge MA: MIT Press, 1993.

29 Niklas Luhmann, *Grundrechte als Institution: Ein Beitrag zur politischen Soziologie*, Berlin: Duncker & Humblot, 1965.

30 Chris Thornhill, *A Sociology of Constitutions: Constitutions and State Legitimacy in Historical-Sociological Perspective*, Cambridge: Cambridge University Press, 2011; Chris Thornhill, 'A Sociology of Constituent Power: The Political Code of Transnational Societal Constitutions', *Indiana Journal of Global Legal Studies*, 2013, 20, issue 2, pp. 551–603.

31 For the internal emergence of rights regimes, see, for example, the development of the regime structuring the Internet. See also Vagias Karavas, *Digitale Grundrechte: Elemente einer Verfassung des Informationsflusses im Internet*, Baden-Baden: Nomos Verlag, 2007.

32 Gunther Teubner, 'A Constitutional Moment? The Logics of "Hitting the Bottom"', in Poul F. Kjaer, Gunther Teubner and Alberto Febbrajo (eds), *The Financial Crisis in Constitutional Perspective: The Dark Side of Functional Differentiation*, Oxford: Hart Publishing, 201, pp. 3–42, at 21; Gunther Teubner: *Constitutional Fragments: Societal Constitutionalism and Globalization*, Oxford: Oxford University Press, 2012, p. 150 *et seq.*

33 Poul F. Kjaer, *Between Governing and Governance: On the Emergence, Function and Form of Europe's Post-national Constellation*, Oxford: Hart Publishing, 2010.

34 Gunther Teubner, *Constitutional Fragments: Societal Constitutionalism and Globalization*, Oxford: Oxford University Press, 2012, p. 88 *et seq.*

35 Niklas Luhmann, 'The Paradoxy of Observing Systems', *Cultural Critique*, 1995, 31, pp. 37–55.

36 Jürgen Habermas, 'Constitutional Democracy: A Paradoxical Union of Contradictory Principles?', *Political Theory*, 2001, 29, pp. 766–81.

37 Niklas Luhmann, *Soziale Systeme: Grundriß einer allgemeinen Theorie*, Frankfurt am Main: Suhrkamp Verlag, 1984, p. 112 *et seq.*

38 Chris Thornhill, 'The Future of the State', in Poul F. Kjaer, Gunther Teubner and Alberto Febbrajo (eds), *The Financial Crisis in Constitutional Perspective: The Dark Side of Functional Differentiation*, Oxford: Hart Publishing, 2011, pp. 357–93, at 390 *et seq.*

9   Conclusion

The starting-point of the inquiry was the observation that the debate on the migration of constitutional concepts and semantics beyond the state has, to date, unfolded within two separate discourses. The dominating approach is, in the main, being advanced by public lawyers and political scientists, and is essentially occupied with the adjustment of the constitutional apparatuses developed in nation-state contexts in order to make it compatible with public international organisations and regimes. The other approach, which adopts a minority position, is dominated by private lawyers, and focuses upon how legal instruments are being deployed in order to stabilise private-law-based social processes normatively through a dual set of limiting and facilitating rules. Both of these perspectives have their blind spots. The latter essentially keeps the core concepts of law and the political constant, and merely assumes that the exercise of law and the political is being transferred to new sites. The former position, on the other hand, has engaged in a challenging exercise of developing a concept of law which is suitable for describing and understanding legal processes unfolding beyond the state. But, in doing so, they systematically ignore or downplay the political aspect of the processes which they describe, and they thereby fail to recognise that a context-adequate concept of the political also needs to be developed. The bridging of the gap between the two positions, furthermore, necessitates the activation of a more complex conceptual apparatus which is capable of linking the evolution and the function of constitutional frameworks to deeper structural transformations. Thus, the development of a theory of constitutionalism suitable for the global realm needs to take the form of a sociological inquiry.

Illuminating the function and location of constitutional set-ups in the global realm implies a need to contextualise them within the still ongoing globalisation processes. Globalisation is, however, not a new phenomenon, but is, instead, a *protracted process*. The ongoing globalisation wave can be traced back to the late nineteenth century when the Eurocentric ordering of the world began to disintegrate. It is this still ongoing structural transformation which provides the overall setting within which the transmutation of constitutionalism into the global realm has unfolded.

From a sociological perspective, this transformation reflects a gradual substitution of centre/periphery differentiation with functional differentiation as the core organisational principle of globally operating structures. Today, social processes with a global reach primarily unfold within functionally delineated regimes related to public and private international organisations, multi-national companies and large-scale non-governmental organisations. The emergence of such regimes is a reflection of the process of de-colonisation, in the sense that the present-day functionally delineated transnational structures serve as 'replacements' for the previous colonial structures which were based on centre/periphery differentiation. Thus, apart from globalisation de-colonisation provides a second structural change, which serves as a basis for the emergence of new constitutional forms of ordering with a global reach.

The vast majority of the existing work on global constitutionalism explicitly or implicitly departs from the assumption that the state, defined as an institution which fulfils the function of taking and implementing collectively binding decisions within a territorially defined segment of world society, has been weakened through the emergence of functionally delineated global regimes. This assumption has been refuted in this volume. In contrast, the state phenomenon has expanded radically since the mid-twentieth century. States only became a global phenomenon in the wake of de-colonisation and no contradiction exists between the emergence and viability of statehood and the emergence of global structures of ordering. On the contrary, a relationship of mutual increase exists between the two forms of social ordering.

It follows that the world consists of a multiplicity of normative orders, and that it is normative orders and not states that are the basic object of social scientific enquiry in world society. Such orders are universes in *their own right*, since their sense of purpose and meaning is not externally derived. The existence of a multiplicity of normative orders automatically brings the character of their interaction to the fore. The transfer of compact social components (in the form of, for example, legal acts, political decisions, scientific knowledge, economic products or capital) is the central form of interaction occurring between such orders. In a more specific sense, network-based governance structures have emerged as the institutionalised form through which transfers between different normative orders take place. Such networks *simultaneously* act as buffer zones, offsetting collisions between different normative orders, and provide a basis for convergence and 'colonisation' through the institutionalisation of asymmetric relations between different normative orders.

A common feature of normative orders is that they rely upon law as the medium through which they structure expectations and norms. The law is, however, not external to the social processes against which it is oriented, but, instead, emerges from *within* such social processes. It is through the hybridity emerging from the combination of a legal frame with a given social structure that normative orders come into existence. But a normative order first becomes autonomous at the moment that its legality is derived from the legitimacy of the social structure that it frames. Since no overarching hierarchy of law exists in world society, a conflict of laws perspective, furthermore, becomes the central mechanism for understanding the interaction between legally condensed normative orders.

The classical understanding of the contribution of law to society is that it solves conflicts between social structures external to the law, while, at the same time, maintaining a counter-factual normative outlook. Primarily in relation to functionally delineated normative orders, a new type of law has emerged which promotes negative integration by reducing barriers to the transfer of condensed social components between different normative orders. The function which it provides to normative orders, as such, is, therefore, to frame and to facilitate learning processes between such orders. Classical law relies upon the supremacy of normative expectations, in the sense that legal imperatives are upheld even in the face of non-realisation. In contrast, the new law is characterised by a structural supremacy of cognitive components, in the sense that the law becomes a learning law which is not only oriented towards facilitating societal-learning processes, but also changes itself when confronted with disappointment.

The change in the set-up of law has emerged hand in hand with a transformation of the political. Two distinct forms of politics can be observed in relation to social processes with a global reach: first, functionally delineated public regimes which remain primarily political regimes, in so far as they operate upon the basis of a political logic; and second, a subordinate form of the political has emerged within private transnational regimes and organisations, such as large-scale non-governmental organisations, multi-national companies and private self-regulatory regimes. The latter form of the political is secondary to the substantial function reproduced by such private structures and in this capacity it remains primarily oriented towards an internal stabilisation of the social processes in question as well as the handling of externalities vis-à-vis other normative orders.

Whereas the nation-state form of the political has a strong normative component, the transnational form of the political is a form of 'managerialism' (Koskenniemi) which, in its self-understanding, is 'technical' and 'rational', characterised by learning and continued adaptation, rather than the promotion of contra-factually upheld values. It stylises itself as a kind of 'non-political' cognitivised form of the political which is directly oriented towards avoiding intensive politicisation. This is also reflected in the substitution of traditional nation-state concepts of the nation, the public sphere and representation with new semantic classifications in relation to stakeholders, transparency and self-representation.

The move towards increased cognitivisation of law and politics is, however, not based upon a zero-sum game in which 'more of one' implies 'less of the other'. The two sides of the normative/cognitive distinction are, instead, *mutually constitutive*, in the sense that increased vibrancy of one dimension implies an increased vibrancy of the other. The migration of constitutional language to the transnational level can be understood as a reflection of this, in that the emergence of mainly cognitivised forms of transnational law and politics creates a *functional* need for a second-order normative stabilisation of such processes.

Against this background, the constitutional concept was re-conceptualised in three steps.

First, the linking of law and a multitude of organisations is the central feature of modern global society both at the national, as well as the transnational, level. Thus, in *praxis*, the constitution of normative orders takes the form of organisational constitutions. This makes it possible to argue that the constitutional object is formal organisations, as such, and *not* states, and that this remains *irrespective* of their location in world society.

The *internal function* of constitutions is double edged: in their political function, constitutions frame the body of rules and norms which establishes the formal structure, decisional competences and a hierarchical *locus* of authority within the formal organisations of normative orders. In their legal function, they lay down principles for the structuring of conflicts between norms *within* such organisations. Constitutions, in this sense, lay down the enabling and the limiting rules which internally guide normative orders relying on formal organisation through the institutionalisation of a specific kind of *double reflexivity*, in which the internal perspectives of law and politics are bound to each other and mutually stabilised at the same time as hierarchy is established within the two dimensions.

Second, in modern society crisis and *anomie* are synonymous with de-differentiation processes in which the operational ability, integrity and coherency of normative orders become strained or disintegrate due to processes of coalescence unfolding between one or more normative orders and the rest of society. In particular, it is the transfers of social components that create the danger of boundary dissolutions. It is against this background that the category of rights has emerged. Rights regimes are filters through which social components are transformed into potential subjects of transfer and given a specific condensed form. Thus, one can speak of *external* constitutionalisation processes when legal mechanisms are deployed in order to regulate the transfer of social components, and, in particular, the constitutional values and objectives which are internally developed within a normative order, into other segments of world society. In such cases, a particular form of *double prestation*, unfolds, since a normative order through such processes is made compatible with a limited segment of its surrounding society.

Third, the *counter-factual narratives of constitutionalism* fulfil the function of overcoming the contradiction between the internal and external dimensions by externalising the difference into a constantly reproduced vision of the future. Through recourse to the time dimension, the promise of a future which reconciles the internal and external dimensions of normative orders is constantly reproduced, thereby establishing a comprehensive perspective on the world within each normative order. Constitutionalism, in other words, fulfils the function of establishing a *double function*, in the sense that it develops a comprehensive view of the world within a given normative order through the development of a constitutional consciousness.

Bibliography

Amstutz, Marc (2011) 'Eroding Boundaries: On Financial Crisis and an Evolutionary Concept of Regulatory Reform', in Poul F. Kjaer, Gunther Teubner and Alberto Febbrajo (eds), *The Financial Crisis in Constitutional Perspective: The Dark Side of Functional Differentiation*, Oxford: Hart Publishing, pp. 223–68.

——(2009) 'Métissage. Zur Rechtsform in der Weltgesellschaft', in Andreas Fischer-Lescano, Florian Rödl and Christoph U. Schmid (eds), *Europäische Gesellschaftsverfassung: Zur Konstitutionalisierung sozialer Demokratie in Europa*, Baden-Baden: Nomos Verlag, pp. 333–263.

——(2005) 'In-Between Worlds: Marleasing and the Emergence of Interlegality in Legal Reasoning', *European Law Journal*, 11, pp. 766–84.

——(2002) 'Rechtsgeschichte als Evolutionstheorie: Anmerkungen zum Theorierahmen von Marie Theres Fögens Forschungsprogramm', *Rechtsgeschichte*, 1, pp. 26–31.

——(2001) *Evolutorisches Wirtschaftsrecht: Vorstudien zum Recht und seiner Methode in den Diskurskollissionen der Marktgesellschaft*, Baden-Baden: Nomos Verlag.

Amstutz, Marc and Vaois Karavas (2009) 'Weltrecht: Ein Derridasches Monster', in Gralf-Peter Calliess, Andreas Fischer-Lescano, Dan Wielsch and Peer Zumbansen (eds), *Soziologische Jurisprudenz: Festschrift für Gunther Teubner zum 65. Geburtstag*, Berlin: Walter de Gruyter, pp. 645–72.

——(2006) 'Rechtsmutation: Zu Genese und Evolution des Rechts im transnationalen Raum', *Rechtsgeschichte*, 8, pp. 14–32.

Andersen, Torben M. and Thor T. Herbertsson (2003) 'Measuring Globalization', *IZA Discussion Paper Series*, p. 807.

Anderson, Benedict ([1983] 2006) *Imagined Communities: Reflections on the Origin and Spread of Nationalism*, London: Verso.

Archibugi, Daniele and David Held (eds) (1995) *Cosmopolitan Democracy: An Agenda for a New World Order*, Cambridge: Polity Press.

Augsberg, Ino (2013) 'Observing (the) Law: The "Epistemological Turn", in Public Law and the Evolution of Global Administrative Law', in Paulius Jurčys, Poul F. Kjaer and Ren Yurakami (eds), *Regulatory Hybridization in the Transnational Sphere*, Leiden: Brill Publishing, pp. 11–27.

Backer, Larry Catá (2007) 'Economic Globalization and the Rise of Efficient Systems of Global Private Lawmaking: Wal-Mart as Global Legislator', *University of Connecticut Law Review*, 37, pp. 1739–84.

Baecker, Dirk (2011) 'The Culture Form of a Crisis', in Poul F. Kjaer, Gunther Teubner and Alberto Febbrajo (eds), *The Financial Crisis in Constitutional Perspective: The Dark Side of Functional Differentiation*, Oxford, Hart Publishing, pp. 173–88.

Balibar, Étienne (2001) *Nous, citoyens d'Europe? Les frontières, l'État, le peuple*, Paris: La Découverte.

Basedow, Jürgen (1992) *Von der deutschen zur europäischen Wirtschaftsverfassung*, Tübingen: J.C.B. Mohr.

Baumann, Zygmunt (1989) *Modernity and Holocaust*, Cambridge: Polity Press.

Beck, Ulrich (1986) *Risikogesellschaft: Auf dem Weg in eine andere Moderne*, Frankfurt am Main: Suhrkamp Verlag.

Beck, Valentin (2010) 'Theorizing Fairtrade from a Justice-related Standpoint', *Global Justice: Theory, Practice, Rhetoric*, 3, pp. 1–21.

Berman, Paul Schiff (2012) *Global Legal Pluralism: A Jurisprudence of Law beyond Borders*, New York: Cambridge University Press.

Black, Jeremy (1991) *A Military Revolution? Military Change and European Society, 1550–1800*. Basingstoke: Macmillan.

Borch, Christian (2012) *The Politics of Crowds: An Alternative History of Sociology*, Cambridge: Cambridge University Press.

——(2005) 'Systemic Power. Luhmann, Foucault and Analytics of Power', *Acta Sociologica*, 48, pp. 155–67.

Bourdieu, Pierre (1994) 'Rethinking the State: Genesis and Structure of the Bureaucratic Field', *Sociological Theory*, 12, pp. 1–18.

——(1989) *La Noblesse d'état: grandes écoles et esprit de corps*, Paris: Les Editions de Minuit.

——(1979) *La Distinction. Critique sociale du jugement*, Paris: Les Editions de Minuit.

Brunkhorst, Hauke (2011) 'The Return of Crisis', in Poul F. Kjaer, Gunther Teubner and Alberto Febbrajo (eds), *The Financial Crisis in Constitutional Perspective: The Dark Side of Functional Differentiation*, Oxford: Hart Publishing, pp.131 – 171.

——(2010) 'Constitutionalism and Democracy in the World Society', in Petra Dobner and Martin Loughlin (eds), *The Twilight of Constitutionalism?*, Oxford: Oxford University Press, 2010, pp. 179–98.

——(2010) 'Cosmopolitanism and Democratic Freedom', in Chris Thornhill and Samantha Ashenden (eds), *Legality and Legitimacy – Normative and Sociological Approaches*, Baden-Baden: Nomos Verlag, pp. 171–96.

——(2009) 'Machbarkeitsillussionen, feierliche Erklärungen und Gesänge. Zum Verhältnis von Evolution und Revolution im Recht', in Gralf-Peter Calliess, Andreas Fischer-Lescano, Dan Wielsch and Peer Zumbansen (eds), *Soziologische Jurisprudenz: Festschrift für Gunther Teubner zum 65. Geburtstag am 30. April 2009*, Berlin: Walter de Gruyter, pp. 447–64.

——(2002) *Solidarität: Von der Bürgerfreundschaft zur globalen Rechtsgenossenschaft*, Frankfurt am Main: Suhrkamp Verlag.

Buckel, Sonja (2007) *Subjektivierung und Kohäsion: Zur Rekonstruktion einer materialististischen Theorie des Rechts*, Weilerswist: Velbrück, 2007.

Bundesverfassungsgericht (BVerfGE) (1993) 89, 155 vom 12, Oktober. Available at: www.servat.unibe.ch/dfr/bv089155.html.

Buzan, Barry and Mathias Albert (2010) 'Differentiation: A Sociological Approach to International Relations Theory', *European Journal of International Relations*, 16, 3, pp. 315 – 337.

Caldwell, Peter C. (2000) 'Is a Social *Rechtsstaat* Possible? The Weimar Roots of a Bonn Controversy', in Peter C. Caldwell and William E. Scheuerman (eds), *From Liberal Democracy to Fascism: Legal and Political Thought in the Weimar Republic*, Boston, MA, Leiden: Brill/Humanities Press, pp. 136–53.

Caldwell, Peter C. and William E. Scheuerman (eds) (2000) *From Liberal Democracy to Fascism: Legal and Political Thought in the Weimar Republic*, Boston, MA, Leiden: Brill/Humanities Press.

Carporaso, James and Sidney Tarrow (2009) 'Polanyi in Brussels: Supranational Institutions and the Transnational Embedding of Markets', *International Organization*, 64, pp. 593–620.

Cassirer, Ernst ([1946] 1977) *The Myth of the State*, New Haven, CT: Yale University Press.

Chalmers, Damian (2003) 'Food for Thought: Reconciling European Risks and Traditional Ways of Life', *Modern Law Review*, 66, pp. 532–62.

Chernilo, Daniel (2007) *A Social Theory of the Nation-state: The Political Forms of Modernity beyond Methodological Nationalism*, London: Routledge.

——(2006) 'Social Theory's Methodological Nationalism. Myth and Reality', *European Journal of Social Theory*, 9, pp. 5–22.

Clam, Jean (2006) 'What is Modern Power?', in Michael King and Chris Thornhill (eds), *Luhmann on Law and Politics: Critical Appraisals and Applications*, Oxford: Hart Publishing, pp. 145–62.

Cohen, Joshua and Charles F. Sabel (2005) 'Global Democracy?', *New York University Journal of International Law and Politics*, 37, pp. 763–97.

Constitution of Fairtrade Labelling Organizations International. Available at: www.fairtrade.net/our_vision.html.

Cover, Robert M. (1983) 'Nomos and Narrative', *Harvard Law Review*, 97, pp. 4–68.

Dahrendorf, Ralf (1957) *Soziale Klassen und Klassenkonflikt in der industriellen Gesellschaft*, Stuttgart: Ferdinand Enke Verlag, 1957.

Deakin, Simon (2009) 'The Return of the Guild? Network Relations in Historical Perspective', in Marc Amstutz and Gunther Teubner (eds), *Networks: Legal Issues of Multilateral Co-operation*, Oxford: Hart Publishing, pp. 53–73.

Deitelhoff, Nicole (2006) *Überzeugung in der Politik. Grundzüge einer Diskurstheorie internationalen Regierens*, Frankfurt am Main: Suhrkamp Verlag.

de Wet, Erika (2009) 'The Role of European Courts in the Development of a Hierarchy of Norms within International Law: Evidence of Constitutionalisation?', *European Constitutional Law Review*, 5, pp. 284–306.

——(2006), 'The International Constitutional Order', *International and Comparative Law Quarterly*, 55, pp. 51–72.

Dilling, Olaf, Martin Herberg and Gerd Winter (eds) (2008) *Responsible Bussiness. Self-Governance and Law in Transnational Economic Transactions*, Oxford: Hart Publishing.

Donahue, Charles (2008) 'Private Law without the State and during its Formation', *American Journal of Comparative Law*, 56, pp. 541–66.

Dupuy, Pierre-Marie (2007) 'A Doctrinal Debate in the Globalisation Era: On the 'Fragmentation' of International Law', *European Journal of Legal Studies*, 1, pp. 1–19.

Durkheim, Émile ([1893] 1973) *De la division du travail social*, Paris: Presses universitaires de France.

Eder, Klaus (1992) *Geschichte als Lernprozeß? Zur Pathogenese politischer Modernität in Deutschland*, Frankfurt am Main: Suhrkamp Verlag.

Elias, Norbert ([1969] 2002) *Die höfische Gesellschaft*, Frankfurt am Main: Suhrkamp Verlag.

——([1938] 1976) *Über den Prozeß der Zivilisation, Band 1*, Frankfurt am Main: Suhrkamp Verlag.

——([1938] 1976): *Über den Prozeß der Zivilisation, Band 2*, Frankfurt am Main: Suhrkamp Verlag.

Enderlein, Henrik, Sonja Walti and Michael Zürn (eds) (2011) *Handbook on Multi-level Governance*, Cheltenham: Edward Elgar Publishing.

European Commission (2012) 'Communication from the Commission to the European Parliament, the Council, the European Economic and Social Committee and the Committee of the Regions. A Re-inforced European Research Area Partnership for Excellence and Growth, Brussels', 17.7.2012, European Commission, COM(2012) p. 392 final.

Fahey, Elaine and Ester Herlin-Karnell (eds) (2012) 'Deciphering Regulatory and Constitutional Competence between EU Environmental Law and Global Governance. Special issue of German Law Journal', *German Law Journal*, 13, pp. 1147–1268.

Fairtrade International website. Available at: www.fairtrade.net.

Fischer-Lescano, Andreas (2009) 'Kritische Systemtheorie Frankfurter Schule', in Gralf-Peter Calliess, Andreas Fischer-Lescano, Dan Wielsch and Peer Zumbansen (eds), *Soziologische Jurisprudenz: Festschrift für Gunther Teubner zum 65. Geburtstag*, Berlin: Walter de Gruyter, pp. 49–68.

——(2005) *Globalverfassung: Die Geltungsbegründung der Menschenrechte*, Weilerswist: Velbrück.

Fischer-Lescano, Andreas, and Gunther Teubner (2006) *Regime-Kollisionen: Zur Fragmentierung des Weltrechts*, Frankfurt am Main: Suhrkamp Verlag.

——(2004) 'Regime-Collisions: "The Vain Search for Legal Unity in the Fragmentation of Global Law"', *Michigan Journal of International Law*, 25, pp. 999–1046.

Fleck, Ludwig ([1935] 1980) *Entstehung und Entwicklung einer wissenschaftlichen Tatsache: Einführung in die Lehre vom Denkstil und Denkkollektiv*, Frankfurt am Main: Suhrkamp Verlag.

Forst, Rainer (2007) *Das Recht auf Rechtfertigung: Elemente einer konstruktivistischen Theorie der Gerechtigkeit*, Frankfurt am Main: Suhrkamp Verlag.

Foucault, Michel (1997) *Il faut défendre la Société: Cours au Collége de France, 1975–76*, Paris: Gallimard, 2007.

——(1982) 'The Subject and Power', in Hubert Dreyfus and Paul Rabinow (eds), *Michel Foucault: Beyond Structuralism and Hermeneutics*, Chicago: Chicago University Press, pp. 208–26.

Fraser, Nancy (1992) 'Rethinking the Public Sphere: A Contribution to the Critique of Actually Existing Democracy', in Craig Calhoun, *Habermas and the Public Sphere*, Cambridge, MA: MIT Press, pp. 109–42.

Garnett, Richard (2007) 'The Freedom of the Church', *Journal of Catholic Social Thought*, 4, pp. 59–86.

Graber, Christoph B. (2009) 'Aboriginal Self-Determination vs. the Propertisation of Traditional Culture: The Case of Sacred Wanjina Sites', *Australian Indigenous Law Review*, 13, pp. 18–34.

Grimm, Dieter (2005) 'The Constitution in the Process of Denationalization', *Constellations*, 12, pp. 447–63.

Habermas, Jürgen (2008) *Ach, Europa*, Frankfurt am Main: Suhrkamp Verlag.

——(2008) 'The Constitutionalization of International Law and the Legitimation Problems of a Constitution for World Society', *Constellations*, 15, pp. 444–55.

——(2008) 'A Political Constitution for the Pluralist World Society', in Jürgen Habermas, *Between Naturalism and Religion*, Cambridge: Polity Press, pp. 312–52.

——(2001) 'Constitutional Democracy: A Paradoxical Union of Contradictory Principles?', *Political Theory*, 29, pp. 766–81.

——(1992) *Faktizität und Geltung: Beiträge zur Diskurstheorie des Rechts und des demokratischen Rechtsstaats*, Frankfurt am Main: Suhrkamp Verlag.

——([1962] 1990) *Strukturwandel der Öffentlichkeit: Untersuchungen zu einer Kategorie der bürgerlichen Gesellschaft*, Frankfurt am Main: Suhrkamp Verlag.

——(1987) 'Geschichtsbewußtsein und posttraditionale Identität: Die Westorientierung der Bundesrepublik', in *Eine Art Schadensabwicklung: Kleine politische Schriften IV*, Frankfurt am Main: Suhrkamp Verlag, pp. 159–79.

——(1985) *Der philosophische Diskurs der Moderne: Zwölf Vorlesungen*, Frankfurt am Main: Suhrkamp Verlag.

——(1981) *Theorie des kommunikativen Handelns, Band 1 Handlungsrationalität und gesellschaftliche Rationalisierung*, Frankfurt am Main: Suhrkamp Verlag.

——(1981) *Theorie des kommunikativen Handelns, Band 2, Zur Kritik der funktionalistischen Vernunft*, Frankfurt am Main: Suhrkamp Verlag, 1981.

——(1977) 'Hannah Arendt's Communications Concept of Power', *Social Research*, 44, pp. 3–24.

——(1973) *Legitimationsprobleme im Spätkapitalismus*, Frankfurt am Main: Suhrkamp Verlag.

Hall, Peter A. and David Soskice (eds) (2001) *Varieties of Capitalism: The Institutional Foundations of Comparative Advantage*, Oxford: Oxford University Press.

Haltern, Ulrich (2007) *Was bedeutet Souveränität?* Tübingen: Mohr Siebeck.

Harste, Gorm (1997) *Modernitet og Organisation*, Copenhagen: Politisk Revy.

——(1996) 'Kant und Luhmann über Teleologie in politischer Kommunikation und Natur', in Gorm Harste, Thomas Mertens and Thomas Scheffer (eds), *Immanuel Kant über Natur und Gesellschaft*, Odense: Odense University Press, pp. 169–83.

——(1974) '"Haus" and "Haushalt"', in *Historisches Wörterbuch der Philosophie, Band 3*, Basel/Stuttgart: Schwabe & Co. Verlag, pp. 1007–20, 1020–21.

Hegel, Georg W.F. ([1800–802] 1971) *Die Verfassung Deutschlands, Werke 1*, Frankfurt am Main: Suhrkamp Verlag.

——([1821] 1970) *Grundlinien der Philosophie des Rechts oder Naturrecht und Staatswissenschaft im Grundrisse, Werke Band 7*, Frankfurt am Main: Suhrkamp Verlag.

Held, David (2004) *Global Covenant: The Social Democratic Alternative to the Washington Consensus*, Cambridge: Polity Press.

Held, David and Mathias Koenig-Archibugi (eds) (2005) *Global Governance and Public Accountability*, Oxford: Blackwell Publishing.

Heller, Agnes (1990) 'Death of the Subject', *Thesis Eleven*, 25, pp. 22–38.

Herberg, Martin (2008) 'Global Legal Pluralism and Interlegality: Environmental Self-Regulation in Multinational Enterprises as Global Law-making', in Olaf Dilling, Martin Herberg and Gerd Winter (eds), *Responsible Business: Self-Governance and Law in Transnational Economic Transactions*, Oxford: Hart Publishing, pp. 17–40.

——(2007) *Globalisierung und private Selbstregulierung: Umweltschutz in multinationalen Unternehmen*, Frankfurt am Main: Campus Verlag.

Hirst, Paul and Grahame Thompson (2001) *Globalization in Question: The International Economy and the Possibilities of Governance*, 2nd edition, Cambridge: Polity Press.

Höffe, Otfried (1999) *Demokratie im Zeitalter der Globalisierung*, Munich: C.H. Beck Verlag.

Howse, Robert and Kalypso Nicolaidis (2001) 'Legitimacy and Global Governance: Why Constitutionalizing the WTO is a Step to Far', in Roger B. Poter, Pierre Suave and Arvind Subramian (eds), *Efficiency, Equity, Legitimacy and Governance: The Multilateral Trading System at the Millennium*, Washington, DC: Brookings Institution, pp. 227–152.

International Non Governmental Organizations Accountability Charter. Available at: www.realizingrights.org/pdf/INGO_Accountability_Charter.pdf.

Ipsen, Hans Peter (1984) *Europäisches Gemeinschaftsrecht in Einzelstudien*, Baden-Baden: Nomos Verlag.

Jaffee, Daniel (2007) *Brewing Justice. Fair Trade Coffee, Sustainability and Survival*, Berkeley, CA: University of California Press.

Jellum, Linda (2011) 'Lessons to Be Learned: Public Participation and Transparency in Norm Creation within the European Union and United States', *FSU College of Law, Public Law Research Paper No. 562*.

Jessup, Philip C. (1956) *Transnational Law*, New Haven, CT: Yale University Press.

Joerges, Christian (2011) 'A New Type of Conflicts Law as the Legal Paradigm of the Postnational Constellation', in Christian Joerges and Josef Falke (eds), *Karl Polanyi: Globalisation and the Potential of Law in Transnational Markets*, Oxford: Hart Publishing, pp. 465–501.

——(2010) '*Rechtsstaat* and Social Europe: How a Classical Tension Resurfaces in the European Integration Process', *Comparative Sociology*, 9, pp. 65–85.

——(2004) 'What is Left of the European Economic Constitution', *EUI Working Paper Law*, p. 13.

——(1997) 'The Market without the State? The "Economic Constitution" of the European Community and the Rebirth of Regulatory Politics', *European Integration online Papers (EIoP)*, 1, 19.

——(1997) 'States Without a Market? Comments on the German Constitutional Court's Maastricht-Judgement and a Plea for Interdisciplinary Discourses', *European Integration online Papers (EIoP)*, 1, 20.

Joerges, Christian and Navraj Singh Ghaleigh (eds) (2003) *Darker Legacies of Law in Europe: The Shadow of National Socialism and Fascism over Europe and its Legal Traditions*, Oxford: Hart Publishing.

Joerges, Christian, Poul F. Kjaer and Tommi Ralli (eds) (2011) 'A New Type of Conflicts Law as Constitutional Form in the Postnational Constellation. Special Issue of Transnational Legal Theory', *Transnational Legal Theory*, 2, pp. 152–285.

Joerges, Christian and Florian Rödl (2009) 'Zum Funktionswandel des Kollisionsrechts II. Die kollisionsrechtliche Form einer legitimen Verfassung der post-nationalen Konstellation', in Gralf-Peter Callies, Andreas Fischer-Lescano, Dan Wielsch and Peer Zumbansen (eds), *Soziologische Jurisprudenz: Festschrift für Gunther Teubner zum 65. Geburtstag*, Berlin: Walter de Gruyter, pp. 765–78.

Joerges, Christian, Bo Stråth and Peter Wagner (eds) (2005) *The Economy as Polity: The Political Constitution of Contemporary Capitalism*, London: UCL Press.

Joerges, Christian and Michael Zürn (eds) (2005) *Law and Governance in Postnational Europe. Compliance Beyond the Nation-State*, Cambridge: Cambridge University Press, 2005.

Kaelble, Hartmut (2002) 'The Historical Rise of a European Public Sphere?', *Journal of European Integration History*, 8, pp. 9–22.

Kant, Immanuel ([1790] 1996) *Kritik der Urteilskraft: Werkausgabe Band X*, Frankfurt am Main: Suhrkamp Verlag.

——([1795] 1992): *Zum ewigen Frieden*, Hamburg: Felix Meiner Verlag.

Kantorowicz, Ernst ([1957] 1997) *The King's Two Bodies: A Study in Mediaeval Political Theology*, Princeton, NJ: Princeton University Press.

Karavas, Vagias (2007) *Digitale Grundrechte: Elemente einer Verfassung des Informationsflusses im Internet*, Baden-Baden: Nomos Verlag.

Kennedy, Duncan (1982) 'The Stages of the Decline of the Public/Private Distinction', *University of Pennsylvania Law Review*, 130, pp. 1349–57.

Kingsbury, Benedict, Nico Krisch and Richard B. Stewart (2005) 'The Emergence of Global Administrative Law', *Law and Contemporary Problems*, 68, pp. 15–62.

Kjaer, Poul F. (2013) 'Transnational Normative Orders: The Constitutionalism of Intra- and Trans-Normative Law', *Indiana Journal of Global Legal Studies*, 20, issue 2, pp. 777–803.

——(2012) 'Law of the Worlds – Towards an Inter-Systemic Theory', in Stefan Keller and Stefan Wipraechtiger (eds), *Recht zwischen Dogmatik und Theorie: Marc Amstutz zum 50. Geburtstag*, Zürich: Dike Verlag, pp. 159–75.

——(2011) 'The Concept of the Political in the Concept of Transnational Constitutionalism', in Christian Jorges (ed.), in co-operation with Tommi Ralli, *After Globalisation: New Patterns of Conflict and their Sociological and Legal Re-construction*, Oslo: Arena, pp. 285–321.

——(2011) 'Law and Order within and beyond National Configurations', in Poul F. Kjaer, Gunther Teubner and Alberto Febbrajo (eds) *The Financial Crisis in Constitutional Perspective: The Dark Side of Functional Differentiation*, Oxford, Hart Publishing, pp. 395–430.

——(2011) 'The Political Foundations of Conflicts Law', *Transnational Legal Theory*, 2, pp. 227–41.

——(2011) 'The Structural Transformation of Embeddedness', Christian Joerges and Josef Falke (eds), *Karl Polanyi: Globalisation and the Potential of Law in Transnational Markets*, Oxford: Hart Publishing, pp. 85–104.

——(2010) *Between Governing and Governance: On the Emergence, Function and Form of Europe's Post-national Constellation*, Oxford: Hart Publishing, 2010.

——(2010) 'Constitutionalizing Governing and Governance in Europe', *Comparative Sociology*, 9, pp. 86–119,

——(2010) 'Formalization or De-formalization through Governance?' in Rainer Nickel (ed.), *Conflict of Laws and Laws of Conflict in Europe and Beyond – Patterns of Supranational and Transnational Juridification*, Antwerp: Intersentia Publishing, pp. 189–200.

——(2010) 'A Hybrid within a Hybrid. Contextualizing REACH in the process of European Integration and Constitutionalization', *European Journal of Risk Regulation*, 1, pp. 383–96.

——(2010) 'The Metamorphosis of the Functional Synthesis: A Continental European Perspective on Governance, Law and the Political in the Transnational Space', *Wisconsin Law Review*, 2010, 2, pp. 489–533.

——(2009) 'Embeddedness through Networks – a Critical Appraisal of the Network Concept in the Oeuvre of Karl-Heinz Ladeur', *German Law Journal*, 10, pp. 483–99.

——(2009) 'Post-Hegelian Networks: Comments on the Chapter by Simon Deakin', in Marc Amstutz and Gunther Teubner (eds), *Networks: Legal Issues of Multilateral Co-operation*, Oxford: Hart Publishing, pp. 75–85.

——(2009) 'Three-dimensional Conflict of Laws in Europe', *ZERP – Discussion Papers*, 2.

——(2007): 'The Societal Function of European Integration in the Context of World Society', *Soziale Systeme: Zeitschrift für Soziologische Theorie*, 13, pp. 369–80.

——(2006) 'Systems in Context: On the Outcome of the Habermas/Luhmann Debate', *Ancilla Iuris*, September, pp. 66–77.

Klabbers, Jan (2013) 'Of Round Pegs and Square Holes: International Law and the Private Sector', in Paulius Jurčys, Poul F. Kjaer and Ren Yurakami (eds), *Regulatory Hybridization in the Transnational Sphere*, Leiden: Brill Publishing, pp. 29–48.

Klabbers, Jan, Anne Peters and Geir Ulfstein (2009) *The Constitutionalization of International Law*, Oxford: Oxford University Press.

Koskenniemi, Martti (2011) 'Empire and International Law: The Real Spanish Contribution', *University of Toronto Law Journal*, 61, pp. 1–36.

——(2011) *The Politics of International Law*, Oxford: Hart Publishing.

——(2009) 'Legal Fragmentation(s) – An Essay on Fluidity and Form', in Gralf-Peter Callies, Andreas Fischer-Lescano, Dan Wielsch and Peer Zumbansen (eds) *Soziologische Jurisrudenz: Festschrift für Gunther Teubner zum 65. Geburtstag*, Berlin: Walter de Gruyter, pp. 795–810.

——(2007) 'Constitutionalism, Managerialism and the Ethos of Legal Education', *European Journal of Legal Studies*, 2007, 1, pp. 1–18.

——([1989] 2005) *From Apology to Utopia: The Structure of International Legal Argument*, Cambridge: Cambridge University Press.

——(2001) *The Gentle Civilizer of Nations. The Rise and Fall of International Law 1870–1960*, Cambridge: Cambridge University Press.

Koselleck, Reinhart (2006) *Begriffsgeschichten: Studien zur Semantik und Pragmatik der politischen und sozialen Sprache*, Frankfurt am Main: Suhrkamp Verlag.

——(2006) 'Begriffsgeschichtliche Probleme der Verfassungsgeschichtsschreibung', in *Begriffsgeschichten: Studien zur Semantik und Pragmatik der politischen und Sozialen Sprache*, Frankfurt am Main: Suhrkamp Verlag, pp. 365–82.

—— ([1959] 1973) *Kritik und Krise: Eine Studie zur Pathogenese der bürgerlichen Welt*, Frankfurt am Main: Suhrkamp Verlag.

Krisch, Nico (2010) *Beyond Constitutionalism: The Pluralist Structure of Postnational Law*, Oxford: Oxford University Press.

——(2010) 'Pluralism in Postnational Risk Regulation: The Dispute over GMOs and Trade', *Transnational Legal Theory*, 1, pp. 1–29.

——(2001) *Selbstverteidigung und kollektive Sicherheit*, Berlin, Heidelberg: Springer-Verlag.

Kuhn, Thomas S. ([1962] 1996) *The Structure of Scientific Revolutions*, Chicago: Chicago University Press.

Kumm, Mattias (2010) 'The Best of Times and the Worst of Times: Between Constitutional Triumphalism and Nostalgia', in Petra Dobner and Martin Loughlin (eds) *The Twilight of Constitutionalism?* Oxford: Oxford University Press, pp. 201–19.

——(2009) 'The Cosmopolitan Turn in Constitutionalism: On the Relationship between Constitutionalism in and Beyond the State', in Jeffrey L. Dunoff and Joel. P. Trachtman (eds), *Ruling the World? International Law, Global Governance, Constitutionalism*, Cambridge: Cambridge University Press, pp. 258–326.

Ladeur, Karl-Heinz (2006) *Der Staat gegen die Gesellschaft: Zur Verteidigung der Rationalität der Privatrechtsgesellschaft*, Tübingen: Mohr Siebeck Verlag.

——(1997) 'Towards a Legal Theory of Supranationality – the Viability of the Network Concept', *European Law Journal*, 3, pp. 33–54.

Legrand, Pierre (1997) 'The Impossibility of Legal Transplants', *Maastricht Journal of Comparative Law*, 4, pp. 111–24.

Leibfried, Stephan and Michael Zürn (eds) (2005) *Transformations of the State?* Cambridge: Cambridge University Press.

Liekweg, Tania (2003) *Das Recht der Weltgesellschaft: Systemtheoretische Perspektiven auf die Globalisierung des Rechts am beispiel der lex mercatoria*, Stuttgart: Lucius & Lucius, 2003.

Lindahl, Hans (2007) 'Constituent Power and Reflexive Identity: Towards an Ontology of Collective Selfhood', in Martin Loughlin and Neil Walker (eds), *The Paradox of Constitutionalism: Constituent Power and Constitutional Form*, Oxford: Oxford University Press, pp. 9–24.

Loughlin, Martin (2010) *What is Constitutionalisation?*, in Petra Dobner and Martin Loughlin (eds), *The Twilight of Constitutionalism?*, Oxford: Oxford University Press, pp. 47–69.

——(2009) 'In Defence of Staatslehre', *Der Staat*, 48, 1, pp. 1–28.

Luhmann, Niklas (2011) *Organisation und Entscheidung*, Wiesbaden: Verlag für Sozialwissenschaften.

——([1975] 2009) 'Die Weltgesellschaft', *Archiv für Rechts-und Sozialphilosophie*, 1971, 57, pp.1–35. Reprinted in *Soziologische Aufklärung 2: Aufsätze zur Theorie der Gesellschaft*, Opladen: Westdeutsche Verlag, pp. 51–71.

——(2000) *Politik der Gesellschaft*, Frankfurt am Main: Suhrkamp Verlag.

——(1997) *Die Gesellschaft der Gesellschaft*, Frankfurt am Main: Suhrkamp Verlag.

——(1996) 'Quod Omnes Tangit: Remarks on Jürgen Habermas' Legal Theory', *Cardozo Law Review*, 17, pp. 883–99.

——(1995) 'The Paradoxy of Observing Systems', *Cultural Critique*, 31, pp. 37–55.

——(1995) 'Die Soziologie und der Mensch', in *Soziologische Aufklärung Band 6: Die Soziologie und Mensch*, Opladen: Westdeutscher Verlag.

——(1994) 'Europa als Problem der Weltgesellschaft', *Berliner Debatte*, 1994, pp. 3–7.

——(1994) 'Die Zukunft der Demokratie', in *Soziologische Aufklärung, Band 4: Beiträge zur Funktionalen Differenzierung der Gesellschaft*, Opladen: Westdeutscher Verlag, pp. 131–38.

——(1993) *Das Recht der Gesellschaft*, Frankfurt am Main: Suhrkamp Verlag.

——(1992) 'Die Beobachtung der Beobachter im politischen System: Zur Theorie der Öffentlichen Meinung'', in Jürgen Wilke (eds), *Öffentliche Meinung, Theorie, Methoden, Befunde: Beiträge zu Ehren von Elisabeth Noelle-Neumann*, Freiburg: Verlag Karl Alber, pp. 77–86.

——(1990) 'Verfassung als evolutionäre Errungenschaft', *Rechtshistorisches Journal*, 9, pp. 176–220.

——(1989) *Die Wirtschaft der Gesellschaft*, Frankfurt am Main: Suhrkamp Verlag.

——([1975] 1988) *Macht*, Stuttgart: Ferdinand Enke Verlag.

——(1985) 'Einige Probleme mit "reflexivem Recht"', in *Zeitschrift für Rechtssoziologie*, 6, pp. 1–18.

——(1984) *Soziale Systeme. Grundriß einer allgemeinen Theorie*, Frankfurt am Main: Suhrkamp Verlag.

——([1972], 1983) *Rechtssoziologie. 2 Bände*, Opladen: Westdeutscher Verlag.

——(1983) 'Der Wohlfahrtsstaat zwischen Evolution und Rationalität', in Peter Koslowski, Philipp Kreuzer and Reinhard Low (eds), *Chancen und Grenzen des Sozialstaats*, Tübingen: J.C.B. Mohr, pp. 26–40.

——(1980) 'Gesellschaftliche Struktur und semantische Tradition', in *Gesellschaftsstruktur und Semantik. Studien zur Wissenssoziologie der modernen Gesellschaft, Band 1*, Frankfurt am Main: Suhrkamp Verlag, pp. 9–71.

——(1974) 'Der politische Code. "Konservativ" und "progressiv" in systemtheoretischer Sicht', *Zeitschrift für Politik*, 21, pp. 253–71.

——([1968] 1973) *Zweckbegriff und Systemrationalität: Über die Funktion von Zwecken in sozialen Systemen*, Frankfurt am Main: Suhrkamp Verlag.

——(1971) 'Sinn als Grundbegriff der Soziologie', in Jürgen Habermas and Niklas Luhmann (eds) *Theorie der Gesellschaft oder Sozialtechnologie: Was leistet die Systemforschung?* Frankfurt am Main: Suhrkamp Verlag, pp. 25–100.

——(1965) *Grundrechte als Institution: Ein Beitrag zur politischen Soziologie*, Berlin: Duncker & Humblot.

Mac Amhlaigh, Cormac (2011) 'The European Union's Constitutional Mosaic: Big "C" or Small "c", is That the Question?', in Neil Walker, Jo Shaw and Stephen Tierney (eds), *Europe's Constitutional Mosaic*, Oxford: Hart Publishing, pp. 21–48.

McBain, Howard Lee (1927) *The Living Constitution, a Consideration of the Realities and Legends of our Fundamental Law*, New York: Workers Education Bureau Press, 1927.

McNeish, John-Andrew and Owen Logan (eds) (2012) *Flammable Societies: Studies on the Socio-economics of Oil and Gas*, London: Pluto Press.

Marx, Karl and Friedrich Engels ([1888] 1975) 'Ludwig Feuerbach und der Ausgang der Klassischen Deutschen Philosophie', in *Marx & Engels: Werke, Band 21*, Berlin: Dietz Verlag, pp. 262–307.

Mascareño, Aldo (2008) 'La Cultura chilena como ficción real', in Maximiliano Figueroa and Manuel Vicuña (eds), *El Chile del Bicentenario*, Santiago de Chile: Ediciones Universidad Diego Portales, pp. 183–220.

Mauss, Marcel ([1925] 2007) *Essai sur le don: Forme et raison de l'échange dans les sociétés archaïques*, Paris: Presses universitaires de France.

Meyer, John W., John Boli, George M. Thomas and Francisco O Ramirez (1997) 'World Society and the Nation-State', *American Journal of Sociology*, 103, pp. 144–81.

Milward, Alan S. (2000) *The European Rescue of the Nation-State*, 2nd edition, London: Routledge.

Moravcsik, Andrew (1999) *The Choice for Europe: Social Purpose and State Power from Messina to Maastricht*, Ithaca, NY: Cornell University Press.

Morgenthau, Hans (revised by Kenneth Thompson) ([1948] 2005): *Politics Among Nations. The Struggle for Power and Peace*, 7th edition, New York: McGraw-Hill.

Neumann, Franz L. ([1944] 1983) *Behemoth: The Structure and Practice of National Socialism 1933–1944*, Washington, DC: Octagon.

Neyer, Jürgen (2012) *The Justification of Europe: A Political Theory of Supranational Integration*, Oxford: Oxford University Press.

——(2010) 'Justice, Not Democracy. Legitimacy in the European Union', *Journal of Common Market Studies*, 48, pp. 903–21.

Nicholls, Alex, and Charlotte Opal (2004) *Fair Trade, Market-driven Ethical Consumption*, Thousand Oaks, CA: Sage Publications.

Nickel, Rainer (2006) 'Participatory Transnational Governance', in Christian Joerges and Ernst-Ulrich Petersmann (eds) *Constitutionalism, Multilevel Trade Governance, and Social Regulation*, Oxford: Hart Publishing, 2006, pp. 157–95.

Nicol, Danny (2010) *The Constitutional Protection of Capitalism*, Oxford: Hart Publishing.

Nipperday, Hans Carl (1961) *Soziale Marktwirtschaft und Grundgesetz*, Cologne: Heymann.

Parsons, Talcott (1971) *The System of Modern Societies*, Englewood Cliffs, NJ: Prentice-Hall.

Perez, Oren (2006) 'Facing the Global Hydra: Ecological Transformation at the Global Financial Frontier: The Ambitious Case of the Global Reporting Initiative', in Christian Joerges and Ernst-Ulrich Petersmann (eds), *Constitutionalism, Multilevel Trade Governance and Social Regulation*, Oxford: Hart Publishing, pp. 459–87.

——(2004) 'The Many Faces of the Trade-Environment Conflict: Some Lessons for the Constitutionalisation Project', in Christian Joerges, Inger-Johanne Sand and Gunther Teubner (eds), *Constitutionalism and Transnational Governance*, Oxford: Hart Publishing, pp. 233–55.

Peters, Anne (2012) 'Are we Moving towards Constitutionalization of the World Community?', in Antonio Cassese (ed.), *Realizing Utopia: The Future of International Law*, Oxford: Oxford University Press, pp. 118–35.

——(2009) 'The Merits of Global Constitutionalism', *Indiana Journal of Global Legal Studies*, 16, pp. 397–411.

Petersmann, Ernst-Ulrich (2009) 'Constitutional Theories of International Economic Adjudication and Investor-State Arbitration', in Pierre-Marie Dupuy, Francesco Francioni and Ernst-Ulrich Petersmann (eds), *Human Rights in International Investment Law and Arbitration*, Oxford: Oxford University Press, pp. 137–94.

——(2008) 'Multilevel Judicial Governance as Guardian of the Constitutional Unity of International Economic Law', *Loyola International and Comparative Law Review*, 30, pp. 101–52.

Pogge, Thomas (2008) *World Poverty and Human Rights: Cosmopolitan Responsibilities and Reforms*, 2nd edition, Cambridge: Polity Press.

Poggi, Gianfranco (1978) *The Development of the Modern State: A Sociological Perspective*, Stanford, CA: Stanford University Press.

Polanyi, Karl ([1944] 2001) *The Great Transformation: The Political and Economic Origins of our Time*, Boston, MA: Beacon Press.

Ponte, Stefano and Timothy Sturgeon (2013) 'Explaining Governance in Global Value Chains: A Modular Theory-Building Effort', *Review of International Political Economy*. Available at: www.tandfonline.com/doi/abs/10.1080/09692290.2013.809596.

Porter, Bruce D. (1994) *War and the Rise of the State: The Military Foundations of Modern Politics*, New York: Free Press.

Preuß, Ulrich K. (2010) 'Disconnecting Constitutions from Statehood. Is Global Constitutionalism a Promising Concept?', in Petra Dobner and Martin Loughlin (eds), *The Twilight of Constitutional Law?*, Oxford: Oxford University Press, pp. 23–46.

Randeria, Shalini (2005) 'Eisenstadt, Dumont and Foucault: The Challenge of Historical Entanglements for Comparative Civilization as Analysis', *Erwägen Wissen Ethik*, 17, pp. 59–62.

Rawls, John (1972) *A Theory of Justice*, Oxford: Oxford University Press.

Renner, Moritz (2013) 'Occupy the System! Societal Constitutionalism and Transnational Corporate Accounting', *Indiana Journal of Global Legal Studies*, 20, issue 2, pp. 941–961.

——(2011) 'Death by Complexity – The Crisis of Law in World Society', in Poul F. Kjaer, Gunther Teubner and Alberto Febbrajo (eds), *The Financial Crisis in Constitutional Perspective: The Dark Side of Functional Differentiation*, Oxford: Hart Publishing, pp. 93–111.

——(2011) *Zwingendes transnationales Recht: Zur Struktur der Wirtschaftsverfassung jenseits des Staates*, Baden-Baden: Nomos Verlag.

Rhodes, R.A.W. (2007) 'Understanding Governance: Ten Years On', *Organization Studies*, 28, pp. 1243–64.

Roberts, Michael (1956) *The Military Revolution, 1560–1660*, Belfast: Boyd.

Ronchi, Loraine (2002) 'The Impact of Fairtrade on Producers and their Organisations: A Case Study with Coocafé in Costa Rica', 11, *PRUS Working Paper*.

Rosa, Hartmut (2005) *Beschleunigung: Die Veränderung der Zeitstrukturen in der Moderne*, Frankfurt am Main: Suhrkamp Verlag.

Ross, Robert N. (1975) 'Ellipsis and the Structure of Expectation', *San José State Occasional Papers in Linguistics*, 1, November.

Rousseau, Jean-Jacques ([1762] 2005) *Du Contract Social ou Principes du Droit Politique*, Paris: Hachette Littératures.

Rubin, Edward L. (2001) 'Getting Past Democracy', *University of Pennsylvania Law Review*, 149, pp. 711–92.

Rupp, Hans H. (1974) *Grundgesetz und 'Wirtschaftverfassung'*, Tübingen: J.C.B. Mohr.

Sabel, Charles, and Joshua Cohen (2005) 'Global Democracy?', *NYU Journal of International Law and Politics*, 37, pp. 763–97.

Sand, Inger-Johanne (2009) 'Hybrid Law – Law in a Global Society of Differentiation and Change', in Gralf-Peter Calliess, Andreas Fischer-Lescano, Dan Wielsch and Peer Zumbansen (eds), *Soziologische Jurisprudenz: Festschrift für Gunther Teubner zum 65. Geburtstag*, Berlin: Walter de Gruyter, pp. 871–86.

Sassen, Saskia (2006) *Territory, Authority, Rights: From Medieval to Global Assemblages*, Princeton, NJ: Princeton University Press.

Schäfer, Armin (2005) *Die neue Unverbindlichkeit: Wirtschaftspolitische Koordinierung in Europa*, Frankfurt am Main: Campus Verlag.

Scharpf, Fritz W. (2010) 'Legitimacy in the Multi-level European Polity', in Petra Dobner and Martin Loughlin (eds), *The Twilight of Constitutionalism?*, Oxford: Oxford University Press, pp. 89–119.

——(2002) 'The European Social Model: Coping with the Challenges of Diversity', *Journal of Common Market Studies*, 40, pp. 645–70.

Schepel, Harm (2005) *The Constitution of Private Governance – Product Standards in the Regulation of Integrating Markets*, Oxford: Hart Publishing.

Scheuerman, William E. (2004) *Liberal Democracy and the Social Acceleration of Time*, Baltimore, MD: Johns Hopkins University Press.

Schmalz-Bruns, Rainer (1999) 'Deliberativer Supranationalismus: Demokratisches Regieren jenseits des Nationalstaates', *Zeitschrift für Internationale Beziehungen*, 6, pp. 185–244.

Schmid, Christoph Ulrich (2000) 'Diagonal Competence Conflicts between European Competition Law and National Law: The Example of Book Price Fixing', *European Review of Private Law*, 8, pp. 155–72.

Schmitt, Carl ([1942] 2008) *Land und Meer: Eine Weltgeschichtliche Betrachtung*, Stuttgart: Klett-Cotta.

——(1950) *Der Nomos der Erde: Im Völkerrecht des Jus Publicum Europaeum*, Berlin: Duncker & Humblot.

Schmitter, Philippe C. (1981) 'Still the Century of Corporatism?', in Philippe C. Schmitter and Gerhard Lehmbruch (eds), *Trends Toward Corporatist Intermediation*, London, Beverly Hills, CA: Sage Publications, pp. 7–52.

Schulz-Forberg, Hagen and Bo Stråth (2010) *The Political History of European Integration: The Hyprocrisy of Democracy-Through-Market*, London: Routledge.

Schwöbel, Christine (2012) 'Whither the Private in Global Governance?', *International Journal of Constitutional Law*, 10, pp. 1106–33.

Sciulli, David (2001) *Corporate Power: An Application of Societal Constitutionalism*, New York: New York University Press.

——(1992) *Theory of Societal Constitutionalism: Foundations of a Non-Marxist Critical Theory*, Cambridge: Cambridge University Press.

Scott, Joanne, and Susan P. Storm (2007) 'Courts as Catalysts: Rethinking the Judicial Role in New Governance', *Columbia Journal of European Law*, 13, pp. 565–94.

Scott, Joanne, and David M. Trubek (2002) 'Mind the Gap: Law and New Approaches to Governance in the European Union', *European Law Journal*, 8, pp. 1–18.

Simmel, Georg ([1890] 1989) 'Über soziale Differenzierung. Sociologische und psychologische Untersuchungen', in *Aufsätze 1887–1890*, Frankfurt am Main: Suhrkamp Verlag.

Sinzheimer, Hugo (1976) *Arbeitsrecht und Rechtssoziologie, Vol. 1*, Frankfurt am Main: Europäische Verlagsanstalt.

Slater, Donald (2003) 'Would Chocolate by Any Other Name Taste as Sweet? A Brief History of the Naming of Generic Foodstuffs in the EC with Regard to the Recent Chocolate Cases (Case C-12/00, Commission *v*. Spain and Case C-[14/00], Commission *v*. Italy)', *German Law Journal*, 4, pp. 571–87.

Slaughter, Anne-Marie (2004) *A New World Order*, Princeton, NJ: Princeton University Press.

Somek, Alexander (2010) 'Administration without Sovereignty', in Petra Dobner and Martin Loughlin (eds), *The Twilight of Constitutionalism?* Oxford: Oxford University Press, pp. 267–78.

Somers, Margaret R. (1995) 'What's Political or Cultural about Political Culture and the Public Sphere? Toward an Historical Sociology of Concept Formation', *Sociological Theory*, 13, pp. 113–44.

Soros, George (2008) *The New Paradigm for Financial Markets: The Credit Crisis of 2008 and What it Means*, New York: Public Affairs.

Stäheli, Urs (1998) 'Die Nachträglichkeit der Semantik: Zum Verhältnis von Sozialstruktur und *Semantik*', *Soziale Systeme: Zeitschrift für Soziologische Theorie*, 4, pp. 315–40.

Steffek, Jens (2011) 'Tales of Function and Form: The Discursive Legitimation of International Technocracy', *Normative Orders Working Paper*, 02.

Stichweh, Rudolf (2012) 'The History and Systematics of Functional Differentiation in Sociology'. Paper 02. Available at: www.unilu.ch/deu/prof._dr._rudolf_stichwehpublikationen_38043.html.

——(2009) 'Centre and Periphery in a Global University System'. Paper 08. Available at: www.unilu.ch/deu/prof._dr._rudolf_stichwehpublikationen_38043.html.

——(2008): 'Das Konzept der Weltgesellschaft: Genese und Strukturbildung eines globalen Gesellschaftssystems', *Rechtstheorie*, 39, pp. 329–55.

——(2007) 'Dimensionen der Weltstaat im System der Weltpolitk', in Mathias Albert and Rudolf Stichweh (eds), *Weltstaat und Weltstaatlichkeit: Beobachtungen globaler politischer Strukturbildung*, Wiesbaden: Verlag für Sozialwissenschaften, pp. 25–36.

——(2006) 'Strukturbildung in der Weltgesellschaft – Die Eigenstrukturen der Weltgesellschaft und die Regionalkulturen der Welt', in Thomas Schwinn (eds), *Die Vielfalt und Einheit der Moderne: Kultur-und strukturvergleichende Analysen*, Wiesbaden: Verlag für Sozialwissenschaften, pp. 239–57.

——(2005) *Inklusion und Eksklusion: Studien zur Gesellschaftstheorie*, Bielefeld: Transcript Verlag.

——(2005) 'Transfer in Sozialsystemen: Theoretische Überlegungen'. Paper 12. Available at: www.unilu.ch/deu/prof._dr._rudolf_stichwehpublikationen_38043.html.

——(2002) 'Die Entstehung einer Weltöffentlichkeit', in Hartmut Kaelble, Martin Kirsch and Alexander Schmidt-Gernig (eds), *Transnationale Öffentlichkeiten und Identitäten im 20. Jahrhundert*, Frankfurt am Main: Campus Verlag, pp. 57–66.

——(2000) *Die Weltgesellschaft. Soziologische Analysen*, Frankfurt am Main: Suhrkamp Verlag.

Stichweh, Rudolf and Paul Windolf (eds) (2009) *Inklusion und Exklusion: Analysen zur Sozialstruktur und sozialen Ungleichheit*, Wiesbaden: Verlag für Sozialwissenschaften.

Streeck, Wolfgang (2009) *Re-Forming Capitalism: Institutional Change in the German Political Economy*, Oxford: Oxford University Press.

Supiot, Alain (2009) 'The Territorial Inscription of Laws', in Gralf-Peter Calliess, Andreas Fischer-Lescano, Dan Wielsch and Peer Zumbansen (eds), *Soziologische Jurisprudenz: Festschrift für Gunther Teubner zum 65. Geburtstag am 30. April 2009*, Berlin: Walter de Gruyter Verlag, pp. 375–93.

Teubner, Gunther (2012) *Constitutional Fragments: Societal Constitutionalism and Globalization*, Oxford: Oxford University Press.

——(2011) 'A Constitutional Moment? The Logics of "Hitting the Bottom"', in Poul F. Kjaer, Gunther Teubner and Alberto Febbrajo (eds), *The Financial Crisis in Constitutional Perspective: The Dark Side of Functional Differentiation*, Oxford: Hart Publishing, pp. 3–42.

——(2011) 'Constitutionalising Polycontexturality', *Social and Legal Studies*, 20, pp. 17–38.

——(2001) 'Das Recht hybrider Netzwerke', *Zeitschrift für das gesamte Handelsrecht und Wirtschaftsrecht*, 165, pp. 550–75.

——(ed.) (1997) *Global Law without a State*, Aldershot: Ashgate-Dartmouth Publishing.

——(1996) 'Globale Bukowina: Zur Emergenz eines transnationalen Rechtspluralismus', *Rechtshistorisches Journal*, 15, pp. 255–90.

——(1993) 'The "State" of Private Networks: The Emerging Legal Regimes of Polycorporatism in Germany', *Brigham Young University Law Review*, 2, pp. 553–75.

——(1982) 'Reflexives Recht: Entwicklungsmodelle des Rechts in vergleichender Perspektive', *Archiv für Rechts-und Sozialphilosophie*, 68, pp. 13–59.

——(1978) *Organisationsdemokratie und Verbandsverfassung: Rechtsmodelle für politisch relevante Verbände. Tübinger Habilitationsschrift, Tübinger Rechtswissenschaftliche Abhandlungen, Band 47*, Tübingen: Mohr/Siebeck.

Thompson, Grahame F. (2012) *The Constitutionalization of the Global Corporate Sphere?*, Oxford: Oxford University Press.

Thornhill, Chris (2013) 'A Sociology of Constituent Power: The Political Code of Transnational Societal Constitutions', *Indiana Journal of Global Legal Studies*, 20, issue 2, pp. 551–603.

——(2011) 'The Future of the State', in Poul F. Kjaer, Gunther Teubner and Alberto Febbrajo (eds), *The Financial Crisis in Constitutional Perspective: The Dark Side of Functional Differentiation*, Oxford: Hart Publishing, pp. 357–93.

——(2011) *A Sociology of Constitutions. Constitutions and State Legitimacy in Historical-Sociological Perspective*, Cambridge: Cambridge University Press.

——(2008) 'Towards a Historical Sociology of Constitutional Legitimacy', *Theory and Society*, 37, pp. 161–97.

Tilly, Charles (1990): *Coercion, Capital, and European States, AD 990–1990*, Oxford: Blackwell Publishing.

Trenz, Hans-Jörg and Eder, Klaus (2005) 'The Democratizing dynamics of a European Public Sphere. Towards a Theory of Democratic Functionalism', *European Journal of Social Theory*, 7, pp. 5–25.

Trubek, David M. and Patrick Cottrell (2008) 'Robert Hudec and the Theory of International Economic Law: The Law of the Global Space', *Society of International Economic Law, Working Paper*, No. 02.

Trubek, David M. and Louise G. Trubek (2005) 'Hard and Soft Law in the Construction of Social Europe: the Role of the Open Method of Co-ordination', *European Law Journal*, 11, pp. 343–64.

Tully, James (2007) 'The Imperialism of Modern Constitutional Democracy', in Neil Walker and Martin Loughlin (eds), *The Paradox of Constitutionalism: Constituent Power and Constitutional Form*, Oxford: Oxford University Press, pp. 315–38.

Verfassung (I) (1990) in Otto Brunner, Werner Conze and Reinhart Koselleck (eds), *Geschichtliche Grundbegriffe. Historisches Lexikon zur politisch-sozialen Sprache in Deutschland, Band 6*, Stuttgart: Klett-Cotta, pp. 831–62.

Verfassung (II) (1990) in Otto Brunner, Werner Conze and Reinhart Koselleck (eds), *Geschichtliche Grundbegriffe. Historisches Lexikon zur politisch-sozialen Sprache in Deutschland, Band 6*, Stuttgart: Klett-Cotta, pp. 863–99.

Virilio, Paul (1977) *Vitesse et Politique: essai de dromologie*, Paris: Galilée.

von Savigny, Friedrich Carl (1974) *System des heutigen römischen Rechts*, Bearb. von O. L. Heuser – 2. Aufl, Berlin, private publishing.

——(1961) *Geschichte des römischen Rechts im Mittelalter. Band 5*, Bad Homburg, private publishing.

Wai, Robert (2008) 'The Interlegality of Transnational Private Law', *Law and Contemporary Problems*, 71, pp. 107–27.

Walk, Heike (2004) 'Formen Politischer Institutionalisierung: NGOs als Hoffnungsträger globaler Demokratie', in Jens Beckert, Julia Eckert, Martin Kohli and Wolfgang Streeck (eds), *Transnationale Solidarität. Chancen und Grenzen*, Frankfurt am Main: Campus Verlag, pp. 163–80.

Walker, Neil (2010) 'Out of Place and Out of Time: Law's Fading Co-ordinates', *Edinburgh Law Review*, 14, pp. 13–46.

——(2008) 'Beyond Boundary Disputes and Basic Grids: Mapping the Global Disorder of Normative Orders', *International Journal of Constitutional Law*, 6, pp. 373–96.

——(2006) 'A Constitutional Reckoning', *Constellations*, 13, pp. 140–502.

Wallerstein, Immanuel (2000) 'Globalization or the Age of Transition?', *International Sociology*, 2, pp. 249–65.

Walter, Christian (2001) 'Constitutionalizing (Inter)national Governance: Possibilities for and Limits to the Development of an International Constitutional Law', *German Yearbook of International Law*, 44, pp. 170–201.

Weber, Eugen (1976) *Peasants into Frenchmen: The Modernization of Rural France, 1870–1914*, Stanford, CA: Stanford University Press.

Weber, Max ([1946] 2007) 'Bureaucracy', in Hans H. Gerth and Charles Wright Mills (eds), *From Max Weber*, London: Routledge, pp. 196–244.

Weiler, Joseph H.H. (1999) *The Constitution of Europe: Do the New Clothes Have an Emperor?*, Cambridge: Cambridge University Press.

——(1999) 'Epilogue: "Comitology" as Revolution – Infranationalism, Constitutionalism and Democracy', in Christian Joerges and Ellen Vos (eds), *EU Committees: Social Regulation, Law and Politics*, Oxford: Hart Publishing, pp. 337–50.

Werron (2010) *Tobias (2010): Der Weltsport und sein Publikum. Zur Autonomie und Entstehung des modernen Sports*, Weilerswist: Velbrück.

Wiener, Antje (2008) *The Invisible Constitution of Politics: Contested Norms and International Encounters*, Cambridge: Cambridge University Press.

Wilke, Helmut (2006) *Global Governance*, Bielefeld: Transcript Verlag.

——(1998) *Systemtheorie III: Steuerungstheorie, 2. Auflage*, Stuttgart: Lucius & Lucius.

——(1992) *Ironie des Staates: Grundlinien einer Staatstheorie polyzentrischer Gesellschaft*, Frankfurt am Main: Suhrkamp Verlag.

Wobbe, Theresa (2000) *Weltgesellschaft*, Bielefeld: Transcript Verlag.

Yearbook of International Organisations (2001). Available at: www.uia.org/statistics/organisations/11.1.1a.pdf.

Zillman, Donald N., Alistair Lucas and George Pring (eds) (2002) *Human Rights in Natural Resource Development: Public Participation in the Sustainable Development of Mining and Energy Resources*, New York: Oxford University Press.

Zumbansen, Peer (2013) 'Law and Legal Pluralism: Hybridity in Transnational Governance', in Paulius Jurčys, Poul F. Kjaer and Ren Yurakami (eds), *Regulatory Hybridization in the Transnational Sphere*, Leiden: Brill Publishing, pp. 49–70.

Index